"For the disciples living in the first century, Jesus's teachings were tangible, practical, and real. That sense of immediacy has often become lost amidst voluminous commentaries on the Gospels that have overstuffed bookshelves in the twenty centuries since. John A. Beck's newest book, *A Walking Tour of the Gospels*, makes Jesus's words accessible again. Each chapter is concise, to the point, and relevant, bringing a breath of fresh air to the divine-human touch of Jesus. Start your day with a stroll through *A Walking Tour of the Gospels*. Your journey will be blessed on the way."

—PAUL WRIGHT, president emeritus, Jerusalem University College

"Weaving important cultural, geographical, and historical elements to each story, Dr. Beck has an extraordinary gift for reaching and communicating the heart of the gospel.... Offers a wealth of wonder, hope, comfort, and peace."

—MARILYN STULL, trainer and Bible study teacher,
Precept Ministries International

"By pairing the background to the meaning of each gospel story, Beck has created a field guide to the Bible, brilliantly incorporating Jesus's invitational challenge of 'Come, follow me' in a way that will serve to benefit any Bible reader!"

—JIM HALBERT, founding pastor, Crossroads Church, Nampa, Idaho

"Dr. John Beck has the unique ability to combine geographical insights with the practical application of biblical truth. His experience in the land of the Bible has equipped him well to share his personal insights in a way that will impact the spiritual lives of his readers. I have been personally blessed by John's books and enthusiastically recommend *A Walking Tour of the Gospels*. Reading his new book is like taking a hike through the Gospels with an experienced guide and spiritual leader."

—J. CARL LANEY, professor emeritus,
Western Seminary, Portland, Oregon

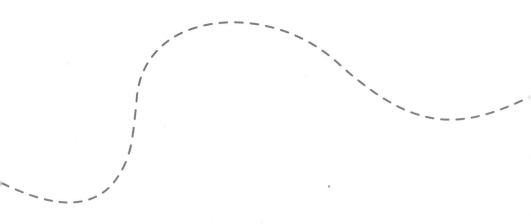

"Brief and yet powerful exposition of numerous gospel accounts relating to Jesus's earthly ministry. . . . Jack helps us see good ways to connect the realities of the land of the Bible with our understanding of God's Word."

—**MICHAEL A. GRISANTI, PhD, Old Testament department chair, distinguished research professor of Old Testament, The Master's Seminary, Los Angeles, California**

"It is good to follow a Bible teacher going through the Bible and understanding the historical and geographical settings of the biblical text. I am so happy to see this book in print for our devotional reading, too. I highly recommend this book. You will be blessed as you read through 150 key events of the Gospels."

—**REV. TAN ENG BOO, pastor, Life Bible-Presbyterian Church, Singapore**

"In short vignettes, Jack tours some 150 gospel stories using a simple format of asking who and where, what is this text about, and what does this text teach? Along the way, this consummate geographer and biblical scholar offers some memorable and pithy insights sure to find their way into any preacher's message. . . . This is a book that will stay on my desk and will be opened countless times."

—**C. CHAPPELL TEMPLE, PhD, lead pastor, Christ Church, Sugar Land, Texas**

A
Walking Tour
of the
Gospels

Experience the
Life and Lessons of Jesus

JOHN A. BECK

Our Daily Bread
Publishing™

Requests for permission to quote from this book should be directed to: Permissions Department, Our Daily Bread Publishing, PO Box 3566, Grand Rapids, MI 49501, or contact us by email at permissionsdept@odb.org.

Cover design by Patti Brinks
Interior design by Faceout Studio, Paul Nielsen

ISBN: 978-1-64070-165-6

Library of Congress Cataloging-in-Publication Data

Names: Beck, John A., 1956- author.
Title: A walking tour of the gospels : experience the life and lessons of
 Jesus / John A. Beck.
Description: Grand Rapids, MI : Our Daily Bread Publishing, [2023] |
 Summary: "Change the way you understand the stories of Jesus as you walk
 alongside John A. Beck while he points out the who, what, and where of
 150 key events of the gospels"-- Provided by publisher.
Identifiers: LCCN 2022022086 | ISBN 9781640701656
Subjects: LCSH: Bible. Gospels--Criticism, interpretation, etc. | Jesus
 Christ--Biblical teaching.
Classification: LCC BS2555.52 .B43 2023 | DDC 226.06--dc23/eng/20220630
LC record available at https://lccn.loc.gov/2022022086

Printed in China
23 24 25 26 27 28 29 30 / 8 7 6 5 4 3 2 1

Dedicated to my compassionate and loving soul mate, Marmy,
and to our gifted and adventurous grandchildren

Contents

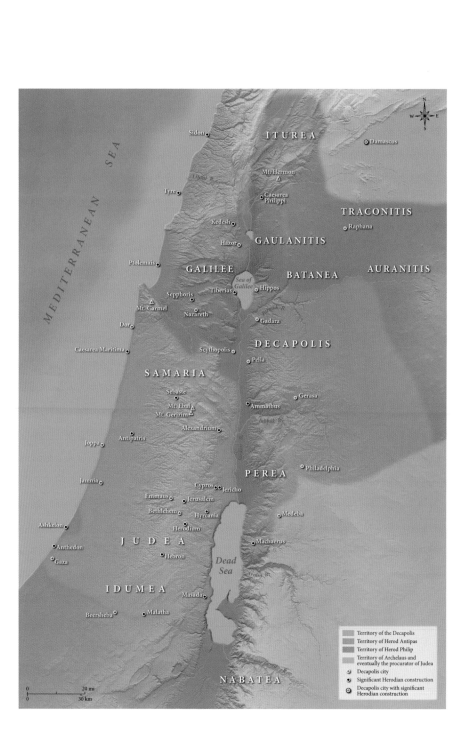

MEDITERRANEAN SEA

Sidon
Damascus

ITUREA

Mt. Hermon

Tyre
Caesarea Philippi

TRACONITIS

Kedesh
Raphana

Hazor
GAULANITIS

Ptolemais
GALILEE
Sea of Galilee
BATANEA
AURANITIS

Sepphoris
Tiberias
Hippos

Mt. Carmel
Nazareth

Dor
Gadara

Caesarea Maritima
Scythopolis
DECAPOLIS

Pella

SAMARIA

Sebaste
Gerasa

Mt. Ebal
Mt. Gerizim
Ammathus

Alexandrium
Jabbok R.

Joppa
Antipatris

Philadelphia

Jamnia
PEREA

Cypros
Jericho

Emmaus
Jerusalem

Bethlehem
Hyrcania
Medeba

Herodium

Ashkelon
Machaerus

JUDEA

Anthedon
Dead Sea

Gaza
Hebron

IDUMEA

Masada

Beersheba
Malatha

NABATEA

0   20 mi
0   30 km

Territory of the Decapolis
Territory of Herod Antipas
Territory of Herod Philip
Territory of Archelaus and eventually the procurator of Judea
Decapolis city
Significant Herodian construction
Decapolis city with significant Herodian construction

Abbreviations

Old Testament

Gen.	➤ Genesis	Eccl.	➤ Ecclesiastes
Ex.	➤ Exodus	Song	➤ Song of Songs
Lev.	➤ Leviticus	Isa.	➤ Isaiah
Num.	➤ Numbers	Jer.	➤ Jeremiah
Deut.	➤ Deuteronomy	Lam.	➤ Lamentations
Josh.	➤ Joshua	Ezek.	➤ Ezekiel
Judg.	➤ Judges	Dan.	➤ Daniel
Ruth	➤ Ruth	Hos.	➤ Hosea
1 Sam.	➤ 1 Samuel	Joel	➤ Joel
2 Sam.	➤ 2 Samuel	Amos	➤ Amos
1 Kings	➤ 1 Kings	Obad.	➤ Obadiah
2 Kings	➤ 2 Kings	Jonah	➤ Jonah
1 Chron.	➤ 1 Chronicles	Mic.	➤ Micah
2 Chron.	➤ 2 Chronicles	Nah.	➤ Nahum
Ezra	➤ Ezra	Hab.	➤ Habakkuk
Neh.	➤ Nehemiah	Zeph.	➤ Zephaniah
Est.	➤ Esther	Hag.	➤ Haggai
Job	➤ Job	Zech.	➤ Zechariah
Ps(s).	➤ Psalm(s)	Mal.	➤ Malachi
Prov.	➤ Proverbs		

New Testament

Matt.	▶ Matthew	1 Tim.	▶ 1 Timothy
Mark	▶ Mark	2 Tim.	▶ 2 Timothy
Luke	▶ Luke	Titus	▶ Titus
John	▶ John	Philem.	▶ Philemon
Acts	▶ Acts	Heb.	▶ Hebrews
Rom.	▶ Romans	James	▶ James
1 Cor.	▶ 1 Corinthians	1 Peter	▶ 1 Peter
2 Cor.	▶ 2 Corinthians	2 Peter	▶ 2 Peter
Gal.	▶ Galatians	1 John	▶ 1 John
Eph.	▶ Ephesians	2 John	▶ 2 John
Phil.	▶ Philippians	3 John	▶ 3 John
Col.	▶ Colossians	Jude	▶ Jude
1 Thess.	▶ 1 Thessalonians	Rev.	▶ Revelation
2 Thess.	▶ 2 Thessalonians		

Introduction

Part of me is from there. I was not born in Israel. But each year, I spend months in the Holy Land studying its geography and exploring its ancient culture. I have walked the trails Jesus walked, contemplated the views he used to teach, enjoyed the scent of the soil and flowers he smelled, felt the soft rain and hard stone he touched. These experiences have changed me and changed the way I read the story of Jesus in the Gospels.

My students at Jerusalem University College have shared in this learning adventure and changed as well. With every walk and through every experience, their Bible reading transformed. Now, it's your turn. I will take you on a tour of more than 150 gospel stories, each seen through the lens of the Holy Land.

In less time than it takes to share a cup of coffee, I will put the spotlight on a verse or set of verses that best captures the heart of the story. I will remind you who is involved and where the story is taking place. In a phrase, I will explain what the text is talking about. And in a sentence, I will summarize what the text teaches. Then I will take you on a tour of the story, highlighting what I see as someone who is from there.

Of course, it's impossible to see it all or say all there is to say about a given story. So I will limit our tour to places that offer the most significant insights. And I will direct most of the presentation to how those places impact our understanding of what Jesus said and did. That means I will leave a lot unsaid. So, what I have chosen not to do in this book is just as important as what I have chosen to do. First, you will note that I have not followed a published harmony of the Gospels but developed a harmony of my own. As a result, the cross-references in your Bible may not fully match mine. Also, I have chosen to comment sparingly on the differences we sometimes find between gospel accounts that recount the same event. If those differences are of interest, I encourage you to consult other reference works on that topic. Having covered these preliminaries, it's time to get started!

John walked this land with Jesus, and the experience changed him. "That which was from the beginning, which we have heard, which we have seen with our eyes, which we have looked at and our hands have touched—this we proclaim concerning the Word of life" (1 John 1:1). John encountered the message of Jesus bonded to the soil, scenery, and people of the Holy Land. We seek the same in this guided tour of the Gospels.

CHAPTER 1

Birth and Early Years of Jesus

GENEALOGIES OF JESUS

Matthew 1:1–17; Luke 3:23–38

"... and Jacob the father of Joseph, the husband of Mary,
and Mary was the mother of Jesus who is called the Messiah."
(Matthew 1:16)

▶ **WHO**

Adam, Abraham, Judah, David, Joseph, Jesus

▶ **WHAT IS THIS TEXT TALKING ABOUT?**

The family tree of Jesus

▶ **WHAT DOES THIS TEXT TEACH?**

Jesus qualifies as the Savior from sin because he has the
necessary family tree.

Y ou must be kidding. The first words from God, after four hundred years of silence, are a genealogy! Why should I bother reading a list of names, many of which I can't even pronounce? Before you surrender, let's see if I can convince you that a slow, thoughtful reading of the genealogy of Jesus has much to offer.

First, the reading of the genealogies helps us appreciate how long the world had waited for Jesus and how perilous the wait had been. Each name represents a full generation. Read the verses slowly and sense the hundreds of years slipping by. Think of the sin-debt accumulating over all those centuries. And consider the challenges that threatened the plan of salvation at every turn. It navigated past childless couples, unfaithful husbands, murders, and even exile from the Promised Land. The genealogies help us appreciate the world's long wait for Jesus and the many challenges the Lord overcame.

Second, notice the names that stand out in the list. Matthew includes four women. In Bible times, your relationship to the extended family was determined by your father or stepfather. So why does Matthew include Tamar, Rahab, Ruth, and Uriah's wife (Bathsheba)? Perhaps it anticipates the countercultural inclusion of women championed in Jesus's ministry, one that even counted women among his disciples (Luke 8:2–3). And what is more, two (Rahab and Ruth, if not all four women) were Gentiles! This reminds us that Jesus came to pay the sin-debt for all people.

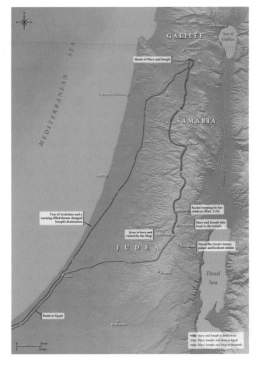

And finally, a careful reading of the genealogies demonstrates that Jesus is qualified to be the Savior from sin promised in the Old Testament. This Savior could not merely simulate the human experience; he had to be fully human, a descendant of Adam and Eve born through Mary. But not just any mortal would do. Jesus had to have the correct family tree. The genealogies demonstrate that Jesus counted Adam and Eve, Abraham and Sarah, Judah, and David as his forebears. And the very last male in the list before Jesus was key to it all. Joseph was not the biological father of Jesus. But as Jesus's stepfather, he gave Jesus the legal connection to the correct family tree.

For Further Reference: **Genesis 3:15; 12:1–3; 21:12; 28:3–4; 49:10; 2 Samuel 7:8–17; Psalm 89:35–37**

THE CONCEPTION OF JOHN THE BAPTIST ANNOUNCED

Luke 1:5–25

"And he will go on before the Lord, in the spirit and power of Elijah, to turn the hearts of the parents to their children and the disobedient to the wisdom of the righteous—to make ready a people prepared for the Lord." (Luke 1:17)

▶ **WHO**

Zechariah, Elizabeth, John the Baptist

▶ **WHAT IS THIS TEXT TALKING ABOUT?**

The birth of John the Baptist

▶ **WHAT DOES THIS TEXT TEACH?**

John the Baptist is the promised "Elijah" whose birth signals the imminent arrival of the Messiah.

Zechariah and Elizabeth lived an ordinary life. Zechariah was a priest, but not one of the aristocratic priests who worked full-time at the Temple in Jerusalem. He was among the common priests eligible to work two weeks a year at lower-level Temple tasks. A late eighth-century tradition says the couple lived in En Kerem, a tiny village about four miles (6.5 kilometers) west of the sacred precinct in Jerusalem. Like so many others in Judah, they farmed and raised livestock to meet their family's needs.

What most stood out was that this couple was childless. That was a big deal in a culture where your children were vital to your identity and well-being. And now that both were advanced in age, what would happen when time robbed them of their ability to care for themselves? We feel pity for but expect little from this challenged couple.

That brings us to the moment this ordinary story takes several extraordinary turns. First, Zechariah was chosen by lot to refresh the incense that smoldered on the altar of incense within the Temple itself. This was an exceptional honor that put him within arm's reach of the ark of the covenant, the throne of the Lord on earth. Given the thousands of ordinary priests available for such service, it's unlikely Zechariah had experienced this honor before. And given his advanced age, Zechariah's first opportunity would be his last.

As Zechariah was standing before the incense altar, watching the smoke rise that symbolized the prayers of the Lord's people, the angel Gabriel appeared. The Lord sent this celestial messenger to announce that Zechariah's prayer had been heard. He and Elizabeth would have a son!

And just when we think we have arrived at the pinnacle of the story, it takes another remarkable turn. Their son would be "Elijah." Elijah was an outstanding prophet in the Old Testament. But this was not that Elijah.

The very last thing we read in the book of Malachi is that the Lord would send a new "Elijah" to prepare people to meet the promised Savior from sin. Zechariah and Elizabeth's son, John, was that Elijah. And that meant the world was about to witness the redeeming work of the Messiah in real time.

For Further Reference: Exodus 30:7–8; Malachi 3:1; 4:5–6; Matthew 7:7–14

THE CONCEPTION OF JESUS ANNOUNCED TO MARY

Luke 1:26–38

"You will conceive and give birth to a son,
and you are to call him Jesus." (Luke 1:31)

▶ WHO & WHERE

Mary, Jesus, Nazareth

▶ WHAT IS THIS TEXT TALKING ABOUT?

The conception of Jesus

▶ WHAT DOES THIS TEXT TEACH?

Mary would conceive Jesus in a miraculous way.

If there was one person who needed to know the plan, it was Mary. Within her body the Spirit would weld together the human and divine natures of Jesus. And because this miracle occurred in Nazareth, it guaranteed that this great honor would come with grave distain.

Nazareth was a small, rural village whose topography limited its size and shaped its culture. It sat atop a near-vertical 1,100-foot (335-meter) ridge. But residents did not enjoy the commanding view offered by the ridge because the village itself was recessed into the bottom of a valley on top of that ridge. The fertility of this pleasant valley provided just enough resources to sustain a village of about three hundred residents. And the isolation of this valley attracted a certain kind of resident, those who wished to remain faithful to the Lord and separate themselves from the pagan influence of the world beyond. Here, marriages were arranged between local families, like that of Mary and Joseph. This indicates something about Mary's age. She was a young teen, twelve to thirteen years of age, who was excited about her coming wedding and anxious to raise a family with her beloved Joseph. But her excitement was about to give way to shock.

God sent the angel Gabriel to Mary to deliver a birth announcement, her birth announcement. It is peppered with language related to the coming Messiah. Mary's son would be named Jesus, a name which means "the Lord saves." He would not be the biological son of Joseph but the "Son of the Most High," a descendant of David who would rule an eternal kingdom. There was no mistaking the message. Mary would give birth to the promised Savior from sin. What a privilege!

But this is not the kind of news easily broken to your family, your village, and your husband. No one had ever conceived a child like this. And while a pregnancy prior to marriage might be glanced over with a wink and a nod in other places, culturally conservative Nazareth was not that place. It was a good thing Gabriel was going to go with her to share the news. Oh wait! "Then the angel left her" (Luke 1:38). In a place where chastity was championed and shame was shared, this young teen had to deliver this news alone.

If you have not appreciated the gravity of her assignment, this is the moment. If you have not paused to give thanks for her, now is the time. Mary's incredible honor came with a grave challenge because this was a Nazareth story.

For Further Reference: 2 Samuel 7:8–16; Isaiah 7:14; 9:6–7; Romans 1:3–4; Galatians 4:4–5; Hebrews 1:8

MARY VISITS ELIZABETH

Luke 1:39–56

"Blessed are you among women, and blessed is
the child you will bear!" (Luke 1:42)

▶ WHO & WHERE
Mary and Elizabeth, hill country of Judea

▶ WHAT IS THIS TEXT TALKING ABOUT?
Mary's humility

▶ WHAT DOES THIS TEXT TEACH?
Mary's humble origins did not prevent the Lord from doing
extraordinary things through her.

Could it really be so? This question was circulating through the house-holds of Nazareth. One of their own, a young teen was pregnant prior to her wedding night. She claimed an angel visited her to tell her that her conception was special. She would give birth to Jesus the Savior. Really? The doubts of her family and friends likely motivated Mary's quick dash south to visit her cousin Elizabeth. We follow along because their initial conversation answers the question raised in Nazareth. Could it really be so?

Elizabeth's words carry weight. She was a descendant of Aaron living near Jerusalem who was married to the priest Zechariah. She was a senior citizen who'd experienced a miraculous pregnancy of her own. But beyond that, the Holy Spirit filled her when Mary's greeting reached her ears. The infant Elizabeth carried in her womb signaled the Spirit's arrival and the next words we hear are the Lord's own. In them, Elizabeth repeatedly utters the word "blessed."

The traditional home of Elizabeth was En Kerem, located on the distant ridge.

That is significant. Different forms of the word "bless" appear five times in Genesis 12:1–3 building in force and emphasis until we come to the last. "All peoples [or nations] on earth will be blessed" through one of Abraham's descendants. Elizabeth's repeated use of "blessed" assures us and Mary that she is now connected with this long-standing promise. Her son would restore the blessing lost in Eden.

Then it was Mary's turn. She bursts into the magnificent song that became known as the Magnificat. The same Spirit who filled Elizabeth now led Mary to weave a song from the songs and psalms of the Old Testament. Mary acknowledged she was a humble person from a humble place. No one important came from Nazareth and nothing of consequence happened there. Yet her song reminds us of the Lord's long-standing habit of using humble people to accomplish magnificent things. And Mary concludes, like her cousin, by declaring that the promise given to Abraham was being realized in her.

That is why the Lord took us on this trip with Mary. Here we see two amazing ladies, one from Galilee and one from Judea, rise above the ordinariness of their humble circumstances to answer God's call. Their words carry us back to the first promises of a Savior given to Abraham and knit that story into their own.

For Further Reference: **Genesis 12:1–3; 1 Samuel 2:1–10; Psalms 103:17; 107:9; 138:6; James 1:9**

THE BIRTH OF
JOHN THE BAPTIST

Luke 1:57–80

"What then is this child going to be?" (Luke 1:66)

▶ WHO

Elizabeth, Zechariah, John the Baptist

▶ WHAT IS THIS TEXT TALKING ABOUT?

The identity of Zechariah and Elizabeth's son

▶ WHAT DOES THIS TEXT TEACH?

John is the promised prophet who would prepare the world for
the Messiah's arrival.

As parents, we gaze into the eyes of our newborn daughter or son and
ask, "Who will you grow up to be?" In this case, the entire hill country of Judea was asking the question and with good reason.

This story is filled with the unexpected. The most ordinary thing about
it was the boy's circumcision. This was what Jewish parents did for their
sons on the eighth day according to the Lord's command (Gen. 17:9–14).
But everything else about it was out of the ordinary, starting with the fact
that Elizabeth had given birth. She had gone through menopause. And
yet here the family was celebrating the birth of her son. Elizabeth used the
family gathering to announce the child's name. This also was unexpected.
Typically, a child was named on the day of birth and Dad was the one who
officially announced it. Then there was the name itself, John. It was the correct name; the name God had assigned to him (Luke 1:13). But it upset the

family because a child was typically named after someone in the extended family. This ignited a family squabble. A consensus emerged that the child should be named Zechariah after his father. At this, Dad picked up a writing tablet, likely a wooden board covered with wax, and used a stylus to write, "His name is John." With that, Zechariah's voice instantly returned. Given how unique this day was, it is no wonder people were asking what would become of this child.

Zechariah provides the answer. He had been thinking all those months that he had been unable to speak. And once his voice returned, he had a lot to say. His first words were a poem or song that became known as the Benedictus (the Latin word used to translate the first word of the song, "praise"). Zechariah praised the Lord for advancing the plan of salvation given to Abraham, a plan that promised to deliver precious cargo, the forgiveness of sins (Luke 1:68–75). Then the inspired poem put the focus on the baby boy. John was a "prophet," someone who spoke on behalf of the Almighty. And more than that, he was the promised prophet who would "prepare" Israel to meet the promised Messiah (vv. 76–79). That is what would become of him.

For Further Reference: Genesis 12:1–3; Isaiah 9:2, 6; 40:3; 60:1; Malachi 4:5–6

THE BIRTH OF JESUS ANNOUNCED TO JOSEPH

Matthew 1:18–25

"Joseph son of David, do not be afraid to take Mary home as your wife, because what is conceived in her is from the Holy Spirit."
(Matthew 1:20)

▶ **WHO & WHERE**
Joseph, Mary, Nazareth

▶ **WHAT IS THIS TEXT TALKING ABOUT?**
Joseph's role in the story of Jesus

▶ **WHAT DOES THIS TEXT TEACH?**
Joseph's role was to connect Jesus with the correct family tree.

The news crushed Joseph. His bride-to-be was pregnant. He did not know how, but he knew he must take extreme action, action that could have had grave implications for the plan of salvation.

What else could he do? Joseph was a righteous man. And he knew the rules. Their parents had arranged a marriage. An agreement had been signed. For the next year, he and Mary were to spend time together growing their relationship while avoiding sexual intimacy. Now Joseph was reeling from the news of Mary's pregnancy.

He quickly dismissed the thought of going ahead with the marriage. This would be tantamount to acknowledging he was the father, something that would bring shame on him and on his family in the small village of Nazareth. He loved Mary but needed to end the marriage contract. But how? The first option was a public divorce during which he would stand before the village elders and denounce Mary for her infidelity. This would exonerate him but expose Mary to

Statue depicting Joseph and Jesus from the Church of Saint Joseph in Nazareth.

public shaming or worse. Instead, he chose to divorce her "quietly." This would end it without dragging Mary into the public eye. Just two or three witnesses would give testimony and the marriage contract would be annulled. He knew that this would leave questions about his role in her pregnancy. But it would spare Mary the worst of it.

As he considered this, an angel appeared to him in a dream and changed his mind. Yes, Mary was pregnant. But it was not because she had been unfaithful to Joseph. For Jesus to accomplish his mission, he needed to be both divine and human. The Holy Spirit would be the child's father. Mary's job was to give Jesus the mortality that made him both "Jesus" (the Lord saves) and "Immanuel" (God with us).

So what was Joseph's role in all this? He would be Jesus's stepfather. And as a "son of David," he gave Jesus something Mary could not. Within the Jewish cultural orbit, the father or stepfather established a child's relationship to the extended family tree. Many challenged Jesus's claim to be the Messiah. But the Gospels do not record a single challenge to Jesus's family ancestry. He was a descendant of David, thanks to Jesus's other father, Joseph.

For Further Reference: Deuteronomy 24:1; 2 Samuel 7:11–16; Isaiah 7:14; 11:1; Acts 13:34; Romans 1:3; Revelation 22:16

THE BIRTH
AND ORIGIN OF JESUS

Luke 2:1–20; John 1:1–18

"Today in the town of David a Savior has been born to you." (Luke 2:11)
"The Word became flesh and made his dwelling among us." (John 1:14)

> ### WHO & WHERE
Jesus, Bethlehem

> ### WHAT IS THIS TEXT TALKING ABOUT?
The origins of Jesus

> ### WHAT DOES THIS TEXT TEACH?
Jesus was present at creation and born in Bethlehem.

W here to begin? That is the question both Luke and John had to answer as they told the story of Jesus. And although they start in different places, they end up telling stories that complement one another and that meet our deepest need.

Luke starts the story of Jesus's unique life on earth with his birth in Bethlehem. In fact, this detail is so important to Luke that he men-

This star in Bethlehem's Church of the Nativity marks the traditional location of Jesus's birth.

tions it repeatedly. Mary and Joseph left Nazareth and traveled to "Bethlehem the town of David" (Luke 2:4). "While they were there," Jesus was born (v. 6). The angel announced to shepherds that a big story was breaking in the "town of David" (v. 11), which led the shepherds to travel to "Bethlehem" (v. 15).

With all the details that Luke leaves out about this special day, why does he put so much emphasis on the location? It is because Bethlehem communicates the significance of Jesus's birth. Throughout the Old Testament, this town was the place where the Lord provided solutions for people in need. When the widowed Naomi and Ruth returned to Bethlehem, they were in trouble—socially disconnected and without access to food. But here, the Lord provided this family with a solution. The kindly Boaz made sure Ruth had grain to take home and eventually brought Ruth and Naomi into his own household (Ruth 1–4). Several generations later, we read about a nation in need. Israel's first king had failed to be the leader the Lord needed him to be. As Israel languished under Saul's poor leadership, the Lord used Bethlehem to provide a solution. Here Samuel anointed David as Saul's successor (1 Sam. 16:1–13). But the best was yet to come. This town that had provided a solution for a family and nation in need was poised to provide a solution for a world in need. Micah foretold that Bethlehem would be the birthplace of the Savior (Mic. 5:2). And that is why Luke elevates Bethlehem to a place of prominence in starting the story of Jesus. Like the other Bethlehem stories, the birth of Jesus is a solution story, one that provides hope to a world separated from the Lord by sin.

When John tells the story of Jesus's origins, he does not take us to Bethlehem, the animal shelter, or the field in which the shepherds are watching their sheep. He starts the story of Jesus's personhood where Genesis starts its story, "In the beginning" (Gen. 1:1; John 1:1). In the murky scenes of this world's first days, Jesus is the very Word that the Lord used to call this world into being and bring it to life. He is the Word that became flesh so that the Creator could live within his creation (John 1:14). He came to his own, "but his own did not receive him" (v. 11). But he pressed past all rejection to accomplish his mission of making us children of God (v. 12).

Luke and John place the story of Jesus's origins in different places. But their stories complement one another. And in the end, they tell the story that meets our deepest need—the need for the Word who became flesh, born in Bethlehem as Jesus, our Savior.

For Further Reference: Genesis 1:1; Micah 5:2; Galatians 4:4; Philippians 2:6–8; Revelation 19:13

THE PRESENTATION OF JESUS AT THE JERUSALEM TEMPLE

Luke 2:22–40

"Sovereign Lord, as you have promised, you may now dismiss
your servant in peace. For my eyes have seen your salvation."
(Luke 2:29–30)

▶ **WHO & WHERE**

Jesus, Simeon, Anna, Temple in Jerusalem

▶ **WHAT IS THIS TEXT TALKING ABOUT?**

Jesus's first visit to the Temple in Jerusalem

▶ **WHAT DOES THIS TEXT TEACH?**

Jesus's first Temple visit fulfilled the Old Testament promise of
the Lord's return to his Temple.

Jesus was a little more than one month old when Mary and Joseph made
the five-mile walk from Bethlehem to the Temple in Jerusalem. They
traveled in response to directives given in the Old Testament law code.
Mary had to undergo purification rites after childbirth (Lev. 12:2–8). And
because Jesus was their firstborn son, Mary and Joseph had to formally
present and redeem Jesus at the Temple (Ex. 13:11–13). But something
much bigger was brewing.

That becomes clear when we meet Simeon and Anna. They were regu-
lars at the Temple. Both were seniors who had lived a full life and were now
focused on what mattered most in life. They were awaiting the coming of
the Messiah. Luke says it like this. Simeon was awaiting the "consolation

of Israel" (Luke 2:25, cf. Isa. 40:1). Anna joined him in looking for the "redemption of Jerusalem" (Luke 2:38). Of course, they could have been waiting anywhere, but they chose to wait at the Temple in Jerusalem.

There was good reason for them being there. Centuries earlier, King Solomon built the Temple in Jerusalem. During the dedication of that building, the visible presence of the Lord filled the place (2 Chron. 7:1–2). The Lord used his special, visible presence to assure Israel that he was with them. But when Israel abandoned the Lord and began to worship other gods, we watch the slow and painful departure of the Lord from his Temple in advance of its destruction by the Babylonians (Ezek. 9:3; 10:4, 18–19; 11:22–23). Only when we appreciate the devastating nature of this departure can we appreciate how passionately God's people awaited his return. That return was promised but never realized in the Old Testament era (Zech. 1:16; 8:3; Mal. 3:1). And so, faithful believers like Simeon and Anna remained in the Temple watching for the moment.

Simeon and Anna were two senior citizens who spent their days in the Temple courtyards, waiting for the Lord's promised return to his Temple.

It happened when Mary and Joseph brought Jesus to Jerusalem. Lest we miss the power of the moment, we experience it through the lens of Simeon and Anna. These senior citizens represent all those who had been waiting ever since Jerusalem fell to Babylon. That's more than six hundred years! The Lord promised Simeon he would not die before he had seen the Messiah. As he held the infant Jesus in his arms, he and the world knew the Lord had returned to his Temple.

For Further Reference: **2 Chronicles 7:1–2; Isaiah 40:1–5; Zechariah 1:16; 8:3; Malachi 3:1**

THE MAGI FIND
JESUS IN BETHLEHEM

Matthew 2:1–12

"Where is the one who has been born king of the Jews?"
(Matthew 2:2)

▶ **WHO & WHERE**

Magi, Bethlehem

▶ **WHAT IS THIS TEXT TALKING ABOUT?**

The location of Jesus's birth

▶ **WHAT DOES THIS TEXT TEACH?**

Nonpartisan witnesses confirm Jesus was born in Bethlehem.

Many questions linger around this story. Who were the wise men? From which country did they come? What was the "star" they were following? But the question Matthew cares about most is *where*. Where was Jesus born? The matter takes center stage in the first two verses. And Matthew won't allow us to take our eyes off the topic. He mentions "Bethlehem" four times in these first twelve verses—half the number of times the word appears in the New Testament.

Matthew makes the case for the Bethlehem birth by using a variety of unrelated witnesses. Let's start with the Magi. We have only indirect evidence of their origins. A case can be made for Babylon, Persia, or Arabia. What we know for sure is why they have come. They were looking for the newborn king, guided by an aberration in the night sky that eventually brings them to Bethlehem. But not before their search takes a temporary detour to the capital city of Jerusalem where they seek the assistance of Herod the Great. He was the Roman-appointed king of Judea but had no information on the whereabouts of this newborn king. Eventually, he too would point us to Bethlehem but using the tips of his soldiers' spears. Herod brings in the third set of witnesses, the respected Jewish teachers at the Temple. They pointed to the prophecy in Micah 5:2, which stated that this special child would be found in nearby Bethlehem. Note that none of these individuals had something to gain by lying about the birthplace of Jesus. Consequently the Magi, Herod, and Jewish scholars become unbiased witnesses who confirm that the birthplace of Jesus was Bethlehem.

Why all the effort? Matthew cared because only someone born in Bethlehem of Judea qualified as the Messiah, the promised Savior from sin. Because Jesus grew up and spent most of his life in Nazareth, many living in the first century lost sight of the fact that Jesus was born in Bethlehem. Consequently, many concluded that "Jesus of Nazareth" was not qualified to be the Messiah (John 7:41–42). And that is why Matthew privileges this question above the others we might ask. In this story, he uses nonpartisan witnesses to confirm that Jesus was born in Bethlehem.

For Further Reference: **Numbers 24:17; Isaiah 60:1–3, 6; Micah 5:2; John 7:42**

EGYPT AGAIN!

Matthew 2:13–18

"And so was fulfilled what the Lord had said through the prophet:
'Out of Egypt I called my son.'" (Matthew 2:15)

▶ **WHO & WHERE**

Jesus, Egypt

> ### WHAT IS THIS TEXT TALKING ABOUT?

Jesus's trip to and from Egypt

> ### WHAT DOES THIS TEXT TEACH?

Jesus's trip to and from Egypt connected him with Israel's story and mission.

Egypt again!

That had to be the furthest thing from the minds of Mary and Joseph. Things were looking up. They had moved into a house in Bethlehem and the Magi's gifts promised this family a bit of economic relief. But the night of the Magi's departure, an angel's warning sent the holy family fleeing toward Egypt. What had happened? Earlier the Magi's visit, which revealed Jesus's birthplace, stoked Herod's paranoia. When the wise men returned to their country without giving the king the coordinates of the child's home, Herod flew into a rage and ordered the execution of every baby boy in Bethlehem two years of age and under. Bethlehem had helped define Jesus as the Messiah. Now being there put his life at risk.

This scene from Rekhmire's tomb in Thebes recalls the significant connection between the story of salvation and Egypt.

An angel visited Joseph to sound the alarm, setting into motion the quick retreat to Egypt. This put them beyond Herod's lengthy reach. But it also created a geographic link between Jesus and his forebears. The Lord had called the family of Abraham and Sarah to serve a vital role in the redemption of the world. But life was not always easy for this family. At the time of Jacob, a severe famine gripped the Promised Land, a threat so great that it precipitated the migration of Jacob's family to Egypt (Gen. 46:1–7). Similarly, when Jesus's life was threatened in the Promised Land, he fled to Egypt. Centuries after Jacob's family had traveled to Egypt, a new threat emerged (Ex. 1:1–22). This led to the exodus from Egypt and eventual return to the Promised Land (Ex. 3:7–8). This powerful moment lingered in the memory of Israel, spoken of by the authors, poets, and prophets of the Old Testament including Hosea. "Out of Egypt I called my son" (Hos. 11:1). Jesus's return from Egypt to the Promised Land is an echo of his forebears' return.

And that is why Matthew quotes Hosea 11:1. It is not a prophecy of what Jesus would do. It declares that the return of Jesus was analogous to his forebears' return from Egypt. And in this way, geography becomes a tool that connects the stories and the mission of Israel and Jesus.

For Further Reference: **Genesis 46:6; Exodus 1:16, 22; 3:7–8; Hosea 11:1; Acts 13:17**

JESUS OF NAZARETH

Matthew 2:19–23

"So was fulfilled what was said through the prophets, that he would be called a Nazarene." (Matthew 2:23)

▶ WHO & WHERE
Jesus, Nazareth

▶ WHAT IS THIS TEXT TALKING ABOUT?

Jesus's connection with Nazareth

▶ WHAT DOES THIS TEXT TEACH?

Jesus's connection with Nazareth enshrined his life with the low expectations that fulfilled Old Testament prophecy about him.

After the holy family's stay in Egypt, the Lord directed them away from Bethlehem and toward Nazareth where Jesus lived out most of his days on earth. Like any hometown, Nazareth left its mark on him.

The geography of Nazareth shaped life in this village as well as the expectations that lingered around those who lived there. It was an exceedingly small village recessed into the bottom of a valley at the top of a ridge. The limited natural resources kept the village small, and its geographic isolation kept it out of the world's view. No one expected people of Nazareth to amount to much. This sleepy village goes unmentioned in the Old Testament and in other first-century writings because it hosted no major event and produced no one of renown prior to Jesus. Because he spent his first thirty years of life here, the label "Jesus of Nazareth" bathed him with low expectations. Nathanael gives us the local perspective. "Nazareth! Can anything good come from there?" (John 1:46).

Ironically, those low expectations fulfilled Old Testament prophecy. But where do we find this language in the Old Testament? There are no passages that speak of Jesus the Nazarene, or one from Nazareth as being the Messiah. This is where we must read Matthew's words very carefully. He is not quoting a specific prophet (singular) but says that Jesus's origins in Nazareth fulfill what the prophets (plural) said about him. So, it is best for us to look for a theme developed in more than one Bible passage rather than a singular reference.

In many places (see the Bible references below), the Messiah is said to be someone who will call attention to himself by the very fact that he will call so little attention to himself. That is the very definition of someone who called first-century Nazareth home. Ironically, the very location that caused others to expect so little of him provokes us to expect much from him. We know precious little about what Jesus's day-to-day life was like in Nazareth. But it accomplished one important thing and Matthew insists we notice. The low expectations of Nazareth create high expectations for Jesus.

For Further Reference: Psalms 22:6–8; 69:8, 20–21; Isaiah 49:7; 53:1–3; Romans 15:3; Philippians 2:6–8

JESUS PURSUES UNDERSTANDING AT THE TEMPLE

Luke 2:40–52

"Didn't you know I had to be in my Father's house?" (Luke 2:49)

▶ **WHO & WHERE**

Jesus, Temple in Jerusalem

▶ **WHAT IS THIS TEXT TALKING ABOUT?**

Jesus's education

▶ **WHAT DOES THIS TEXT TEACH?**

Jesus had to be at the Temple in Jerusalem in order to grow in wisdom.

This story is unique. It is the only story we have from Jesus's youth. It is the first story in which we hear Jesus speak. And it is the first story in which we find Jesus insist that he must be in a specific location. So, what is it about?

Luke signals that this story is about Jesus's pursuit of wisdom in two ways. First, he brackets the story with the idea of Jesus's intellectual growth. Jesus was "filled with wisdom" (Luke 2:40) and "Jesus grew in wisdom" (v. 52). When we examine the verses in between these bookends, we find the language of learning. Jesus was "sitting among the teachers," "listening," and "asking them questions" (v. 46). It is a story about "understanding" (vv. 47, 50), "answers" (v. 47), "searching" (vv. 48, 49), and "knowing" (v. 49). Because this story is saturated with educational terms, we can safely conclude it is a story about Jesus's education.

And that is why this story is set in the Temple courts. When Mary and Joseph upbraid Jesus for remaining behind at the Temple, he asserted the necessity of being where he was. To understand that, we need to understand the tiers within Israel's education system in Jesus's day. It began in the home where Jesus learned the basics from Mary and Joseph. Questions that could not be answered at home were directed to the rabbi at the synagogue in Nazareth. But what about those questions that no one in Nazareth could answer? This is where the Temple comes in. The Temple in Jerusalem was not just a place of worship but a place of higher education where the senior scholars lectured. Jesus

These steps were the southern entry to the Temple in Jerusalem at the time of Jesus. They are known as the "rabbi's teaching steps."

"had to be" there (v. 49) because it was the only place where the questions unanswered in Nazareth could find answers.

This story of Jesus's education confronts us with the mystery of Jesus the God-man. As true God, he knew everything. But as a mortal, he needed to journey through the process of self-discovery and learning known to each of us. Jesus could not merely simulate the human experience. He had to be authentically mortal, engaging the full range of the human experience, to be our redeeming substitute. The fact that he "grew in wisdom" signals that Jesus is that person.

For Further Reference: **Isaiah 11:2; John 5:39; Philippians 2:6–8; Hebrews 2:17**

JOHN PREPARES THE WAY

Matthew 3:1–12; Mark 1:1–8; Luke 3:1–20; John 1:19–28

"And so John the Baptist appeared in the wilderness, preaching a
baptism of repentance for the forgiveness of sins." (Mark 1:4)

▶ WHO & WHERE
John the Baptist, Judean Wilderness, Jordan River

▶ WHAT IS THIS TEXT TALKING ABOUT?
Repentance

▶ WHAT DOES THIS TEXT TEACH?
Those who wish to meet God face-to-face must prepare for the meeting with repentance.

His ministry was short but vital. John preached for less than two years, preparing those living in Israel to meet God face-to-face, work that was intimately bound with wilderness and water.

The gospel writers place John in the Judean Wilderness (Matt. 3:1; Mark 1:4; Luke 3:2; John 1:23). This region lies east of Jerusalem draping

John the Baptist prepared people to meet the Messiah in the austere Judean Wilderness.

the western shoreline of the Dead Sea for some sixty miles (ninety-seven kilometers). It is a rugged and dry landscape, hostile to the human experience, a place that lacks water, food, and people. This is not where we expect John to be. We anticipate that John would follow in the footsteps of his father, Zechariah, a priest serving in the Temple at Jerusalem. But John was likely disillusioned with the rampant corruption of the Temple in his day. So, he went to the place people would go to be alone and rethink the direction of their life—the wilderness. But the Lord had his own reasons for bringing John into this forbidding ecosystem. He had promised that a forerunner would precede the coming of the Messiah, a forerunner who would prepare the way for the Lord's arrival "in the wilderness" (Isa. 40:3–4). This preparation involved a message as austere as the pale slopes of the wilderness. He called for his listeners to repent—to change the way they thought and lived—in preparation to meet the Lord face-to-face.

Water was also part of John's story. The gospel writers link his ministry to the Jordan River (Matt. 3:5; Mark 1:5; John 1:28). The wilderness lacked the water for baptism, so John also spent time along the tributaries and banks of the Jordan River. His form of water baptism is a bit puzzling. It does not strictly follow any of the water rites described in the Old Testament and is unlike the baptism that Jesus commanded at the close of his time on earth (Matt. 28:19). It is best to see John's baptism as a unique, one-time water ceremony, marking the moment his listeners signaled their agreement with John's teaching and their willingness to repent. Thus, through wilderness and water John called for repentance that prepared his listeners to meet the Messiah face-to-face.

For Further Reference: Isaiah 40:3–5; Malachi 3:1; 4:5–6; 2 Corinthians 7:10; 2 Peter 3:9

CHAPTER 2

Baptism and Early Ministry of Jesus

THE BAPTISM OF JESUS

Matthew 3:13–17; Mark 1:9–11; Luke 3:21–22; John 1:29–34

"This is my Son, whom I love; with him I am well pleased."
(Matthew 3:17)

▶ **WHO & WHERE**

Jesus, John the Baptist, Jordan River

▶ **WHAT IS THIS TEXT TALKING ABOUT?**

The baptism of Jesus

▶ **WHAT DOES THIS TEXT TEACH?**

The baptism of Jesus signals his transition into public ministry.

The first thirty years of Jesus's life were quiet, private years. The next three were anything but. The baptism of Jesus marks the transition between the two.

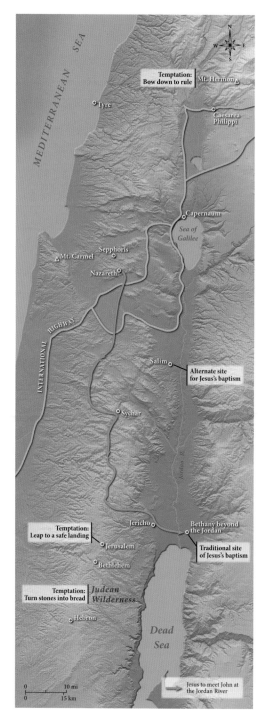

At first, John wanted nothing to do with baptizing Jesus. John's call was to prepare the way for Jesus, summoning sinners to repent and urging them to receive the "baptism of repentance" (Mark 1:4; Luke 3:3). It is no wonder he objected when Jesus asked John to baptize him. This could create confusion, signaling to some that Jesus had become John's student or that Jesus had sinned and needed to repent. John's role was to reveal Jesus's identity (John 1:31), baptizing him would only muddy the water.

But Jesus insisted and John relented. What followed did not confuse but confirmed Jesus's identity. For the first time since the angels sang at Jesus's birth, heaven commented directly on him. The Spirit of God descended on Jesus in the form of a dove and the voice of the Father boomed, "This is my Son, whom I love; with him I am well pleased" (Matt. 3:16–17). The quiet years in Nazareth were over. He was making the transition into public life and ministry.

It was not just the event but the place of Jesus's baptism that signals this baptism is about transition. Rather than wait for John to come to him in Galilee or meet John halfway between Galilee and the Dead Sea, Jesus walked for several days to meet John about five miles (eight kilometers) north of the Dead Sea at a ford in the Jordan River opposite Jericho. The gospel of John calls it, "Bethany on the other side of the Jordan" (1:28). Jesus wanted to be baptized at this spot because it was a place intimately connected with others in transition. This is where Joshua transitioned into his role as Israel's leader after Moses (Josh. 1). This is where Israel transitioned into the Promised Land (Josh. 3–4). And this is where Elisha transitioned into leadership after Elijah (2 Kings 2). Bethany beyond Jordan witnessed some of the most significant transitions in the story of salvation. But none as powerful as the one that marked Jesus's transition from private life into public ministry.

For Further Reference: **Psalm 2:7; Isaiah 11:2; 42:1**

WILDERNESS TEMPTATION

Matthew 4:1–4; Mark 1:12–13; Luke 4:1–4

"Man shall not live on bread alone, but on every word that comes from the mouth of God." (Matthew 4:4)

▶ WHO & WHERE

Jesus, wilderness

▶ WHAT IS THIS TEXT TALKING ABOUT?
Temptation

▶ WHAT DOES THIS TEXT TEACH?
Jesus faced the same temptations we face, but as our substitute, he succeeded in those places we fail.

Jesus's temptation in the wilderness does much more than show us what to do when faced by one of Satan's temptations. It shows us what Jesus did to fix our relationship with the Father when we fail.

The first thing to note is that the temptation of Jesus in the wilderness parallels the temptation of Israel in the wilderness in five ways. First, neither Israel nor Jesus chose to enter this space on their own but rather were led there by God. Second, they did not end up in the same geographic location, but both entered the same ecosystem: wilderness. Third, they remained there for a period of forty, forty years for Israel and forty days for Jesus. Fourth, while there in the wilderness, both Israel and Jesus were ravaged by hunger. Fifth and finally, isolated and challenged by the wilderness setting, both Israel and Jesus faced the same challenging question: will you trust the Father when the fundamentals for survival are not in view?

Ancient Israel and Jesus answered the question differently. To appreciate Israel's answer, we need to understand the purpose behind Israel's extended stay in the wilderness. God sought to mature their character and faith using this ecosystem to humble them, to test them, and to teach them about the Father's ability to provide in all circumstances (Deut. 8:2–3). The Father offered to provide all the things that the wilderness lacked: food, water, security, and a clear direction in which to travel. The question means something here in the wilderness that it does not mean in well-resourced places: "Will you trust me now?" Unfortunately, Israel answered with a resounding, "No!" (Ex. 16:3; Num. 20:2–5).

Jesus's first temptation took place in the forbidding folds of the Judean Wilderness.

Jesus was different. He allowed the Father to put him in the same harsh ecosystem as his forebears. He then succeeded in the very place and ways that Israel failed. Satan tried his best to get Jesus to abandon trust in the Father by attempting to induce the Son of God to satisfy his hunger by making his own bread. In reply, Jesus quoted the words of Deuteronomy 8 that state the purpose of a wilderness experience and affirmed that a promise from his Father is better than bread in the hand.

To be sure, Jesus shows us how to defeat temptation using the Word of God. That is a valuable lesson. But more than that, Jesus lived the obedient life we owed to God but could not deliver. Then as our saving substitute, he covered our failures with his obedience. The wilderness temptation of Jesus shows that substitution in action.

For Further Reference: **Deuteronomy 8:2–3; 1 Corinthians 10:13; Hebrews 2:18; 4:15**

TEMPLE TEMPTATION

Matthew 4:5–7; Luke 4:9–13

"Do not put the Lord your God to the test." (Matthew 4:7)

▶ **WHO & WHERE**

Jesus, Temple in Jerusalem

▶ **WHAT IS THIS TEXT TALKING ABOUT?**

Integrity of the Father's words

▶ **WHAT DOES THIS TEXT TEACH?**

The Father's words have integrity and do not require validation using a manufactured test.

"Prove it!" At his baptism, the Father declared that Jesus was the Son of God. In this temptation, the Devil essentially said to Jesus, "Prove it!"

The place of the temptation is significant. The Devil takes Jesus to the Temple in Jerusalem—the holiest site in the Holy Land. It no longer consisted of a single building set on a hill but was a sprawling campus with courtyards, covered walkways, and auxiliary buildings. We walk with Jesus up one staircase after the next until we arrive at one of the highest places in the compound, the southwest corner of the campus. Jesus likely stood on a small platform known as "the place of trumpeting," the place from which public announcements echoed throughout Jerusalem given via blasts on a ram's horn. On this spot, Jesus stood a dizzying fifteen stories above the busy shopping street immediately below him.

The Devil took Jesus to this spot to tempt him. It was the perfect, public place to demonstrate the validity of the words spoken at Jesus's baptism. All he had to do was take one more step. Gravity would send him plummeting toward the valley floor. An ordinary man would be killed by the fall. But if he were really God's Son, the angels would catch him in their hands and gently lower him unharmed to the pavement below (Ps. 91:11–12). The temptation assumed that the Father's words were deficient in and of themselves and needed a test to validate them.

Jesus responded to the temptation with Old Testament language associated with ancient Israel's struggle to trust the words and promises of God. When facing a water shortage, they demanded that the Lord do something to prove the validity of his presence and promises (Ex. 17:2, 7). This was a sin and Moses cautioned later generations against repeating it. "Do not put the LORD your God to the test as you did at Massah" (Deut. 6:16). This lesson remains. The words of the Father do not require validation, only trust.

For Further Reference: Exodus 17:2, 7; Deuteronomy 6:13, 16; Psalm 91:11–12; Hebrews 4:15

MOUNTAIN TEMPTATION

Matthew 4:8–11; Luke 4:5–8

"Worship the Lord your God, and serve him only."
(Matthew 4:10)

▶ WHO & WHERE
Jesus, Mount Hermon

▶ WHAT IS THIS TEXT TALKING ABOUT?
The object of our worship

God is the only legitimate object of our worship.

It is human nature to avoid unpleasant experiences. The Devil sought to exploit this instinctual response during a mountain-based temptation. In it, the Devil offered Jesus a path to kingship without the cross, a path that required Jesus to recognize the Devil as a legitimate object of worship.

Matthew says that the temptation occurred on a "very high mountain" (Matt. 4:8). The Promised Land is filled with mountains. But as our eyes scan the horizon, one stands out above the others. North of the Sea of Galilee, Mount Hermon rises to 9,232 feet (2,814 meters) in elevation, towering well above its nearest competitor (Mount Meron at 3,963 feet [1,208 meters]). Its profile fills the horizon, covering an area of 270 square miles (700 square kilometers). Merchants moving trade goods between world markets wanted nothing to do with the tundra and snowfields on its towering summit. So, they squeezed past using the well-worn paths they traveled below its sprawling flanks. Their choice compressed merchants and their commodities into a narrow line of travel, making it the perfect place for the Devil to show Jesus representatives of all nations and their splendor.

The Devil quickly put this location to work in a temptation filled with lies. The fallen angel presented himself as a legitimate object of worship who had the ability to give Jesus what the Father had promised to give his Son. "Ask me, and I will make the nations your inheritance, the ends of the earth your possession" (Ps. 2:8). In the end, the Father and the Devil offered Jesus the same thing, kingship, but by different paths. The Devil offered Jesus

Mount Hermon was the setting for Jesus's third temptation that took place on a "very high mountain."

kingship without the cross so long as Jesus would recognize him as a legitimate object of worship.

This was a violation of the very first commandment and Jesus would have nothing to do with it. Alluding to the language of Deuteronomy 6:13, he asserted that God alone was a legitimate object of worship. The temptation comes to a quick close. The Devil would not be worshipped. And there would be no kingship without the cross.

For Further Reference: **Deuteronomy 5:7; 6:13; Psalm 2:7–8; Philippians 2:9–11; Hebrews 4:15**

FIRST MIRACLE AT CANA

John 2:1–11

"And his disciples believed in him." (John 2:11)

▶ WHO & WHERE
Jesus, the disciples, Cana in Galilee

▶ WHAT IS THIS TEXT TALKING ABOUT?
The credibility of Jesus

▶ WHAT DOES THIS TEXT TEACH?
Jesus established his credibility by turning water into wine.

The host at the wedding in Cana had a problem. But Jesus had an even bigger problem. His first miracle solved both.

This story takes us to Cana in Galilee (Khirbet Kana, 8.5 miles [13.7 kilometers] north of Nazareth). John emphasizes the location by mentioning

it in both the first and last verses of this short story. Cana was Nathanael's
hometown (John 21:2). And his voice helps us understand that Jesus had a
credibility problem because he was from Galilee (John 1:46).

Where did this come from? It likely was a product of Galileans, like
Nathanael, internalizing the view Judeans had of Galileans. Judeans in the
south of Israel tended to view Galileans who lived in the north as rural,
unsophisticated, and spiritually suspect. The Judean hubris was fueled by
the fact that their region hosted the founding stories of the faith, particularly
those associated with Abraham's family in places like Hebron and Beersheba.
Judeans had the Temple in Jerusalem. And what is more, they knew that
the Messiah would be born in Bethlehem of Judea (Mic. 5:2). By contrast,
Galilee had been part of the northern kingdom of Israel. This kingdom had a
checkered past whose Old Testament stories are filled with spiritual failings.
This led Judeans to question the spiritual integrity of Galileans. And it led
Galileans like Nathanael to project this negative stereotype on themselves.
This meant Jesus of Nazareth, a Galilean, had a credibility problem.

That is why Jesus did his first miracle in Cana of Galilee. During a
weeklong wedding celebration, the host of the party faced an embarrass-
ing dilemma. Custom dictated that he provide food and beverages for the
guests through the week. But the wine had run out. Jesus responded with a
miracle. This was not a public miracle, performed in front of all the guests,
for his time had not yet come (John 2:4; compare with John 17:1). Rather,
he walked into a small room with the servants and at least some of his disciples. There he turned the water in six, large stone jars into exceptional wine.

The miracle solved two problems. The reputation of the host was saved.
But more importantly, this miracle accomplished what Jesus intended for his
disciples. He needed to have their confidence despite his Galilean heritage.
This miracle was for them. John drives the point home by saving it for last:
"and his disciples believed in him" (John 2:11).

For Further Reference: Exodus 14:31; John 1:44–46; 7:52; 1 Corinthians 1:18

DISCUSSION WITH NICODEMUS

John 3:1–21

"For God so loved the world that he gave his one and only Son, that whoever believes in him shall not perish but have eternal life. For God did not send his Son into the world to condemn the world, but to save the world through him." (John 3:16–17)

▶ WHO & WHERE
Jesus, Nicodemus, Jerusalem

▶ WHAT IS THIS TEXT TALKING ABOUT?
The purpose of Jesus's coming

▶ WHAT DOES THIS TEXT TEACH?
Jesus came to save a perishing world.

What we see is often what we expect to see. That created a problem for Nicodemus because Jesus was not what Nicodemus expected. He himself was a well-educated, influential person—a Pharisee and member of the Jewish ruling council. This made him unique. However, Jesus spent most of his time among those who lived at the other end of the social ladder. But the heady conversation with Nicodemus allowed Jesus to do something particularly important, which was to highlight the purpose he had come to earth.

Nicodemus had expectations of how the conversation with Jesus would go. Pharisees like Nicodemus put a high premium on living a righteous life. They invested copious amounts of time defining righteous living, policing those with whom they interacted, and correcting those who strayed. For Nicodemus, this was what the kingdom of God was about. He

This nineteenth-century print depicts the significant meeting between Jesus and Nicodemus.

expected Jesus to share that view and make that his life's purpose.

Jesus and John join forces to correct this misunderstanding. Jesus emphasized that the kingdom was about what God did in people rather than what people could do to gain entry. To be in the kingdom required rebirth. Unthinkable! Mortals cannot experience physical birth more than once. Spiritual rebirth was even more impossible. But that was the pathway into the kingdom, rebirth through water and the Spirit.

John picks up where Jesus left off, highlighting the role Jesus plays in spiritual rebirth. The very purpose of his coming was not to become another religious teacher condemning those who failed to live according to the Pharisees' code of conduct. This would not open the door to the kingdom of God. John summarizes the purpose of Jesus's coming in twenty-six memorable words: "For God so loved the world that he gave his one and only Son, that whoever believes in him shall not perish but have eternal life" (John 3:16). Belief in Jesus was the rebirth that opened the door of the kingdom.

This is not what Nicodemus expected, but it is what he and we most need to know. Salvation is a gift from God made possible by Jesus.

For Further Reference: Exodus 34:5–7; Ezekiel 36:25–27; Romans 6:23; Titus 3:5; 1 Peter 1:23; 1 John 1:7

JOHN THE BAPTIST REMAINS ON MISSION

John 3:22–36

"He must become greater; I must become less." (John 3:30)

> ## WHO & WHERE

Jesus, John the Baptist, Aenon

> ## WHAT IS THIS TEXT TALKING ABOUT?

The mission of John the Baptist

> ## WHAT DOES THIS TEXT TEACH?

John the Baptist resisted the temptation to compete with Jesus.

It is nice to be popular. But popularity can lead to pride. And pride can lead to inappropriate competition. John the Baptist faced this temptation as his followers expressed concern about the risk Jesus posed to John's popularity. Would John succumb to temptation and abandon his mission?

John had moved north. He had been baptizing and teaching at Bethany just a few miles north of the Dead Sea (John 1:28). Now we find him at Aenon near Salim. Its exact location is debated. But both the label Aenon (place of springs) and its characterization as a place with "plenty of water" support the early church's identification of this site in the Jordan River valley about forty-two miles north of the Dead Sea. This means that for the moment, John had left behind the rural Judean countryside in which he had been teaching.

Jesus also had changed locations. He had left the city of Jerusalem and entered the rural setting in which John had been working. Here Jesus began teaching, his disciples were baptizing (see John 4:2), and the crowds kept growing. John's followers saw this as a problem. Everyone in Judea was now giving attention to Jesus rather than to their beloved teacher, John. They were concerned about John's popularity and legacy.

How would John respond? He resisted the pride-fueled temptation that could have sent him south to reclaim the crowds and the attention now diverted to Jesus. Instead, John repeatedly expressed the distinct role given to him. He was not the Messiah but the one sent ahead of the Messiah (John 3:28). He was not the groom but the friend or best man of the groom (v. 29). He was not from heaven but earth (v. 31). Eternity did not hinge on him but on faith in Jesus (v. 36). What is more, he gladly accepted his role in the story of salvation. John's joy was complete. "He must become greater; I must become less" (v. 30).

This is a powerful moment. If John had not remained in his lane, the ensuing competition with Jesus would have caused great confusion and harm. His life is a wonderful lesson of what it means to shun the pride fueled by popularity and humbly remain on mission.

For Further Reference: Psalm 10:4; Proverbs 8:13; Isaiah 40:3–5; Daniel 4:37; Malachi 3:1; 4:5; Luke 1:76–80; 1 John 2:16

JESUS HEALS THE SON OF A ROYAL OFFICIAL

John 4:43–54

"So he and his whole household believed." (John 4:53)

▶ WHO & WHERE

Jesus, a royal official, Capernaum

▶ WHAT IS THIS TEXT TALKING ABOUT?

The healing of a royal official's child

▶ WHAT DOES THIS TEXT TEACH?

This miracle brought an influential family in Capernaum to faith in Jesus.

We can feel his desperation. A breathless royal official had dashed from Capernaum to Cana to beg Jesus for his help. His child back in Capernaum was near death. Of all the things on his mind at this moment, geography was not one of them. But John uses the healing of the official's son to prepare us for the consequential move Jesus made to Capernaum where he established his base of operations.

Let's start with this question. Where might we expect Jesus to establish the base for his ministry? Judea makes sense. It hosted many of the foundation stories of the Old Testament—stories about Abraham, Sarah, Jacob, and David. What is more, Jerusalem was Israel's religious center. Although Jesus spent the final climactic moments of his life there, it was not his base for ministry. Instead, his stories fill the mountains and lake basin of Galilee where "the Galileans welcomed him" (John 4:45).

But where in Galilee? Nazareth makes sense, the place he called home for the first decades of his life. But Nazareth was isolated and struggled to accept him (Matt. 13:57). How about Cana? This was where Jesus did his first miracle. And unlike Nazareth, it was located along a road system that connected the coast with the Sea of Galilee. In the end, neither Nazareth nor Cana would do. Jesus established his base of operations in Capernaum, a place that become known as his home (Matt. 4:13; 9:1; Mark 2:1).

And that brings us back to this miracle. The royal official coming to Jesus was a man of power and influence. But he was powerless to help his dying child. He had come to Jesus believing he could help. Jesus sent him back with these words, "Go, . . . your son will live" (John 4:50). As the man traveled home, he received word that his son began to improve at the very hour Jesus had spoken these reassuring words.

What we hear next is even more significant. "So he and his whole household believed" (v. 53). Although we don't know their names, this influential household became the nucleus Jesus could count on when he established his base of ministry in Capernaum.

For Further Reference: Matthew 4:13, 23; Mark 1:36–39; 3:7

THE BETHESDA POOLS AND THE AUTHORITY OF JESUS

John 5:1–47

"He was even calling God his own Father, making himself equal with God." (John 5:18)

▶ **WHO & WHERE**

Jesus, Bethesda Pools in Jerusalem

▶ **WHAT IS THIS TEXT TALKING ABOUT?**

The authority of Jesus

▶ **WHAT DOES THIS TEXT TEACH?**

The authority of Jesus is equal to the authority of the Father.

In this chapter, John brings us to a specific location in Jerusalem that prompts an extended conversation about Jesus's authority.

These Jerusalem exchanges take place at the Bethesda Pools. This was part of the city's water collection system designed to capture runoff water

The Bethesda Pools in Jerusalem collected surface runoff water for public use. Here, Jesus healed a man unable to walk for thirty-eight years.

for Jerusalem's residents. It went through several stages of development between the eighth century BC and the first century AD. By the time of Jesus, it consisted of two pools divided from one another by a dam. Four covered porches surrounded the pools and a fifth went down the middle of the dam.

This location is significant to the chapter's message in two ways. First, it brings us into the orbit of the Temple. The Bethesda Pools are just north of the Temple complex, a place not only used for worship but considered the educational center of Judaism. Here the senior scholars of the Jewish world taught the next generation of rabbis and authorized them to teach. When Jesus healed the man who had been unable to walk for thirty-eight years, it was bound to invite comparison between the credentials he carried and those granted by the teachers at the Temple.

Second, popular superstition linked the Bethesda Pools with miraculous healing. In the years to come, the pools would be used by the followers of the pagan god of healing, Asclepius. But the superstitious belief in the healing powers of the pools was alive and well at the time of Jesus. When Jesus healed the disabled man at this spot, it linked him to those superstitious beliefs. Yet another reason for the teachers at the Temple to question his judgment. You can sense their animus when you hear them upbraiding the healed man for carrying his mat on the Sabbath!

If the authority of Jesus did not come from the Temple schools, where did it come from? Jesus pointed to three pieces of evidence that indicated that his authority was greater than that of the Temple teachers no matter what they thought of him. First, he urged his listeners to consider all his works including those to come, namely, the raising of the dead and final judgment (John 5:28–29). Second, he pointed them to the testimony of John the Baptist (vv. 33–34). And third, he directed them to his Father's own words that spoke of the Son's equality with the Father recorded in their Bible (vv. 36–39).

For Further Reference: **Psalm 2:1–7; Daniel 7:13–14; Hebrews 1:1–2; 1 John 5:9**

CHAPTER 3

Jesus's Ministry in Galilee

JESUS'S MOVE FROM NAZARETH TO CAPERNAUM

Matthew 4:12–17

"Leaving Nazareth, he went and lived in Capernaum."
(Matthew 4:13)

▶ **WHO & WHERE**

Jesus, Nazareth, Capernaum

▶ **WHAT IS THIS TEXT TALKING ABOUT?**

Jesus's move from Nazareth to Capernaum

▶ **WHAT DOES THIS TEXT TEACH?**

Jesus's move from Nazareth to Capernaum fulfilled Old Testament prophecy and positioned his ministry for international impact.

The Gospels do not mention all of Jesus's location changes, only those that play a significant role in his story. One of the most important is the shift from his childhood home to a place that became "his own town" (Matt. 9:1), the move from Nazareth to Capernaum.

Nazareth and Capernaum are vastly different places. Nazareth sat on the top of a 1,110-foot (338-meter) ridge, nestled into the bottom of a valley on top of that ridge. Capernaum was situated on a sprawling plain beside the Sea of Galilee. This difference in topography impacted each one's growth. Nazareth could not outgrow its valley, so it remained a small village of three hundred to four hundred residents. Capernaum could stretch out and became a town four times larger. Nazareth's simple economy was based on subsistence farming. Capernaum had a diverse economy that included

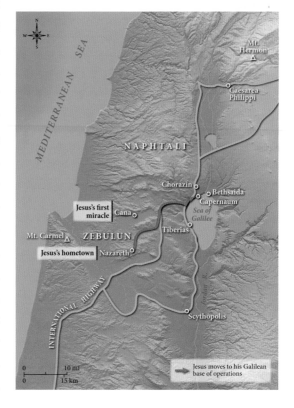

farming, fishing, basalt tool making, as well as the support and taxation of international trade. Nazareth's topography favored isolation, exactly the kind of place that gave observant Jewish families the isolation from Greco-Roman culture they desired. By contrast, Capernaum was fully engaged with the thoughts and culture of the larger world. And finally, Nazareth was part of the tribal territory of Zebulun, while Capernaum was in the tribal territory of Naphtali.

So how was Jesus's ministry advantaged by this shift in location? Matthew begins by highlighting the way in which the shift between tribal territories fulfilled Old Testament prophecy about the Messiah (Isa. 9:1–2). About 750 years before the time of Jesus, the prophet Isaiah indicated that these two tribal territories would have two common experiences. The first was occurring as Isaiah wrote. Zebulun and Naphtali felt the full force of the Assyrian invasion under Tiglath-pileser III whose war machine ravaged the landscape. Isaiah highlights the horror by speaking of the "darkness" of this era when these tribal territories became "Galilee of the Gentiles." But Isaiah also looked ahead to a time when Zebulun and Naphtali would experience a reversal, when "darkness" gave way to "light," the time when the Messiah honored both with his presence. Nazareth is in Zebulun, so the first half of the reversal in fortune happened as Jesus spent his early years in Nazareth. The second was fulfilled when Jesus left Nazareth and moved to Capernaum in Naphtali.

What Matthew does not formally mention but the geography clearly implies is also important. As Jesus moved from the isolation of Nazareth to the international exposure offered by Capernaum, he positioned all that he said and did before the larger world.

For Further Reference: **Genesis 12:3; Isaiah 9:1–2; 60:1–3; John 3:16**

JESUS CALLS
THE FIRST DISCIPLES

**Matthew 4:18–22; 9:9–13; Mark 1:14–20; 2:13–17;
Luke 5:1–11, 27–32; John 1:35–42**

"For I have not come to call the righteous, but sinners."
(Matthew 9:13)

▶ WHO & WHERE
Jesus, Andrew, Peter, James, John, Matthew, Sea of Galilee

▶ WHAT IS THIS TEXT TALKING ABOUT?
The calling of Jesus's first disciples

▶ WHAT DOES THIS TEXT TEACH?
The first disciples of Jesus characterize the core followers of Jesus as ordinary people, broken by sin, and seeking a Savior.

This collection of stories, that detail the calling of Jesus's first disciples, helps us understand the kind of people who flocked to Jesus.

The first thing that stands out is the ordinary circumstances in which we meet them. Peter and Andrew were using cast nets on the shore of the Sea of Galilee. These were circular nets, 18 to 25 feet (5.5 to 7.6 meters) in diameter with stones attached to the perimeter. When the fishermen saw a school of fish in the shallows, they twirled the net above their heads until it had opened to its full diameter and then slung it over the fish to trap them beneath it.

James and John were cleaning their trammel nets on the lakeshore. The trammel net was a multilayer, rectangular net with floats on the top and weights on the bottom. It was deployed from a boat at night, surrounding a school of fish in the deeper water. When the disturbed fish attempted to flee, they become entangled in the multiple layers of the net that surrounded them.

Jesus met Matthew while he was sitting at his tax collection station. Rome hired locals to collect taxes whether from those fishing on the lake or from those traveling on the International Highway. In either case, the tax collectors were permitted to overcharge and keep the extra as a commission.

Modern wooden boat sailing on the Sea of Galilee. The lakeshore was home to many of Jesus's disciples.

In sum, these were ordinary people. But what is more, they were people looking for more from life than they had found. We see it as Andrew,
a student of John the Baptist, quickly leaves John to follow Jesus and then
excitedly tells Peter that he has found the Savior (John 1:35–42). We see
it in Peter. After Jesus delivered a miraculous catch of fish in his trammel
net, Peter exclaimed, "Go away from me, Lord; I am a sinful man!" (Luke
5:8). And we see it at the dinner party hastily arranged by Matthew. As
Jesus sat among other tax collectors and sinners, the Pharisees criticized
him for the company he kept. Jesus replied, "It is not the healthy who need
a doctor, but the sick. . . . For I have not come to call the righteous, but
sinners" (Matt. 9:12–13). In the call of these first disciples, we see the kind
of people who came to follow Jesus in Galilee. They were ordinary people,
broken by their sin, and searching for a Savior.

For Further Reference: **Psalms 32:1–11; 51:5; Isaiah 6:5; Romans 3:10–22**

JESUS'S MINISTRY IN CAPERNAUM

Matthew 8:14–17; Mark 1:21–34; Luke 4:31–41

"The people were amazed at his teaching, because he taught them as one who had authority, not as the teachers of the law."
(Mark 1:22)

▶ WHO & WHERE

Jesus, Capernaum

▶ WHAT IS THIS TEXT TALKING ABOUT?

Jesus's ministry in Capernaum

▶ WHAT DOES THIS TEXT TEACH?

Jesus's teaching and healing miracles in Capernaum established his authority as a Jewish teacher and fulfilled Old Testament prophecy about the Messiah.

Capernaum is one of my favorite places to sit and reflect. Here, it is easier to imagine rubbing shoulders with Jesus as I sit in the pleasant church compound beside the Sea of Galilee.

I suspect that is because we can be confident that we are precisely in the places Jesus was. The gospel writers mention two specific locations in Capernaum that archaeology has certified. The first is the home of Peter (Matt. 8:14). Peter and his extended family shared a living compound in Capernaum. This was where Jesus healed Peter's mother-in-law, who was suffering from a severe fever, and where he likely spent the night while in town. Late in the first century AD, this house became a house church linked to Peter by the graffiti scribed in the walls by

its first visitors. Ever since that
time, a church building has hov-
ered above the spot. The second
location mentioned is the synagogue. A synagogue was a public
building used by the Jews for education and worship. In Capernaum today, the remains of a
fourth- or fith-century-AD synagogue reside over the foundation
of the very building visited by
Jesus (Mark 1:21).

This later-era synagogue was built on the foundation of
the first-century synagogue, the building in which Jesus
regularly taught while in Capernaum.

The Gospels focus on two things Jesus did here. The first is his teaching. The locals noted that he spoke as one with "authority." To understand
that, we need to know something about the way Jewish teachers of this
era were credentialed. A student typically engaged in a multiyear course
of study mastering the methods for interpreting the Bible and the traditional interpretations handed down by the teachers of the law. Only after
demonstrating that mastery was someone authorized to teach. Jesus was
the exception. When he taught, his listeners celebrated the lessons, noting
that they were even better than the teaching of those credentialed in the
usual way (Mark 1:22, 27).

The Gospels also call attention to the healing miracles of Jesus. He
entered a world unlike the one he had created—a world where sickness
and demonic possession damaged the lives of families. So, Jesus repeatedly
used his unique power to restore those who were ill or demon-possessed.
In doing so, he not only validated the authority of his teaching but also
fulfilled Old Testament prophecy about the Messiah (Matt. 8:17).

For Further Reference: **Numbers 27:20; Deuteronomy 1:15; Psalm 103:1–3;
Acts 2:22**

THE GEOGRAPHIC REACH OF JESUS'S GALILEAN MINISTRY

Matthew 4:23–35; Mark 1:35–39; 3:7–12

"Everyone is looking for you!" (Mark 1:37)

▶ **WHO & WHERE**

Jesus, Galilee

▶ **WHAT IS THIS TEXT TALKING ABOUT?**

The geographic reach of Jesus's Galilean ministry

▶ **WHAT DOES THIS TEXT TEACH?**

People came to Jesus from the regions all around Galilee.

Day after day, Jesus did the same things. What changed was the audience. We expect Galileans. If we plot the stories in the Gospels on a map, we find most of Jesus's earthly ministry took place in the Roman district of Galilee. But here we see that the reach of Jesus's Galilean ministry was much broader than just Galilee.

Matthew and Mark offer lists that together present a picture that extends to eight different regions. Of course, Galilee is on the list. But people also came to Jesus from Syria. This is likely a designation for the area north of the Sea of Galilee. Others came to Jesus from the district of Judea and its primary city, Jerusalem. Followers likewise came to Jesus from the Decapolis. This designation points us to those living east of the Sea of Galilee as well as those living on either side of the Jordan River south of the Sea of Galilee. Still others came to Jesus from "the region across the Jordan" (Matt. 4:25). This is likely the district of Perea that extended

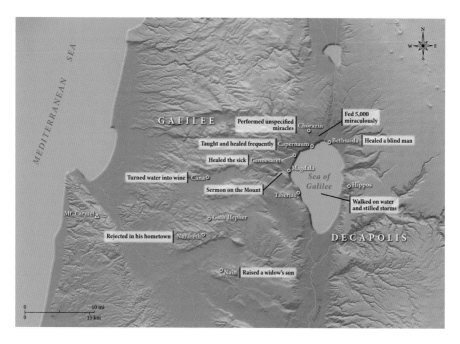

southward from the Decapolis along the eastern side of the Jordan River and the Dead Sea. Mark adds two more regions to the list. The area around Tyre and Sidon takes us to the old haunts of Jezebel in Phoenicia north of the Promised Land. Finally, the label Idumea points us to the portion of the Promised Land from Hebron south that had been overrun by the Edomites (Idumeans) when God's chosen people went into exile in Babylon.

These lists leave us with two impressions. First, the sheer number of places in the list startles us. Jesus, the man from the tiny backwater village of Nazareth, was attracting people from everywhere. A map visually asserts what the disciples said audibly. "Everyone is looking for you!" (Mark 1:37). Second, the list betrays the cultural diversity of those coming to Jesus. Jews from Jerusalem/Judea tended to look down on Galileans as rural, simple, and spiritually compromised. But they came to Galilee to be with Jesus. Gentiles with an affection for all things pagan came to Jesus from as far away as Phoenicia and the Decapolis because the gods whom the people worshipped in those places did not have what Jesus offered.

The geography tells the story. Jesus was building a geographically and culturally diverse kingdom in Galilee.

For Further Reference: Isaiah 42:6–7; Mark 3:20; John 3:16; Colossians 1:6; 1 Timothy 1:15

LIFE LESSONS WITH A COMMANDING VIEW

Matthew 5:1–7:29; Mark 3:13–19; Luke 6:12–49; 11:1–13; 12:22–34

"[Jesus] went up on a mountainside and sat down. His disciples came to him, and he began to teach them." (Matthew 5:1–2)

▶ **WHO & WHERE**

Jesus, disciples, Mount Arbel

▶ **WHAT IS THIS TEXT TALKING ABOUT?**

The blessed life

▶ **WHAT DOES THIS TEXT TEACH?**

We will be blessed when we see ourselves and our lives as God does.

Life! We have our good days, and we have our bad days. But all our days will be better if we come to see ourselves as God does. The wide-ranging discourse that Matthew treats as a whole (and other gospel writers break out and separate in their books) helps us do just that. Both its contents and the location of its delivery are unique.

We sense the difference in content when we read through the discourse recorded by Matthew in one sitting. This lecture is densely packed with advanced information. The primary audience was not the usual crowd that gathered around Jesus but the twelve disciples (Matt. 5:1; Mark 3:13–19; Luke 6:20). Jesus often cautioned these men about saying too much when he sent them out among the people. "As you go, proclaim this message: 'The kingdom of heaven has come near'" (Matt. 10:7). But the day would come when they were to teach "everything" they had learned (Matt. 28:20). Jesus used this moment on the mountain to upload the profound insights they were to share with others when the time was right.

The second thing that is unique is the location of the lecture commonly known as the Sermon on the Mount. While most of Jesus's instruction took place along the shoreline of the Sea of Galilee, this was mountaintop instruction (Matt. 5:1; 8:1; Luke 6:12). The traditional location for the lesson is found just above the western shore of the Sea of Galilee on the modest rise in the terrain known as Mount Eremos where we find the modern Chapel of the Beatitudes. A better candidate is Mount Arbel, a prominent mountain that rises abruptly from the lakeshore and offers a commanding view of the lake basin 1,245 feet (380 meters) below. If I am correct in assuming that Luke is presenting the same event as Matthew, then this is the only mountain near Capernaum whose summit flows into a high plateau that conforms to Luke's other description of the location as a plateau or level place (Luke 6:17).

Why make such a big deal of the setting? Jesus used the view to make the lesson more vivid and memorable. In the Beatitudes when Jesus spoke of people who were blessed, he was not asking the disciples to imagine those who were poor in spirit, mourning, or meek. They were in view below them. And as Jesus turned their eyes around the horizon line, he offered a series of spiritual insights that grew from the things in view. Just below them was Magdala, a town in which salt was used to process and preserve fish. Across the lake was Hippos, a major city set on a high hill that was brilliantly lighted at night. Flowers filled the fields and birds the air. They looked down on wide and narrow roads as well as homes built on solid rock ledges that are set in contrast to the alluvial soils of the valley.

Both content and location made this lecture of Jesus unique. If we leave the plain and hike to the summit, we too can have the experience that allows us to see ourselves the way God does. We are blessed.

For Further Reference: Psalm 1; Isaiah 61:1–3; 2 Corinthians 9:8; Ephesians 1:3; Hebrews 1:1–2; James 1:25

JESUS HEALED A MAN AFFLICTED WITH LEPROSY

Matthew 8:1–4; Mark 1:40–45; Luke 5:12–16

"As a result, Jesus could no longer enter a town openly but stayed outside in lonely places. Yet the people still came to him from everywhere." (Mark 1:45)

▶ **WHO & WHERE**

Jesus, Sea of Galilee basin

▶ **WHAT IS THIS TEXT TALKING ABOUT?**

The healing of a man afflicted with leprosy

▶ **WHAT DOES THIS TEXT TEACH?**

The news of this miracle forced Jesus to restrict the time he spent in the towns of Galilee and move into rural settings.

All of Jesus's healing miracles demonstrate his compassion for the suffering and validate the message he came to share. But how is this miracle unique? It changed the spaces in which Jesus interacted with those who came to him.

Just a few verses earlier, we find those with various maladies coming to Jesus in the town of Capernaum where he was staying (Mark 1:32–34; Luke 4:38–41). Following his time on the mountain (Matt. 8:1), Jesus returned to "one of the towns" (Luke 5:12). At first, Jesus primarily went to where the people were in small towns and villages around the Sea of Galilee.

This story changed that. A man afflicted with leprosy approached Jesus. The Gospels use this term for a variety of skin disorders. Jews of Jesus's day like this man followed the directions given in the Old Testament law. When the skin showed signs of a disease, they went to the priest for evaluation. In some cases, the priest required that they isolate themselves from others while the disorder manifested itself. If their condition improved, they could return to the priest and get the all-clear to return to society (Lev. 13:1–14:32). The man who approached Jesus had a persistent disorder that left him both physically uncomfortable and socially ostracized. Jesus quickly healed him of the disease and then instructed him to seek the all-clear from the priest. He also ordered him to keep the matter to himself.

He did not. And this changed the places Jesus could publicly minister. As expected, the news of the miracle increased the number of people coming to Jesus for healing. The sheer number of those in need increased so dramatically that Jesus could no longer meet them in towns. The limited size of the towns, the modest public space available for a gathering, as well as the limited access to food and water resources caused Jesus to change ministry location. "As a result, Jesus could no longer enter a town openly but stayed outside in lonely places" (Mark 1:45).

For Further Reference: **Leviticus 13:1–14:32; 2 Kings 5:1–19**

JESUS COMMENDS THE CENTURION AT CAPERNAUM

Matthew 8:5–13; Luke 7:1–10

"Lord, I do not deserve to have you come under my roof. But just say the word, and my servant will be healed." (Matthew 8:8)

▶ WHO & WHERE
Jesus, Centurion at Capernaum

▶ WHAT IS THIS TEXT TALKING ABOUT?
Seeking help from Jesus

▶ WHAT DOES THIS TEXT TEACH?
The best way to seek Jesus's help is with humble faith.

Many who approached Jesus for help were ordinary people who lacked power or influence. The centurion at Capernaum was different.

Here is what we know about him. As a centurion, he was an army officer who commanded up to one hundred soldiers. Since Capernaum was a tax and tariff collection station, he likely was responsible for enforcing compliance. This took a special set of skills navigating between locals, his soldiers, tax collectors, and international merchants. He was well paid for his efforts, up to fifteen times that of an ordinary solider. To get the job done, he counted on the respect his position and word carried. "I tell this one, 'Go,' and he goes; and that one, 'Come,' and he comes. I say to my servant, 'Do this,' and he does it" (Matt. 8:9). What's unique is that this centurion was a believer. Although he had not converted to Judaism, he was a God-fearer, someone attracted to the Jewish belief system. He put

The centurion whose servant Jesus healed lived in one of these homes in Capernaum.

his faith into action, building the synagogue in Capernaum and winning the support of the town elders (Luke 7:3–5).

In this story, he is also a man with a problem. His servant was paralyzed and gravely ill. Jesus lived in his town, so the centurion knew of him and his ability to bring miraculous healing. But this man, unlike others, had the authority to compel Jesus's actions. The centurion could have ordered Jesus to come to his home and heal his servant. If Jesus failed to comply, he would do what he normally did: send a contingent of soldiers to force compliance. Or he could have leaned on his influence in the Jewish community of Capernaum. He had done so much for them, was it not time for them to do something for him?

As it turned out, he needed to pull no strings. Jesus was ready to come to his home. The centurion replied, "Lord, I do not deserve to have you come under my roof. But just say the word, and my servant will be healed" (Matt. 8:8). And there it was—the kind of humble faith Jesus so rarely saw among his own people, modeling for us how to humbly seek help from Jesus.

For Further Reference: **Psalm 107:20; Isaiah 25:6–9; 65:13–14; Acts 10:27–29; Hebrews 11:1**

THE COST OF FOLLOWING JESUS

Matthew 8:18–22; Luke 9:57–62

"No one who puts a hand to the plow and looks back is fit for
service in the kingdom of God." (Luke 9:62)

▶ **WHO & WHERE**

Jesus, Galilee

▶ **WHAT IS THIS TEXT TALKING ABOUT?**

Choosing to follow Jesus

▶ **WHAT DOES THIS TEXT TEACH?**

Consider the personal cost before making the commitment to
follow Jesus.

We can feel the excitement of the three individuals we meet in this
story. Jesus was special. They knew it and they were eager to spend
all day, every day with him. Jesus responded to each with a word of caution. Consider the cost before making the commitment.

In the first case, the cost is to one's personal comfort. A well-educated
person like the teacher of the law had a home to live in and a reliable food
plan. Jesus did not. In fact, he contrasted his situation with members of the
animal kingdom. Birds have nests to which they return daily. Jesus did not
have such a home. Foxes have holes. The red fox of Galilee dug multiple
holes in its territory. One served as its primary living space, while the others were for food storage. This was part of its food security plan. If one or
more of the holes was discovered and the food robbed, there were others
where food remained. Jesus did not plant farm fields, raise livestock, or
store food for the future. He relied upon the charity of others. The cost of
following Jesus included the cost to one's personal well-being.

In the second case, Jesus urged a man to follow him. The man asked for a delay so that he could bury his father. This was a son's job in the culture of the Jews living in Galilee, but there is a problem in what he says. It is unlikely his father had died, otherwise he would have been burying him. Death and burial occurred on the same day in this culture, and the son's responsibility for care of the remains would continue for more than a year. The long delay proposed was not going to work. The cost of following Jesus could include a countercultural cost to personal relationships.

A third person announced his willingness to follow Jesus but asked for the opportunity to say goodbye to family. In the request, Jesus apparently saw a lack of single-minded focus. He illustrates the point by speaking about the intense attention required to operate a scratch plow. The operator had to divide his focus between controlling the animal pulling the plow, the angle at which the plow was held, and the amount of pressure placed on the tool to keep it engaged with the soil. The cost of following Jesus included the same single-minded focus.

For Further Reference: 1 Kings 19:19–21; Psalm 37:5–6; Proverbs 16:3; 20:25

THE UNIQUE
AUTHORITY OF JESUS

Matthew 9:1–8; Mark 2:1–12; Luke 5:17–26

"But I want you to know that the Son of Man has authority on earth to forgive sins." (Mark 2:10)

▶ WHO & WHERE

Jesus, paralyzed man, Jerusalem authorities, Capernaum

▷ **WHAT IS THIS TEXT TALKING ABOUT?**
The authority of Jesus

▷ **WHAT DOES THIS TEXT TEACH?**
The authority of Jesus exceeds all mortal authority, even to the
point of forgiving sins.

This was a high-stakes meeting. Religious authorities from Jerusalem had come to Capernaum to correct the behavior of Jesus. Their
schools credentialed those who were "authorized" to interpret Scripture
and to teach. Jesus was operating outside the system. But during the meeting, Jesus doubled down, claiming an authority even greater than theirs.

The meeting was suddenly interrupted as beams of sunlight pierced the
darkness of the dingy room and pieces of the roof fell to the floor. Let's clarify
the setting. They were meeting in a small room of a larger, extended-family
living compound. This compound consisted of a courtyard used for cooking and socializing and a set of smaller rooms that encircled the courtyard
which allowed private time for each nuclear family. Public interest in the
meeting meant the entire living complex was packed, making it impossible
for the friends of the disabled man to get him to Jesus other than by digging
through the roof. The falling dust was soon replaced by the mat of the paralyzed man, which his friends lowered right into the heart of this highly charged meeting.

This style of living compound was the setting for the high-stakes meeting during which Jesus healed a paralyzed man.

Jesus immediately ad-
dressed the man's greatest
problem. "Son, your sins
are forgiven" (Mark 2:5). In
the popular mind of many
first-century Jews, disabil-
ity was linked to sin (John 9:2), imposing an unwarranted guilt on all
those with disabilities. Jesus began there. But in speaking these words of

forgiveness, he raised the stakes of the meeting another notch. Typically, the declaration of forgiveness was given to sinners in Jerusalem by a priest after sacrifice was made. Religious scholars like those in the room with Jesus would never think to speak in this way. Jesus did. And in doing so, he was claiming a level of authority that exceeded theirs.

Jesus did not stop there. The miracle of forgiveness was unseen. "But I want you to know that the Son of Man has authority on earth to forgive sins" (Mark 2:10). Jesus then instructed the disabled man to pick up his mat and walk out. Audible gasps spread through the crowd as they parted to allow the man who had entered through the roof to walk out through the courtyard. And a powerful lesson on Jesus's authority accompanied him.

For Further Reference: Psalm 103:2–3; Isaiah 33:24; 43:25; Jeremiah 31:34; Micah 7:18

THE QUESTION ABOUT FASTING

Matthew 9:14–17; Mark 2:18–22; Luke 5:33–39

"How is it that we and the Pharisees fast often, but your disciples do not fast?" (Matthew 9:14)

▶ **WHO & WHERE**

Jesus, disciples of John the Baptist, Capernaum area

▶ **WHAT IS THIS TEXT TALKING ABOUT?**

Familiar religious practices

▶ **WHAT DOES THIS TEXT TEACH?**

Old and familiar religious practices had to adjust to the era of Jesus's coming.

Jesus had not come to change everything, nor had he come to leave everything the same. Old and familiar practices were bound to change, including fasting.

Fasting was the intentional abstaining from food and drink during the daylight hours. It was only required on the Day of Atonement (Lev. 23:26–32) but was widely practiced at other times as well. Fasting highlighted mortal vulnerability and focused the mind on the Lord's provision. So, people fasted when grieving (2 Sam. 1:12), when praying about significant changes in life (Ezra 8:21), and when seeking assurance of forgiveness (Joel 1:13–15). Jesus fasted prior to engaging in public ministry (Matt. 4:2), and the early church followed suit (Acts 13:2–3).

In this passage, Jesus uses three metaphors to comment on not only fasting but all familiar religious practices. His disciples did not fast on a schedule like the Pharisees or John's disciples. There was a reason for that. This was a special era when God himself walked among mortals. This era was more like a wedding than a funeral, so why would they fast, treating it as something it was not? Some practices had to change.

Jesus expands the conversation beyond fasting to include all familiar religious practices. His listeners could not take something they had always done and assume it would fit seamlessly into this new era. That would be like patching an old garment with a new patch. Because the old and new material would shrink at different rates, the old garment would be damaged again when washed and dried. The old garment had to be discarded not repaired. The same was true of an old, cracked wineskin. Wineskins were containers made from animal skins whose openings were sewn shut. Small holes were strategically placed in the skin to allow fermentation gases to escape while keeping the fluid within. When a wineskin had become old, it lost the elasticity it needed and would rupture during the fermentation process. Jesus's point? Some religious practices needed to be discarded, like a damaged garment or old wine skin, because they simply did not transition into the New Testament era.

For Further Reference: Leviticus 23:26–32; Isaiah 58:1–14; Acts 13:2–3; 1 Corinthians 11:25

BEYOND HOPE, BUT NOT HELP

Matthew 9:18–26; Mark 5:21–43; Luke 8:40–56

"Don't be afraid; just believe." (Mark 5:36)

▶ WHO & WHERE

Jesus, woman with a bleeding disorder, Jairus, Capernaum

▶ WHAT IS THIS TEXT TALKING ABOUT?

Hopeless circumstances

▶ WHAT DOES THIS TEXT TEACH?

Jesus has the power to help those facing hopeless circumstances.

Either of these two stories of Jesus raising Jairus's daughter or healing the bleeding woman is powerful on its own. Together, they join to demonstrate that even people who have come to the horizon of human hope can be helped by the power of Jesus.

These are heart-wrenching stories. First, we meet a nameless woman afflicted with a bleeding disorder that had plagued her for twelve years. Her disorder left her in a perpetual state of ritual impurity (Lev. 15:25–30) and so she was a social outcast. She had exhausted her financial resources seeking a cure. Now impoverished and in persistent pain, she approached Jesus for help. Her feelings of hopelessness drove her to the ground. She approached Jesus from behind, crawling among the legs of the crowd

This mural in the Encounter Chapel at Duc in Altum in Migdal, Israel, captures the hand of the woman seeking healing as she reached for the hem of Jesus's garment.

pressing around Jesus. Without speaking a word, she reached as far as she could to briefly touch the hem of Jesus's garment.

The second person we meet is given a name and celebrated as a person of high social status. Jairus was a leader in Capernaum, one of the synagogue officials. As such, he was accustomed to being in control of things. But not now. Like the nameless woman, he had reached the horizon of human hope. His twelve-year-old daughter was seriously ill and near death. He walked to where Jesus was but quickly assumed a posture that reflected his helplessness. He fell at the feet of Jesus and spoke words no parent wants to contemplate. "My little daughter is dying" (Mark 5:23).

Where others could only voice empathy and offer words of sympathy, Jesus did more. The woman experienced immediate healing and received affirmation that her disorder would no longer define her daily living. "Daughter, your faith has healed you. Go in peace and be freed from your suffering" (Mark 5:34). As Jesus spoke these words, horrible news arrived from the home of Jairus. His beloved daughter had died. Jesus was not fazed. "Don't be afraid; just believe" (v. 36). Jairus did. Then he watched Jesus take the girl's hand and call her back into the land of the living.

These two tragic stories take us beyond the horizon of human hope. And together, they demonstrate that Jesus's power to help does not stop at our horizon.

For Further Reference: **Job 13:15; Psalms 25:3; 33:20; 42:5; 130:5–6; Romans 5:3–5; 1 Thessalonians 4:13**

JESUS STOOD OUT EVEN IN ISRAEL

Matthew 9:27–34

"The crowd was amazed and said, 'Nothing like this
has ever been seen in Israel.'" (Matthew 9:33)

▶ WHO & WHERE

Jesus, two blind men, a demon-possessed man unable to speak,
near Capernaum

▶ WHAT IS THIS TEXT TALKING ABOUT?

Miracles of Jesus

▶ WHAT DOES THIS TEXT TEACH?

In a land that had grown accustomed to seeing miracles, the
miracles of Jesus distinguished him as special.

"We have seen it all before." Or had they?
The land of Israel was special. This was the land that the
Lord chose as the stage for the story of salvation—a story that extended
from Abraham and Sarah through David and Isaiah. This real estate was
accustomed to seeing miracles. The Lord had promised Abraham that he
and Sarah would have a son, even though Sarah had gone through menopause and Abraham was one hundred years old (Gen. 18:10–11; 21:5).
It happened (Gen. 21:1; Heb. 11:11–12). The Lord promised Joshua he
would cause the Jordan River to stop flowing. It did (Josh. 3:8–16). Elisha
fed hundreds with a miraculous multiplication of food (2 Kings 4:42–44),
healed Naaman of his leprosy (2 Kings 5:1–14), and even raised a young

boy from the dead (2 Kings 4:32–37). Miracles like these were known in other places. But per square mile, no place on earth saw more miracles than the land of Israel.

By the time Jesus arrived and began to do miracles here, people could have said, "We have seen it all before." But that is not what happened. When Jesus healed the two blind men and a demon-possessed man who was mute, the crowd was amazed and said, "Nothing like this has ever been seen in Israel" (Matt. 9:33). What? Miracles like this had been seen before in this land.

So what made the miracles of Jesus stand out from the others? It was no longer God enabling others to do the miracles on his behalf, but God himself in the person of Jesus who was doing these miracles. That distinction becomes clear when we listen carefully to the way the two blind men spoke to Jesus when seeking his help. They addressed him as "Son of David." This was more than a statement about Jesus's genealogy. They were using a title the Hebrew Bible had attached to the Messiah. He had arrived. He was doing miracles in this land. And that was something that even Israel had never seen before.

For Further Reference: 2 Samuel 7:12–16; Isaiah 29:18; 35:5–6

JESUS SENT OUT THE TWELVE

Matthew 9:35–11:1; Mark 6:6–13; Luke 9:1–6

"When he saw the crowds, he had compassion on them, because they were harassed and helpless, like sheep without a shepherd. Then he said to his disciples, 'The harvest is plentiful but the workers are few.'" (Matthew 9:36–37)

▶ WHO & WHERE

Jesus, the twelve disciples, Galilee

▶ WHAT IS THIS TEXT TALKING ABOUT?

The urgent need to expand the reach of Jesus's ministry in Galilee

▶ WHAT DOES THIS TEXT TEACH?

Jesus equipped the Twelve with information, power, and confidence to expand his reach in Galilee.

The assignment was urgent and the Twelve were uncertain. This precipitated a long sermon in which Jesus addressed the questions that threatened to delay the disciples from taking immediate action.

Jesus saw it and felt it every day. The people among whom he walked were beset by personal problems and grave misunderstanding. He wanted to reach more people and that meant sending out the Twelve. They were still students, but he needed them to step up and become teachers for a time, on this multiday assignment. That is when the questions came. Matthew's gospel does not preserve those questions. But it does preserve the answers Jesus gave in this extended discourse.

When should we start? Now! Their mission is linked to the image of the grain harvest. Once ripe, the wheat and barley needed to be gathered quickly to prevent theft, loss to wildlife, or rot. Time was so short that the Twelve were not to do any of the things you might think of doing before departing on a multiday mission like bringing along precious metals to purchase supplies or packing extra clothing. The time to start was now.

Where should we go? Go to the people whom you know best, living in the place you know best, Galilee. The time would come when Jesus broadened the geographical scope of their mission. But for now, the focus was on "the lost sheep of Israel" in Galilee (Matt. 10:6).

What should we say or do? Stick to the basics. Jesus had recently given the Twelve advanced instructions in what is called the Sermon on the Mount (Matt. 5–7). For this mission, their focus was to be on the basics. Announce the arrival of Jesus the Messiah and the coming of God's kingdom. To give their message credibility, Jesus provided special power: "Heal the sick, raise the dead, cleanse those who have leprosy, drive out demons" (Matt. 10:8).

What if people respond negatively? Expect it. They were going out like sheep among wolves. As Jesus was rejected, they too would be rejected even by members of their own family. Sometimes the rejection would be accompanied by violence.

What about our misgivings? Focus on your Father's care. If that care extends to the sparrows sold in the marketplace, be assured it extends to you. "So don't be afraid; you are worth more than many sparrows" (Matt. 10:31).

For Further Reference: Isaiah 52:7; Jeremiah 50:6; Zechariah 10:1–2; Romans 8:18; Philippians 1:12–18

UNSTALLING THE JUDEAN MOVEMENT

Matthew 11:2–19; Luke 7:18–35

"Are you the one who is to come, or should we expect someone else?" (Matthew 11:3)

▶ WHO & WHERE
Jesus, John the Baptist, Judea

▶ WHAT IS THIS TEXT TALKING ABOUT?
The stalled movement in Judea

▶ WHAT DOES THIS TEXT TEACH?

The stalled movement in Judea would regain vibrancy when expectations changed to match those established by Old Testament prophecy.

The trouble is evident in the question John the Baptist sent to Jesus. "Are you the one who is to come, or should we expect someone else?" (Matt. 11:3). The movement John started in Judea was stalling out.

The problem? Skewed expectations. John had linked the coming of Messiah with divine judgment and redress for evil: "His winnowing fork is in his hand, and he will clear his threshing floor, gathering his wheat into the barn and burning up the chaff with unquenchable fire" (Matt. 3:12). It did not look like that. Evil flourished, violence continued, and John himself was in prison (Matt. 11:12). Where was divine judgment?

There was also the popular expectation that the Jewish religious leaders in Jerusalem would get on board with this movement. They had not (Luke 7:30). So, the disappointed crowds began to pick at the differences between the teaching of John and Jesus. This fragmented the common message, ramped up dissention, and took the wind out of the movement in Judea.

As it turns out, the problem was not with having expectations but having inaccurate expectations. In response, Jesus sought to realign the Judean expectations with those projected by the Old Testament prophets when they spoke of the coming Messiah.

A winnowing fork like this was used in the process of separating wheat from chaff on the threshing floor.

They spoke of a time in which the physically and socially disadvantaged would be lifted up. This was happening! And Jesus offered a list of recent events in Galilee to affirm it. The blind received sight. The lame walked. Those with leprosy were cleansed. The deaf heard. The dead were raised. And the poor received the good news.

What is more, John himself was evidence that Jesus was the Messiah. Many Judeans had gone out into the wilderness to hear John, the very place that Isaiah promised the Messiah's forerunner would prepare the Lord's people (Isa. 40:3–5). Malachi spoke of this forerunner as a new "Elijah" (Mal. 3:1; 4:5). John was that Elijah.

The movement had stalled in Judea and needed to get unstuck. The path forward flowed from the past as Jesus sought to align Judean expectations with Old Testament promises. Judea had the answer to its question. Jesus was the one.

For Further Reference: Isaiah 26:19; 29:18; 35:4–6; 40:3–5; 61:1–2; Malachi 3:1; 4:5

WARNING!

Matthew 11:20–24; Luke 10:13–15

"Then Jesus began to denounce the towns in which most of his miracles had been performed, because they did not repent."
(Matthew 11:20)

▶ WHO & WHERE
Jesus, Capernaum, Chorazin, Bethsaida

▶ WHAT IS THIS TEXT TALKING ABOUT?
The risk associated with opportunity

▶ WHAT DOES THIS TEXT TEACH?

Those with the best opportunity to hear Jesus proved least likely
to believe him.

T he geography comes fast and furious. In just three verses, Jesus mentions six locations a total of nine times. But this is no ordinary geography lesson. It is a lesson that uses geography to warn three towns of the
risk that came with their opportunity.

Matthew tells us that Jesus invested most of his three years of ministry in Galilee (Matt. 4:23–25). The geography of Matthew 11 tightens the
focus to just three towns—Capernaum, Chorazin, and Bethsaida—often
called the "evangelical triangle." They are not far apart. And if we connect
the dots between them and do the math, we find that Jesus did most of his
teaching and miracle working in just 2.2 square miles (5.7 square kilometers). Those who lived in this small parcel of land had more opportunities
to see, listen to, and personally engage with Jesus than others.

Despite the opportunity they enjoyed, many in those towns failed to
repent. That is why Jesus levels this geographic judgment speech at them.
Capernaum, Chorazin, and Bethsaida would fare worse at the final judgment that three other cities: Tyre, Sidon, and Sodom. Think about what
these three cities have in common. All of them are outside the Promised
Land. Tyre and Sidon are in Phoenicia to the north of Israel. The location
of Sodom is not certain but likely east of the Dead Sea. All were pagan cities
whose attitude and behavior positioned them to receive divine judgment.
Most importantly, all had less frequent and less direct contact with God.

We expect less from them than the three towns within the evangelical
triangle. And that is the punch in this geographic wake-up call for Capernaum, Chorazin, and Bethsaida. Those Gentile, pagan places were getting
what they were missing. Every opportunity to hear Jesus carries that risk.

For Further Reference: Genesis 19:1–29; Isaiah 23:1–18; Ezekiel 28:1–26;
Ephesians 5:16; Hebrews 1:1–2

REST FOR THE LIFE-WEARY

Matthew 11:25–30

"Take my yoke upon you and learn from me, for I am gentle and
humble in heart, and you will find rest for your souls."
(Matthew 11:29)

> ### WHO & WHERE
Jesus, Galilee

> ### WHAT IS THIS TEXT TALKING ABOUT?
Exhaustion

> ### WHAT DOES THIS TEXT TEACH?
The yoke of Jesus brings rest to those exhausted by life.

Life can be exhausting. No group of people in Israel knew this better
than Galileans.

Jesus mentions "yoke" twice in these verses. It is likely that he heard
fellow Galileans using this as a metaphor for their lives. A yoke was a collar
designed to fit around the front shoulders of a draft animal. Its primary
purpose was to transfer a load to the shoulders of the animal so that it
could expend its energy on tasks like plowing, pulling a cart, or dragging
around a threshing sledge. Given the choice, the animal would pursue a
different and more pleasant life. But the yoke harnessed the draft animal
to a difficult task that was not of their own choosing.

Galileans could resonate with the image. A wealthy elite held landed
estates and controlled fishing rights on the Sea of Galilee. Consequently,
most labored at the direction of others and they were poorly paid for their
efforts. Most Galileans lived at or below subsistence level. The length of

Jesus used the image of a yoke on draft animals to highlight the rigors of the life lived without him.

their workday, the amount of pay they received, and what they would do on any given day was determined by those less interested in their well-being than using them to get a job done. The imposed tasks hung on their shoulders like a yoke, robbing them of satisfaction, certainty, and peace.

But that was not the only yoke they carried. Religious leaders also put a yoke on God's people. In particular, the Pharisees taught that God was like those who controlled their work lives. In place of comfort, they offered a rigorous set of rules that also felt like a yoke. Jesus saw it and roundly criticized the Pharisees for linking relationship with God to a long and detailed list of tasks that further wearied an already weary group of people (Matt. 23:4).

To those exhausted by this kind of life, Jesus spoke of a different kind of yoke. To be sure, there was still a yoke. In the kingdom, there was still work to be done, some of it hard. But behind that yoke is a kindly operator who never asks more than can be delivered: "For my yoke is easy and my burden is light" (Matt. 11:30). Jesus offers rest to those exhausted by life.

For Further Reference: Exodus 6:6; Deuteronomy 22:10; Jeremiah 6:16; 2 Corinthians 4:8–9; Galatians 5:1

LESSON ON APPRECIATION

Luke 7:36–50

"Therefore, I tell you, her many sins have been forgiven—as her great love has shown. But whoever has been forgiven little loves little." (Luke 7:47)

▶ **WHO & WHERE**

Jesus, Simon the Pharisee, unnamed "sinful" woman, Galilee

▶ **WHAT IS THIS TEXT TALKING ABOUT?**

Appreciation for Jesus

▶ **WHAT DOES THIS TEXT TEACH?**

The greatest appreciation for Jesus is found among those who comprehend the sin-debt from which Jesus released them.

Jesus spoke of forgiveness frequently and distributed assurance of it equally among the cross section of people he met. But not everyone who heard it responded with the same level of appreciation. This story explains why.

Simon, an influential Pharisee, invited Jesus to a banquet given at his home. As an authorized teacher in Galilee, he cared deeply about order and appearance. And there were things about Jesus that made him uncomfortable. So, he invited Jesus to dinner in order to inspect his teaching and character more closely. He would withhold judgment as well as certain elements of hospitality until he knew more.

A second person rises to prominence in the story. She is not given a name so our thoughts, like those of Simon, go to her character. She was a woman who "lived a sinful life" (Luke 7:37)—someone known to live contrary to the law and to the traditional interpretation of the law championed by the Pharisees. It seems unlikely she was a prostitute, given her presence at the banquet in Simon's home and the fact that she carried an extremely expensive item—a long-necked, alabaster perfume flask. During the meal as the guests reclined at a low table with their feet extended away from the dining surface, she broke the flask and poured its contents on Jesus's feet. This woman supplied the hospitality Simon withheld.

Why did she show such deference and appreciation for Jesus when Simon did not? Jesus uses a metaphor to answer that question. He speaks of an all-too-common situation many faced in Galilee—debt. In Jesus's illustration, one person had a crushing debt of five hundred denarii equaling the wages that a laborer would earn over a year and a half. The other had a more modest debt of fifty denarii equaling wages of a little over two months. Both are equally freed from the debt but reflect unequal appreciation. Jesus saw the same thing in Simon. He treated Jesus more casually and with less appreciation because he, like the man with the smaller debt, did not appreciate the weight of the sin-debt Jesus had forgiven. The woman illustrates the other kind of person. The greatest appreciation for Jesus is found among those who comprehend the sin-debt from which Jesus released them.

For Further Reference: Colossians 3:16–17; 1 John 1:6–10; 4:9–10

LORD OF THE SABBATH

Matthew 12:1–14; Mark 2:23–3:6; Luke 6:1–11
"The Sabbath was made for man, not man for the Sabbath. So the Son of Man is Lord even of the Sabbath." (Mark 2:27–28)

▶ WHO & WHERE
Jesus, Pharisees, Galilee

▶ WHAT IS THIS TEXT TALKING ABOUT?
The tension between Sabbath laws and life

▶ WHAT DOES THIS TEXT TEACH?
The tension between Sabbath laws and life is best resolved by erring on the side of love.

The Old Testament law code is perfect. Life is not. This creates tensions between the law and life.

For first-century Judaism, that tension was most keenly felt in Sabbath observance. It was one of the three defining elements of Judaism (besides circumcision and kosher diet) and is mentioned frequently in the Gospels. In these verses, we read about four conflicts between a rigid observing of Sabbath law and the realities of life. First, no work was to be done on Sabbath (Ex. 20:10), yet the Lord directed Israel's clergy to "work" by offering sacrifices (Num. 28:9–10). Second, livestock wandered into harm's way on Sabbath just as often as any other day of the week. When a sheep fell into a well, people did not wait until Sabbath was over to pull it out. Third, when Jesus's disciples began picking grain, the Pharisees charged them with sinning. They did not accuse them of stealing but of harvesting and processing grain on Sabbath—two of thirty-nine forms of work Judaism came to prohibit on Sabbath. And fourth,

Jesus used the moment his disciples picked grain on Sabbath to teach that he was Lord of the Sabbath.

the Pharisees accused Jesus of "working" by healing a disabled man who was worshipping in the synagogue on Sabbath.

Jesus did not deny the tensions that existed between the directives of the law involving Sabbath and life. Instead, he responded to the accusation of the Pharisees in two powerful ways. First, he spoke of his own identity. He declared that he was "Lord of the Sabbath" (Matt. 12:8). Think about what that means for this conversation. God established the Sabbath day at creation and then put laws in place regarding its observance. Because Jesus is God, he has the right to define what the day means and resolve apparent tensions between the law and life. Second, Jesus provided the governing principle for resolving tensions over what one could do on Sabbath. It was meant as a day of rest, worship, and restoration. But when there was an opportunity to show love for others, love was more important than ritual.

For Further Reference: **Genesis 2:2–3; Micah 6:6–8; Mark 12:28–30; Colossians 2:16–19**

THE HALLMARKS OF JESUS'S MINISTRY

Matthew 12:15–21

"He will not quarrel or cry out; no one will hear his voice in the streets. A bruised reed he will not break, and a smoldering wick he will not snuff out." (Matthew 12:19–20)

▶ WHO & WHERE

Jesus, the servant of Isaiah, rural Galilee

▶ WHAT IS THIS TEXT TALKING ABOUT?

The hallmarks of Jesus's ministry

▶ WHAT DOES THIS TEXT TEACH?

The two outstanding hallmarks of Jesus's ministry were quietness and gentleness.

The path to prominence in the ancient world is the same one taken today by those who long for recognition. Keep yourself in the public eye and attract attention in any way possible. Jesus did just the opposite.

These verses come as an aside in Matthew's account of Jesus's life, a time when he was changing tactics. Jesus had been spending more time in the towns and villages, the places where most people lived and where the Pharisees wielded influence. But now he abandoned the towns and villages to minister in rural Galilee. The crowds followed him. The Pharisees did not.

Matthew uses this moment to comment on the hallmarks of Jesus's ministry fostered by this change in geography. Jesus was quiet. This is not how people typically made a name for themselves. Those who wanted to be someone in the ancient world had to be heard above the din. That meant being as bombastic as possible in the most public arenas possible. Jesus did neither. His ministry was not characterized by loud quarrels conducted with a raised voice. It was conducted quietly, in remote places, so that many did not "hear his voice in the streets" (Matt. 12:19).

Jesus's ministry is also characterized by its gentleness. The ancient world had plenty of sword-wielding crusaders who charged into combat, running over anyone who got in the way. This was not Jesus. To be sure, he attacked injustice but not with slashing sword. Matthew characterizes him in relationship to the most fragile things people encountered in daily life—dry reeds and smoldering wicks. Dry reeds found in wet lowlands were fragile and easily damaged. The wicks of oil lamps that have run out of fuel smolder and smoke. Jesus's ministry is so gentle that the most fragile are not broken and the most hopeless are not snuffed out.

This may not be the kind of person who typically made a name for himself in the ancient world. But it was who Jesus was. That makes him just the kind of person expected by the Old Testament (Isaiah 42) and just the kind of Messiah the world most needed.

For Further Reference: Isaiah 42:1–4; 53:2; Philippians 2:6–11

RESPONDING TO JESUS

Matthew 12:22–37; Mark 3:20–30; Luke 11:14–28

"Whoever is not with me is against me, and whoever does not gather with me scatters." (Matthew 12:30)

▶ **WHO & WHERE**

Jesus, Pharisees and teachers of the law, rural Galilee

▶ **WHAT IS THIS TEXT TALKING ABOUT?**

Responding to Jesus

▶ **WHAT DOES THIS TEXT TEACH?**

With Jesus there is no middle ground; either you believe in him or you don't.

Many followed Jesus as he walked into rural Galilee. But not everyone who followed him responded to his ministry in an appropriate fashion.

Consider the group of Pharisees and teachers of the law who had come all the way from Jerusalem (Mark 3:22). They did not like what Jesus was teaching about Sabbath day because it conflicted with their traditional views. Consequently, they responded by linking what Jesus did to Beelzebul, the name they used for Satan. This response to Jesus was both foolish and gravely dangerous. Satan was the great disruptor of life, the "strong man" Jesus had come to tie up. It made no sense that Jesus was somehow connected to his "household" while working to defeat him. What is more, this response to Jesus was gravely dangerous. The persistent linking of Jesus to Satan worked against the very faith response the Holy Spirit was seeking to build in them. At some unforeseeable moment, this persistent battling against the Spirit's work would become irreversible and saving faith would become impossible.

Jesus's extended family also responded badly to his ministry (Mark 3:21). They thought he had lost his mind. Whether out of concern for his well-being or out of concern over the shame he brought to their household, they came to sweep him off the public stage.

A third group responded to Jesus's ministry with a wait-and-see approach. They were intrigued enough to follow Jesus into the countryside, curious about the miracles he performed, but doubtful that he was the "Son of David" (Matt. 12:23). They were waiting for more evidence. Just one more "sign from heaven" (Luke 11:16) might help them make up their minds.

None of these responses to Jesus are acceptable. And when confronted with them, Jesus drew a clear line in the sand. Either you are in or you are out. "Whoever is not with me is against me, and whoever does not gather with me scatters" (Matt. 12:30). You are a tree bearing either good or bad fruit (v. 33). There is no room for arguing, delay, or wavering. There is only room for unequivocal, unwavering faith.

For Further Reference: **Deuteronomy 30:19; Joshua 24:15; Proverbs 3:5–6; 1 Corinthians 12:3; Hebrews 6:4–6**

JESUS AND THE SIGN OF THE PROPHET JONAH

Matthew 12:38–45; Luke 11:29–32

"A wicked and adulterous generation asks for a sign!
But none will be given it except the sign of the prophet Jonah."
(Matthew 12:39)

▶ **WHO & WHERE**

Jesus, Pharisees and teachers of the law, rural Galilee

▶ **WHAT IS THIS TEXT TALKING ABOUT?**

The best sign of Jesus's authenticity

▶ **WHAT DOES THIS TEXT TEACH?**

The most compelling sign of Jesus's authenticity is his
resurrection from the dead.

Is Jesus the real deal? Some asked with honest hesitation; others asked
with an agenda. The latter included the Jewish religious leaders from
Jerusalem who had come to Galilee demanding that Jesus give them an
authenticating sign. What Jesus offered was the sign of the prophet Jonah.

There are four similarities between Jesus and Jonah. First, both were
Galileans who grew up on the same ridge—Jesus in Nazareth and Jonah
in Gath Hepher just three miles (five kilometers) away (2 Kings 14:25).
Second, both were Galilean prophets who delivered a message meant for
both Jews and Gentiles. Third, both entered a place from which no one
expected them to return. For Jonah, that was three days and nights inside

When asked for a sign, Jesus compared his life to that of the prophet Jonah.

a large fish. For Jesus, it was three days and nights in the tomb. And fourth, both Jesus and Jonah exited those forbidding places no worse for wear.

The sign of Jonah is the last of the four, Jesus's resurrection from the dead. It was not the kind of sign these Jewish religious authorities could accept easily. First, it required that they overcome their regional bias against Galileans. As Judeans, they were very suspicious of the religious convictions and messaging that came from Galilee. They were dismissive of not only Jesus but Jonah as well. We see this in the gospel of John. When Nicodemus urged his colleagues in Jerusalem to give Jesus a fair hearing, they responded, "Are you from Galilee, too? Look into it, and you will find that a prophet does not come out of Galilee" (John 7:52). Jonah was from Galilee. But they discounted him as quickly as they discounted Jesus because he was a Galilean. A second reason that the Jewish religious leaders found the sign Jesus offered hard to accept is because it was a delayed sign.

They wanted something immediate. Jesus offered a sign for which they had to wait.

In the end, even the resurrection did not convince the Jerusalem elites. And for that reason, Gentiles like those in Nineveh and the Queen of the South entered the kingdom of God even though they lived in distant lands, heard the message from a lesser authority, and received a more modest authenticating sign.

For Further Reference: 1 Kings 10:1–13; Jonah 1–4; Luke 10:21–24; Acts 2:22–32; 1 Corinthians 15:12–14

THE BIG FAMILY OF JESUS

Matthew 12:46–50; Mark 3:31–35; Luke 8:19–21

"For whoever does the will of my Father in heaven is my brother and sister and mother." (Matthew 12:50)

▶ **WHO & WHERE**

Jesus, Mary, Jesus's brothers, rural Galilee

▶ **WHAT IS THIS TEXT TALKING ABOUT?**

The family of Jesus

▶ **WHAT DOES THIS TEXT TEACH?**

All those who believe in Jesus as their Savior are members of his family.

Family brings a mix of blessing and challenge to our lives. Jesus knew it all too well. In these verses, he faced one of those challenging moments. But Jesus uses it to teach a lesson about his family that expands the concept well beyond the broad way people thought of family in first-century Galilee.

The more the merrier. That is how people in Bible times thought about family, particularly in rural Galilee. For them, family included everyone in their extended family—aunts, uncles, cousins, second cousins, and beyond. That meant a family could and often did literally expand to include every member of a village! That broad definition of family was fueled by the importance of family to one's survival. Family members were the workforce that allowed the community to raise more grain and tend more livestock. Family was the security force that prevented others from bringing harm to the family compound. And family was the retirement plan for those in their senior years who were unable to care for themselves.

Jesus had a biological family that is mentioned in the Gospels. His mother Mary and brothers are mentioned in this story. (Their names are given in Matthew 13:55. And his sisters are mentioned in Mark 6:3.) After Jesus's resurrection, some, if not all, came to believe that Jesus was their Savior (Acts 1:14; Gal. 1:19). But for the moment, Jesus's actions and words bothered them. He had done the unthinkable in moving away from the family compound, which meant his contribution to the family well-being was lost. And his words suggested to them that he was mentally unstable, so they came to take charge of him (Mark 3:21).

Rather than defend his decision to leave the extended family in Nazareth, Jesus expanded the idea of family. "My mother and brothers are those who hear God's word and put it into practice" (Luke 8:21). That is how Jesus invites us to think too. No matter how we draw the circle that defines our family, Jesus invites us to draw it large enough to include all those who believe that he is their Savior from sin. The more the merrier.

For Further Reference: **Exodus 20:12; Deuteronomy 5:16; Galatians 6:10; 1 Thessalonians 4:10; Hebrews 2:11; 1 Peter 5:9**

PARABLES ABOUT
THE KINGDOM OF GOD

Matthew 13:1–52; Mark 4:1–34; Luke 8:1–18

"Because the knowledge of the secrets of the kingdom
of heaven has been given to you . . ." (Matthew 13:11)

▶ **WHO & WHERE**

Jesus, crowds gathered on the shoreline of the Sea of Galilee

▶ **WHAT IS THIS TEXT TALKING ABOUT?**

The kingdom of God

▶ **WHAT DOES THIS TEXT TEACH?**

The kingdom of God is large, enduring, joy-inducing, and non-discriminating.

Jesus had come to bring in the kingdom of God. But he could not assume everyone understood what it was. So, he often used parables to explain it.

A parable is a story or analogy that uses familiar experiences from life, elements from the natural world, or manufactured items to deliver a spiritual lesson. As Jesus moved along the lakeshore of the Sea of Galilee, he used the seaside setting in two ways. First, he used its coves, over which sound propagated, to expand the reach of his voice. Second, he used scenes from the lakeshore to shape his parables, including those that spoke about the kingdom of God.

Most Galileans grew their own food so they could easily relate to stories of growing grain, starting with the parable of the sower. In this lesson, the same farmer cast the same kind of seed through the air. But this seed landed on different types of soil, producing dramatically different yields. This parable highlights the dramatic growth in the kingdom that occurs when the word of the Lord falls on good soil.

Another agricultural parable features weeds. Weeds naturally invaded the grainfields, competing with the wheat and barley for water and nutrients. In this parable, things were even worse because an enemy sowed additional weed seeds in the field. Pulling them too soon might damage the grain plants. So, the best course of action was to wait until both matured and then separate them at the harvest. This parable explains that the kingdom of God will endure and coexist with evil in this world until the last day.

Three short illustrations all address the surprising growth of the kingdom. The minuscule mustard seed grows into a mighty tree. The small amount of fermenting bread dough (yeast) mixed in with sixty pounds (twenty-seven kilograms) of dough causes the entire batch to rise. And the small seeds scattered in the ground sprout to become acres of swaying grain. Compared to the sprawling Roman Empire that touched all shores of the Mediterranean Sea, the kingdom of God looked puny. But it would become a kingdom that filled the world and outlasted all that Rome was in Jesus's day.

Jesus used everyday images from the fishing and farm life around the Sea of Galilee to teach about God's kingdom.

There were no banks as we know them today, so if a person had items of great value, they might bury them to safeguard them. If someone other than the original owner accidentally discovered this treasure, and was unable to locate the owner, it became their own. The joy felt in joining the kingdom of God exceeded even that experience.

There were several types of net used by fishermen to fish the inland lake on which Jesus was teaching. One of those was the drag net. Through a combination of floats and weights, it stood vertically in the water, corralling fish as the boat moved parallel, then perpendicular to the shore. The drag net gathered indiscriminately and so the catch had to be separated at the end of the process. This parable addresses the job of those within the kingdom. Like the fishermen, they were to gather indiscriminately and leave the separation of the catch until the last day.

For Further Reference: **Psalm 78:1–4; Isaiah 6:9–10; 55:10–11; Acts 1:8; Romans 14:17; 1 John 2:20, 27**

REJECTION OF JESUS IN NAZARETH

Matthew 13:53–58; Mark 6:1–6; Luke 4:14–30

"A prophet is not without honor except in his own town and in his own home." (Matthew 13:57)

▶ **WHO & WHERE**

Jesus, Nazareth

▶ **WHAT IS THIS TEXT TALKING ABOUT?**

Reactions to Jesus

▶ **WHAT DOES THIS TEXT TEACH?**

The people of Nazareth reacted to Jesus with amazement, pride, offense, and angry rejection.

They knew him well. They had watched Jesus grow up, knew his family, and assumed how his visit with them would go. They were wrong.

When Jesus stopped for a visit in Nazareth, his hometown reacted in a variety of ways, starting with amazement (Matt. 13:54; Mark 6:2). They expected Jesus would follow in the footsteps of his stepfather, Joseph, a builder who worked in a variety of materials including wood and stone. Jesus had no formal, advanced training. So, everyone was amazed when this apprenticed builder spoke like a scholar.

They also reacted with pride. "Isn't this Joseph's son?" (Luke 4:22). Nazareth was a small village, topographically isolated from the larger world that expected little from it. This was a backwater that, apart from Jesus, never produced a notable figure. Now, Jesus could change all of that. This possibility fueled an honest pride that Nazareth felt over this hometown hero.

But in the end, most were offended at Jesus. After being invited to read and interpret Scripture in the synagogue, Jesus read Isaiah 61:1–2 (or at least most of it): "The Spirit of the Lord is on me" (quoted in Luke 4:18). This language reminds us of Jesus's baptism when the Holy Spirit descended on him in the form of a dove and marked him as the Messiah. Imagine that, the Messiah from our hometown. But as he read on, they noticed that Jesus left out a portion of the reading, the one that spoke about "the day of vengeance" (Isa. 61:2). In the Targum, the Aramaic translation/interpretation of the Hebrew Bible, this passage speaks about the revenge the Lord would visit on Gentiles. Perhaps Jesus would return to it when he sat down to deliver his interpretation. But instead, he related two stories in which Gentiles are held up as examples of faith. That set the stage for a showdown!

Geography isolated the people of Nazareth from Gentiles. But that did not prevent them from having an opinion about them. Gentiles to them were the foreign occupiers of their homeland, loathsome "others" who were ineligible for inclusion in God's kingdom. Jesus delivered this synagogue sermon to challenge that notion. When he did, Nazareth got the point but refused to accept it. And taking offense, they took Jesus to the high ridge on which he likely played as a child. Their intention was to throw Jesus from the brow of the ridge, using the terrain to execute him. Jesus walked through the crowds and did not return.

For Further Reference: 1 Kings 17:7–24; 2 Kings 5:1–19; Isaiah 58:6; 61:1–2

ARREST AND EXECUTION OF JOHN THE BAPTIST

Matthew 14:1–12; Mark 6:14–29; Luke 3:19–20

"Now Herod had arrested John . . . and had John beheaded in the prison." (Matthew 14:3, 10)

▶ WHO
Herod Antipas, John the Baptist

▶ WHAT IS THIS TEXT TALKING ABOUT?
The arrest and execution of John the Baptist

▶ WHAT DOES THIS TEXT TEACH?
The execution of John demonstrates that political leaders would find the advancing kingdom of God so threatening that they would use extreme measures to stop it.

Herod Antipas was a son of Herod the Great, coming to power after his father's death in 4 BC. The Romans assigned Antipas the duty of ruling the districts of Galilee and Perea. Technically he was not a king but a tetrarch (Matt. 14:1)—ruler of a portion of his father's kingdom. But he had enough of his father's hubris to claim the loftier title (Mark 6:14).

According to Josephus, Herod Antipas executed John the Baptist at the palace-fortress of Machaerus.

This story highlights two character traits of Herod Antipas. First, his worldview was influenced by both his Greco-Roman education and Judaism. In this story, he was hosting his own birthday party—a tradition common in Europe but not within Judaism. Yet, he regarded John as a righteous and holy man to whom he enjoyed listening (Mark 6:20). Second, Antipas was a man guided by sensual pleasures. He fell in love with Herodias, the wife of his half-brother Philip. Seeing Antipas as the brother with the better political future, Herodias divorced her husband of fifteen years and married Antipas. During the birthday party mentioned in this story, Herodias's teenage daughter danced in alluring fashion for Antipas and his male guests. This led Antipas to take an oath he regretted. He offered his stepdaughter the opportunity to ask for whatever she wanted. She asked for what her mother wanted—the head of John served up on a platter!

Why did Herod honor the request? He saw John the Baptist as a threat to his authority and economic well-being. John had boldly attacked

Antipas for marrying Herodias, criticism that threatened his status. In addition, soldiers and tax collectors found the message of John appealing (Luke 3:12–14). The advice John gave them threatened the ability of Antipas to enforce his wishes and compromised the collection of taxes. At first, Herod tried to control this perceived threat by having John arrested. In time, this was not enough. So as the alcohol flowed at the party, Herod made a promise he was unwilling to reverse.

This story, like Herod the Great's slaughter of the children in Bethlehem (Matt. 2:1–16) and the hearings before Antipas and Pilate (Luke 23:6–11), joins to illustrate that the coming of God's kingdom would often meet a forceful and violent response from the kingdoms of this world.

For Further Reference: Leviticus 18:16; 20:21; Psalm 2:1–6; Matthew 2:1–12; Luke 9:7–9

JESUS FEEDS FIVE THOUSAND HOUSEHOLDS

Matthew 14:13–21; Mark 6:30–44; Luke 9:10–17; John 6:1–15

"They all ate and were satisfied, and the disciples picked up twelve basketfuls of broken pieces that were left over."
(Matthew 14:20)

▶ WHO & WHERE

Jesus, Jewish families, rural area near Bethsaida

▶ WHAT IS THIS TEXT TALKING ABOUT?

Jesus's miraculous provision of food

▶ WHAT DOES THIS TEXT TEACH?

This miracle of feeding the five thousand illustrates Jesus's
growing popularity, his connection with the office of prophet,
and his loving care for Israel.

Meals do more than meet our nutritional needs. We dine to celebrate,
to conduct business, and to impress on a date. So it is fair to ask,
how did the meal Jesus hosted for five thousand Jewish families function?

The first thing it did was illustrate Jesus's growing popularity. Although
he had walked to a more remote location, the size of his following grew.
Each of the Gospels reports the size at five thousand men. This language
uses an ancient metric that counts the number of households by identifying
the male leader of each household. The math leaves us with an astonishing
number—some ten to twenty thousand people had gathered around Jesus.
This number exceeds the local population, so it likely included Jewish pilgrims who were traveling the International Highway that arches east to
west across the Fertile Crescent and then south toward Jerusalem for Passover (John 6:4).

The stunning number of people created a problem that gives us a second insight into Jesus's identity. There was insufficient food in the nearby
villages to feed the swelling crowd, so Jesus provided a meal for them using
a miracle like the ones done by Moses and Elisha in remote places (Exodus 16; 2 Kings 4:42–44). Consequently, the miracle connected Jesus with
the office of Old Testament prophet and led many to conclude he was the
Prophet, another title for the Messiah (John 6:14).

The third thing the miracle did was show Jesus's love and care for
the chosen people of God. Another feeding miracle is coming in which
Jesus cared for Gentiles, but this one was for Jews. How do we know
that? First, we suspect this from the demographics. The northwest side
of the Sea of Galilee was home to observant Jewish families and the
road that led to Jerusalem which carried Passover pilgrims. And then

there is the number twelve. Twelve basketfuls of leftovers were gathered at the close of the meal—a number that reminds us of the twelve tribes of Israel.

Apart from the resurrection, this is the only miracle of Jesus reported by all four Gospels. Why? Because it tells us so much about Jesus. He was a rabbi attracting exceptionally large crowds, a teacher connected to the office of prophet, and God himself who had come to personally show care and love for his chosen people.

For Further Reference: Exodus 16; Deuteronomy 18:15; 2 Kings 4:42–44; Psalm 132:15

JESUS WALKS ON WATER

Matthew 14:22–36; Mark 6:45–56; John 6:16–24

"Take courage! It is I. Don't be afraid." (Matthew 14:27)

▶ **WHO & WHERE**
Jesus, the disciples, Peter, Sea of Galilee

▶ **WHAT IS THIS TEXT TALKING ABOUT?**
Imperfect faith

▶ **WHAT DOES THIS TEXT TEACH?**
Jesus comes to rescue people with imperfect faith.

Perfect faith like perfect love dispels all fear (1 John 4:18). I am not that person. All too often I find myself responding like the father seeking help for his son, "I do believe; help me overcome my unbelief!"

(Mark 9:24). This story of Jesus walking on the water teaches us how Jesus responds to people with imperfect faith.

Jesus had just finished feeding five thousand Jewish households with a miraculous meal. He directed his disciples to take a boat from the harbor at Bethsaida on the north side of the lake (Mark 6:45) back to Capernaum on the western shore of the lake (John 6:16–17). While they spent time on the water, Jesus spent time in prayer. Early the next morning, long after they should have arrived in Capernaum, the disciples were still on the lake. They were battling a strong, spring storm whose westerly winds blew them off course. No matter how hard they rowed, they were stuck in the middle of the lake, tired and frustrated (Mark 6:47–48; John 6:19).

While the storm itself does not appear to have stoked their fear, what happened next did. On this dark and stormy night, they saw a ghostly figure moving toward them on the surface of the water. It was Jesus, doing something God can do, leaving unseen footprints on the water (Ps. 77:19). His first words were not meant to correct but comfort: "Take courage! It is I. Don't be afraid" (Matt. 14:27).

As the Sea of Galilee was roiled by a storm that terrified the disciples, Jesus showed his perspective on people with imperfect faith.

In that moment, Peter's faith was stirred into action. He asked to join Jesus and Jesus said come (Matt. 14:28–29). So Peter stepped over the gunnel of the overloaded boat that was riding perilously low in the water. With faith and no small amount of courage, he too walked on the surface of the water! But the farther he got from the boat the more his attention was distracted from Jesus to the wind and waves. What had he done? "Lord, save me!" (Matt. 14:30). Jesus again responded to his quavering faith not with rebuke but with an extended hand that grabbed the sinking Peter and put him back in the boat.

That is how Jesus responds to imperfect faith. "Thanks be to God, who delivers me through Jesus Christ our Lord!" (Rom. 7:25).

For Further Reference: **Job 9:8; Psalm 77:19; Romans 7:21–25; 1 John 4:18; Revelation 1:17–18**

JESUS THE BREAD OF LIFE

John 6:25–71

"I am the living bread that came down from heaven. Whoever eats this bread will live forever. This bread is my flesh, which I will give for the life of the world." (John 6:51)

▷ WHO & WHERE
Jesus, synagogue at Capernaum

▷ WHAT IS THIS TEXT TALKING ABOUT?
Jesus's identity and purpose

▷ WHAT DOES THIS TEXT TEACH?
Jesus is the living bread sent from heaven to provide eternal life.

This story begins with thousands of people searching for Jesus (John 6:24) and ends with many abandoning him (v. 66). What happened?

Jesus had changed locations, and so he likewise changed the way he addressed the topic of bread. When he was in a remote area on the north side of the Sea of Galilee where food was in short supply, he did a miracle that provided bread for five thousand households. Now, Jesus had returned to the synagogue in Capernaum where the markets promised plenty of food. Here, he used bread as a metaphor, likening himself to bread and comparing eating bread to believing in him.

For the crowd that followed Jesus to Capernaum, the connection between their eating bread that Jesus had provided and their forebears' eating manna in the wilderness was natural (v. 31). This led Jesus to compare himself to manna. First, both had the same source: "It is my Father who gives you the true bread from heaven" (v. 32). Second, both were unique. The wilderness bread was truly out of this world. So was Jesus, even though he looked like others from Nazareth (v. 42). And third, both manna and Jesus were vital. Grain and grain products accounted for more than one-third of a person's nutrient intake in Jesus's day. Bread was vital for sustaining life, eaten every day at every meal. Jesus was vital for gaining eternal life (v. 27). That is why his Father had sent him: "For my Father's will is that everyone who looks to the Son and believes in him shall have eternal life, and I will raise them up at the last day" (v. 40).

Manna was good. The literal bread Jesus provided was good. Jesus himself in the flesh was better. But sadly, many just wanted Jesus to be the one who provided miraculous meals like they enjoyed on the north side of the Sea of Galilee. When he spoke of greater things by describing himself as the "bread of life," many found his words too hard to digest. That is why this story begins with thousands of people searching for Jesus (v. 24) and ends with many abandoning him (v. 66).

For Further Reference: Exodus 16:14–36; Ephesians 2:8–9; 1 John 4:13–17

JESUS ON THE RISK OF INAUTHENTIC PIETY

Matthew 15:1–20; Mark 7:1–23

"These people honor me with their lips, but their hearts are far from me. They worship me in vain; their teachings are merely human rules." (Matthew 15:8–9)

▶ WHO & WHERE

Jesus, Jerusalem religious leaders, Galilee

▶ WHAT IS THIS TEXT TALKING ABOUT?

The risk of practicing inauthentic piety

▶ WHAT DOES THIS TEXT TEACH?

Inauthentic piety can masquerade as true piety when it is based on human rules rather than the words of Jesus.

"They are blind guides" (Matt. 15:14). This terse assessment highlights the tension that filled the meeting between the Jerusalem religious leaders and the Galilean Jesus. They were sparring over the topic of pious living.

Jerusalem was regarded as the center for religious study and the source of deep theological insights. By contrast, many Judeans perceived Galileans as lacking intellectual sophistication and religious credibility. This fueled the hubris of the Pharisees and teachers of the law who came to investigate what Jesus was doing in Capernaum.

The Jerusalem religious leaders began by pursuing their greatest concern. Jesus was not honoring the "tradition of the elders." These were the

The Jewish Mishnah captures the long-standing and far-reaching discussion within Judaism on what it means to obey the law.

oral laws of Judaism that in a later era achieved written form in the Mishnah and Talmud. The Pharisees and teachers of the law had an affinity for the oral laws, which went well beyond the written law. It led them to criticize Jesus's disciples for failing to wash their hands before eating. This was not about hygiene but a codicil of the oral law that applied handwashing requirements imposed on the priests to all laypersons (Ex. 30:18–21). For these Jerusalem religious leaders, authentic piety required everyone to obey these oral laws.

Jesus characterized such piety as inauthentic. He ignored their reservations about Galileans and set on three glaring problems with measuring piety with the standard of the oral law. First, this approach elevated human opinion and practice to a place of authority equal to the revealed word of God. Note the contrast between "for God said . . . " and "but you say . . . " (Matt. 15:4–5). Second, the oral law often created problems with obeying the written law. He cites the example of "Corban" (putting money in trust with the Temple) that prevented people from using their resources to care for their needy parents. And third, Jesus observed that some of the written law from which their oral law derived was changing. For example, Jesus was bringing the world into a time of transition when the dietary laws of the Old Testament would no longer be in force (Mark 7:19).

In the end, true piety flowed from following the written revelation of God as interpreted by the Galilean Jesus, rather than in following the oral law of the Jerusalem religious elite.

For Further Reference: **Isaiah 29:13; Galatians 5:19–21; Colossians 2:16–23**

JESUS HEALS THE BLIND MAN AT BETHSAIDA

Mark 8:22–26

"Don't even go into the village." (Mark 8:26)

▶ WHO & WHERE

Jesus, blind man, Bethsaida

▶ WHAT IS THIS TEXT TALKING ABOUT?

Assessing the risk of going back

▶ WHAT DOES THIS TEXT TEACH?

Those who come to know Jesus will avoid places that are a threat to their spiritual well-being, even if those places are dear to us.

Hometowns are wonderful places, full of family, friends, and memories. Although the blind man's "home" was outside of town, Bethsaida was the town he knew. But by the close of this short story, it was the place he was to avoid.

The Bethsaida mentioned here is likely the town linked to the archaeological site of Tel El-Araj on the north shore of the Sea of Galilee. It enjoyed two advantages that made it the ideal place to learn about who Jesus was and what he had come to do on earth. First, it was the hometown of three of the twelve disciples—Philip, Andrew, and Peter (John 1:44). And second, it was one of three towns on the northwest shore of the Sea of Galilee that saw more of Jesus's earthly ministry than others (Matt. 11:20). Sadly, and despite these advantages, Bethsaida squandered the opportunity to repent and believe (Matt. 11:21).

Ironically, the town that had so many opportunities to know Jesus had become a risky place for believers. That impacts how Jesus deals with this man. First, Jesus took the visually impaired man outside of town prior to healing him. The miracle that linked Jesus with the Messiah promised in the Old Testament (Isa. 35:5) would not be seen by those living in town—another opportunity lost. The healing miracle occurred in two stages and between the two, Jesus asks the question, "Do you see anything?" (Mark 8:23). Jesus was asking the man if his sight was returning. But he was also asking if the man "saw" the significance of the miracle, something Bethsaida regularly missed. And finally, Jesus instructed the man not to return to his hometown! "Don't even go into the village," he told the man (v. 26).

This last directive is stunning. Imagine being told that the very place you regarded as your hometown, the place where you had family and friends, was now a threat to your spiritual well-being. What a word of caution! Bethsaida remained blind to what the man could now see.

For Further Reference: Isaiah 29:18; 35:5; 42:7; Matthew 11:21

JESUS ANNOUNCES HIS IMPENDING DEATH AND RESURRECTION

Matthew 17:22–23; Mark 9:30–32; Luke 9:43–45

"The Son of Man is going to be delivered into the hands of men. They will kill him, and after three days he will rise." (Mark 9:31)

▶ WHO & WHERE

Jesus, Galilee

▶ WHAT IS THIS TEXT TALKING ABOUT?

Jesus's death and resurrection

▶ WHAT DOES THIS TEXT TEACH?

The impending death and resurrection of Jesus were significant and essential elements of his mission on earth as the Messiah.

Everything Jesus said and did during his time on earth is important—two are essential to our eternity.

The significance of this brief lesson is marked in three ways. First, this lesson was delivered three times in three different places. Here Jesus gives the lesson in Galilee. Just before this, he gave the same lesson at the base of Mount Hermon (Matt. 16:21–28). And just after this, he would give it en route to Jerusalem (Matt. 20:17–19). Important things like this get said more than once. Second, Jesus intentionally isolated the disciples from the rest of the crowd for this lesson to be sure he had their undivided attention (Mark 9:30–31). And third, he began with these attention-demanding words: "Listen carefully to what I am about to tell you" (Luke 9:44). Together, these combine to elevate the significance of the moment.

With the disciples' focus firmly fixed on him, Jesus spoke about the two difficult but essential elements of his mission on earth—his death and resurrection. Shifting into the third person, he speaks of their importance for the mission of the Messiah. He does not say "I" must have these experiences but that the "Son of Man" must die and rise from the dead. Son of Man is a title used by Daniel for the Messiah (Dan. 7:13–14).

Sadly, the Jewish people in Israel were all too familiar with the execution of Jewish men conducted by their Roman occupiers. Jesus would not be the first or last Jewish man to be tried and executed by Pilate. In fact, the same day he died on the cross, two others were put to death alongside him. But what made Jesus's execution different is that he would not remain in the grave. Three days later he would rise from the dead. And it is these two elements taken together, his death and resurrection, that were essential to the Messiah's mission. The first pays the price for our sin-debt; the second confirms the Father's acceptance of the payment: "He was delivered over to death for our sins and was raised to life for our justification" (Rom. 4:25).

For Further Reference: Isaiah 52:13–53:12; Daniel 7:13–14; Acts 2:23–24; Romans 4:25

JESUS ON THE TEMPLE TAX

Matthew 17:24–27

"Doesn't your teacher pay the temple tax?" (Matthew 17:24)

▶ WHO & WHERE
Jesus, Peter, Capernaum

▶ WHAT IS THIS TEXT TALKING ABOUT?
The two-drachma Temple tax

▶ WHAT DOES THIS TEXT TEACH?
Jesus used a miracle to pay the Temple tax, illustrating his desire to bring changes to the Jewish belief system without causing offense.

Taxes and fees are part of life. The same was true at the time of Jesus. In this case, Jesus turned one of those experiences into a teachable moment. It was precipitated by a question asked by officials from Jerusalem: "Your teacher pays the two-drachma Temple tax, right?"

A Tyrian half shekel, the type of coin used to pay the required annual tax in support of the Temple in Jerusalem.

The Temple played a vital role in the Jewish faith from the time of Solomon until it was destroyed by the Romans about forty years after the time of this story recorded in Matthew 17. The Temple at Jerusalem was the geographic focal point of the Jewish faith—the place where the Lord said most clearly, "I am one. I am with you. I forgive you."

The tax mentioned in the story originated at Mount Sinai when Moses collected a half shekel (the income from two working days) from every Israelite male twenty years of age and older (Ex. 30:13–14). The offering was used to support service conducted at the Tabernacle, the portable version of what would become the Temple in Jerusalem. The First Temple was built by Solomon about one thousand years before the time of Jesus. At the time of King Joash, who reigned about eight hundred years before Jesus, this offering became a tax used to rebuild and reinvigorate worship at the Temple, which had drifted into disuse and disrepair (2 Chron. 24:4–12). The same tax, collected annually, was now called the "two-drachma" tax. It is the subject of the question posed to Peter.

Peter's quick affirmative answer showed the need for clarification. With the coming of Jesus, a new reality was dawning. The Temple, as important as it was, would soon be destroyed (Matt. 24:2). Jesus presented himself as its replacement (Matt. 12:6; John 2:19–22). Given this impending reality, was payment of the tax necessary? Jesus drew a comparison with the political world in which kings do not collect taxes from their own family members. With Jesus as King, there was no need for believers, his family, to pay the tax.

At the same time, Jesus did not want to create an unnecessary obstacle around a building that was so important to the faith of so many. So, he directed Peter to pay the tax but did so by providing the necessary coin in supernatural fashion. In this way, he helped both Peter and those who had yet to make the transition from Temple to Jesus.

For Further Reference: **Exodus 30:11–16; 2 Chronicles 24:4–12; Hebrews 10:1–14**

JESUS ON STATUS IN THE KINGDOM OF GOD

Matthew 18:1–9; Mark 9:33–37; Luke 9:46–48
"For it is the one who is least among you all who is the greatest."
(Luke 9:48)

▶ **WHO & WHERE**
Jesus, the Twelve, Capernaum

▶ **WHAT IS THIS TEXT TALKING ABOUT?**
Status in the kingdom of God

▶ **WHAT DOES THIS TEXT TEACH?**
The greatest in the kingdom of God see themselves as least important and humbly treat the least important as the most important.

We like to feel good about ourselves. Unfortunately, we often seek that sense of status by comparing ourselves to others using metrics like athleticism, intelligence, beauty, popularity, and wealth. What counts for status in the kingdom of God?

The question surfaced among the Twelve, in part, because most of them were Galileans who were hungry for respect. When we look at Galilee stories in the Old Testament, we do not find the powerful founding stories of Judea—stories about Abraham and Sarah, Naomi, Ruth, and David. Rather, we find troubling stories of Israel's apostasy—stories about Jeroboam, Ahab, and Jezebel. This legacy led Galileans to crave recognition and status not provided by their regional backstory. On the way back to Capernaum, an argument broke out among the disciples about who was the greatest.

When they arrived at the house in Capernaum, Jesus answered their question with two illustrations, the first using a child: "Whoever takes the lowly position of this child is the greatest in the kingdom of heaven" (Matt. 18:4). Jesus treated children as valuable members of society much as the Old Testament did (Matt. 19:14; Pss. 127:3–5; 128:3–4). But here he is using the general attitude of his culture that perceived children as second-rate. The extended family needed contributors who played a role in food production and in protecting the household. Little children did little to help with either and so were regarded as of less importance. Jesus uses that perspective to teach a lesson on kingdom status. The highest status in the kingdom of God belonged to those who regarded themselves as if they were a child.

The second related picture is that of host (Matt. 18:5; Mark 9:37; Luke 9:48). In the ancient Near East, any visitor from outside the household received lavish attention from the host. Other household duties gave way to making sure the visitor was well fed, provided with water, aromatics, and protection. But note who receives this attention in Jesus's example—the children within the household rather than the visitor. Thus, the greatest in the kingdom of God are those who see themselves as least important and humbly treat the least important as the most important.

For Further Reference: **Proverbs 11:2; 15:33; 22:4; Philippians 2:3; 1 Peter 5:5**

PARABLES OF THE LOST SHEEP

Matthew 18:10–14; Luke 15:1–7

"In the same way your Father in heaven is not willing that any of these little ones should perish." (Matthew 18:14)

▶ **WHO & WHERE**

Jesus, lost sheep in the wilderness

▶ **WHAT IS THIS TEXT TALKING ABOUT?**

Marginalized members of society

▶ **WHAT DOES THIS TEXT TEACH?**

The Father's love and concern extends to the most marginalized members of society.

The pagan world consistently presented the gods as distant and uncaring. The Old Testament countered by portraying the God of Israel as a caring shepherd (Psalm 23). Jesus uses the same image to further establish the compassion of the Almighty for the most marginalized of society.

The typical family of Jesus's day had its own flock of sheep and goats, so this illustration tapped into an experience they knew well. Sheep and goats are blessed neither with strong defensive skills nor with the ability to quickly flee a predator. So, any time the family's livestock was in open country, and particularly when they were pastured in the Judean Wilderness (Luke 15:4), the shepherd stayed with them. She or he led them to pastures, assured contact with watering stations, and protected them from predators. The job was made a bit easier because sheep and goats are gregarious animals. What they lacked in defensive or flight skills they made up for in numbers. Many eyes and ears were employed to spot and warn of a predator's approach. If one animal moved, every animal moved.

But in this story, we find the exception. A sheep wandered off by itself. Separated from the shepherd and flock, this animal was in real trouble. The shepherd had a choice to make, either pursue the lost animal or write off the loss. Even if the shepherd left the rest of the flock with another caregiver, they could not count on that person offering high quality care. In Jesus's parables, the shepherd took the risk, found the wanderer, and joyfully brought it home.

The lost sheep in these parables represents marginalized members of society. First-century Judaism tended to divide society into those who

Jesus's story of the lost sheep in the wilderness highlights the Lord's love for those whom society has marginalized.

were worth your time and those who were not. People tended to devalue those in the out group: Gentiles, the ritually unclean, children, tax collectors, and public sinners. How did the Father think about them? The Father saw them as people of value. And when one of them wandered, he was quick to pursue and return the lost: "I tell you that in the same way there will be more rejoicing in heaven over one sinner who repents than over ninety-nine righteous persons who do not need to repent" (Luke 15:7).

For Further Reference: **Psalms 23; 28:9; Ezekiel 34:11–16; John 10:1–18**

JESUS ON THE THREE QUALITIES OF GENUINE FORGIVENESS

Matthew 18:15–35

"Shouldn't you have had mercy on your fellow servant just as I had on you?" (Matthew 18:33)

▶ **WHO & WHERE**

Jesus, Peter, Galilee

▶ **WHAT IS THIS TEXT TALKING ABOUT?**

Forgiveness

▶ **WHAT DOES THIS TEXT TEACH?**

Genuine forgiveness has three qualities. It is restorative, persistent, and compassionate.

O n any given day, I have the opportunity to respond to the sins of oth-ers, some of which have personally harmed me. It is easy to say, "I forgive you." But Jesus is looking for more. In Matthew 18, three qualities emerge that characterize genuine forgiveness.

First, genuine forgiveness is restorative (Matt. 18:15–20). Sin damages personal relationships. And it is those relationships that are vital to the well-being of the church. That is why Jesus outlined a set of steps designed to bring healing to the sinner and restoration within the church.

Second, genuine forgiveness is persistent (Matt. 18:21–22). Peter raised a question that was more of a declaration. He thought he was being magnanimous by offering to forgive someone who sinned against him seven times. Traditional Jewish teaching came to define the limit as three times! But Jesus offers a new, more extravagant number (either seventy-seven or seventy times seven), not a literal number but a metaphoric number. Forgiveness is persistent beyond imagination, a forgiveness that "keeps no record of wrongs" (1 Cor. 13:5).

Third, genuine forgiveness is compassionate, as Jesus's parable teaches (Matt. 18:23–35). It is a story with three main characters—none of whom Jesus's audience would have celebrated. The size of the debts mentioned is so astronomical that it removes the story from the realm of ordinary citi-zens and places it in the realm of the king and his tax collection system. A provincial tax official owed him an extraordinary sum of money. A talent equaled twenty years of income earned by an ordinary worker. This tax of-ficial owed the king ten thousand talents! He had no way to cover it. That makes the compassion the king showed him extraordinary. Even though Jesus's listeners would not have celebrated this provincial tax official, they expected him to be grateful for his debt relief and to show compassion to another tax collection worker who owed him a far lesser debt, one hun-dred denarii (a denarius was the wage an ordinary person would earn in one day). The lesson is clear. If we can expect a pagan tax collector shown compassion to pay it forward, how much truer of believers. The mercy the

Father has shown us will always be greater than the mercy we are asked to show others.

And that brings us full circle. The forgiveness I offer others can pulse with the kind of forgiveness I have been shown—forgiveness that is restorative, persistent, and compassionate.

For Further Reference: **Leviticus 19:17–18; Matthew 6:12; Galatians 6:1; 2 Thessalonians 3:14–15; James 2:12–13**

JESUS ON RECOGNIZING ALLIES IN KINGDOM WORK

Mark 9:38–41; Luke 9:49–50

"For whoever is not against us is for us." (Mark 9:40)

▶ **WHO & WHERE**
Jesus, John, Galilee

▶ **WHAT IS THIS TEXT TALKING ABOUT?**
Allies in kingdom work

▶ **WHAT DOES THIS TEXT TEACH?**
The church of Jesus will see allies in all those who confess that Jesus is the Messiah.

Competition! John and the other disciples did not like what they saw— other religious teachers in Galilee.

There were plenty of them because of the way the Old Testament ends. As wonderful as this collection of biblical books is, neither 2 Chronicles (the way the Hebrew Bible ends) nor Malachi brings us to a satisfying conclusion. The Old Testament ends before the end of the story. As a result, many religious teachers in Galilee were offering conclusions. Not all were getting it right. But one of them was, a man who was validating his teaching by driving out demons in Jesus's name. John and the other disciples took pride in the fact that they were Jesus's students and took offense at this competitor encroaching on their territory. They ordered him to stop "because he was not one of us" (Mark 9:38).

They expected a pat on the back, but instead Jesus spoke to the disciples about kingdom allies. To be sure, there were those who lacked a personal relationship with Jesus who used his name in a bid to perform miracles. Just ask the seven sons of Sceva how that worked for them (Acts 19:13–16)! But here, Jesus is speaking about those who understood that he brings conclusion to the story begun in the Old Testament. These are people who belong to the Messiah (Mark 9:41). Jesus urges John and the disciples to see them as coworkers in the kingdom, even if they are not part of the team of the Twelve. He honors their contribution to the kingdom whether they are doing miracles like driving out demons or simple acts of service like offering the thirsty a cup of water.

The church today can fall into the same competitive trap. It is laid when we construct our church according to a business model in which we see ourselves in competition with others for "potential customers." This can lead to jealousy and unhealthy competition. Jesus offers this alternative. All those who call Jesus their Lord and Savior are allies in kingdom work, no matter what their denominational affiliation. They are "one of us" and their work advances the kingdom, "for whoever is not against us is for us" (Mark 9:38, 40).

For Further Reference: **Numbers 11:27–29; Acts 19:13–16; Romans 8:31; 1 Corinthians 12:3**

JESUS ON THE RISK OF CARELESS SINNING

Mark 9:42–50

"It is better for you to enter the kingdom of God with one eye than to have two eyes and be thrown into hell." (Mark 9:47)

> **WHO & WHERE**

Jesus, Galilee

> **WHAT IS THIS TEXT TALKING ABOUT?**

Careless sinning

> **WHAT DOES THIS TEXT TEACH?**

The remedy for careless sinning is careful thought about our sins' eternal consequences.

Well, these images in Mark 9 are disturbing and intentionally so. Jesus is using them to get us to think carefully about the high consequences of careless sinning.

In these verses, Jesus highlights two types of careless sinning starting with sins that bring harm to the vulnerable. The "little ones" (Mark 9:42) could be either children or those like the man mentioned in the previous verses who was driving out demons in Jesus's name (v. 38). Either way, Jesus is talking about harming those who are young, new to the faith, or both—those least able to defend themselves. The image that accompanies this part of the lesson is a donkey mill. This was a heavy, stone mill used to grind grain at the industrial level. It was so heavy that a donkey provided the force needed to operate it. This "large millstone" did not float.

Jesus used the image of an industrial-scale donkey mill to speak about the grave consequences of careless sinning.

Imagine having this millstone tied to your neck and being thrown into the sea. What a horrible experience—helplessly sinking as the growing water pressure drives the last breath from our lungs. This experience is preferable to causing the most vulnerable to stumble.

The second type of careless sin is the kind we impose on ourselves. Jesus highlights the personal nature of these thoughts and actions by mentioning hand, foot, and eye (vv. 43–47). The image that accompanies this lesson is no less disturbing. Imagine intentionally maiming yourself by cutting off a limb or gouging out an eye. That horrific outcome is better than the place that awaits careless sinners.

Of course, Jesus is not suggesting we drown people in the sea or practice self-mutilation. He summons these images to highlight the point that forgiven people can become careless in how they think about sin. This is extremely dangerous because behind every sin lies doubt. Doubt is the opposite of faith and the first step toward unbelief. And unbelief severs us from the forgiveness of Jesus, bringing us to the place of eternal punishment. Vivid pictures of the consequences of our sin keep us from careless sinning, a lifestyle that starts us on the road to a place where "the worms that eat them do not die, and the fire is not quenched" (v. 48).

For Further Reference: Isaiah 66:24; Matthew 5:13; Romans 6:15–18; Galatians 5:19–21; 1 Thessalonians 5:15

CHAPTER 4

Jesus's Ministry beyond Galilee

JESUS RAISED THE WIDOW'S SON AT NAIN

Luke 7:11–17

"'A great prophet has appeared among us,' they said. 'God has come to help his people.'" (Luke 7:16)

▶ **WHO & WHERE**

Jesus, widow's son, Nain

▶ **WHAT IS THIS TEXT TALKING ABOUT?**

The identity of Jesus

▶ **WHAT DOES THIS TEXT TEACH?**

By raising the widow's son at Nain, Jesus established his identity as the great Prophet promised in the Old Testament.

Tragic deaths were an all-too-common feature of life in Israel. Nevertheless, Jesus raised the dead on just three occasions. In each case, the miracle had a unique lesson to teach, a lesson linked to its location.

In this case, the location is Nain—a small agricultural village on the north side of Mount Moreh. As Jesus arrived, a heart-wrenching story was unfolding. The townspeople were somberly walking to the cemetery with a grief-stricken widow whose only son had died. Many offered support. Jesus could offer more. He stopped the funeral procession in its tracks and spoke to the deceased young man as if he had overslept: "Young man, I say to you, get up!" (Luke 7:14). He awakened, sat up, spoke a few words, and then embraced his tearful mother.

But that is not the end of the story. And to appreciate what happens next, we need to remember where we are. Being located on the north side of

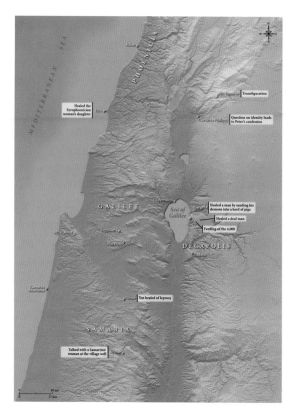

Mount Moreh put Nain a little less than two miles (three kilometers) from Shunem to its south. There, an eerily similar story had played out at the time of Elisha (2 Kings 4:8–37). This Old Testament prophet had asked the Lord to provide his host family with the child they longed for. Within the year, the couple celebrated the birth of a son. And within a few verses, we read of the boy's death. When word of the tragedy reached Elisha, he hurried to Shunem where the Lord used him to bring the young man back to life and place him into his mother's arms. This stunning miracle validated Elisha as a prophet, one who spoke for the Lord.

This is the kind of story that sticks to a place. So, when Jesus set foot on this mountain and did a companion miracle, the people made the connection with the raising of the boy at Shunem. "A great prophet has appeared among us," they said. "God has come to help his people" (Luke 7:16). This miracle not only showcased the compassion and power of Jesus but also led people to a greater understanding of who he was. Jesus was the long-awaited Prophet (Deut. 18:15)—not just someone who spoke for God but God himself who had come to speak to us.

For Further Reference: Deuteronomy 18:15; 2 Kings 4:8–37; John 1:19–21; 7:40

JESUS AND THE SAMARITAN WOMAN AT SYCHAR

John 4:1–42

"The woman said, 'I know that Messiah' (called Christ) 'is coming. When he comes, he will explain everything to us.'
Then Jesus declared, 'I, the one speaking to you—I am he.'"
(John 4:25–26)

▶ WHO & WHERE

Jesus, Samaritan woman, Sychar

▶ WHAT IS THIS TEXT TALKING ABOUT?

The identity of Jesus

▶ WHAT DOES THIS TEXT TEACH?

Jesus is the Messiah, the Savior of the world.

This story is unique because of what Jesus said and where he said it. Jesus was thirsty. And his simple request for a drink turned into a lengthy conversation ranging over a wide array of topics. Jesus and the Samaritan woman who came to draw water at midday spoke about water rights, the woman's history of scarred relationships, and the appropriate place to worship. As the conversation became more personal and more uncomfortable, the Samaritan woman kept changing the topic to no avail. So, she looked for a way to bring it to a close and thought she had the perfect out: "Let's wait for the arrival of the Messiah and let him provide the answers to all the questions." A powerful revelation follows. Jesus does something that the Gospels report him doing only twice. He verbally identified himself as the Messiah: "I, the one speaking to you—I am he" (John 4:26).

It is not just what Jesus said but where he said it that increases the power of this one-sentence sermon. From the start, this story signals that place is important. John tells us that Jesus was traveling between two non-adjacent Roman districts, Judea and Galilee. And although Jesus had several other route options, John says that Jesus "had to" travel through the district of Samaria (John 4:3–4). That raises the unasked question, what was so important for him to do in Samaria? Meeting a woman at a well also signals that the location is important. She reminds us that there is an Old Testament history to this place involving Jacob (vv. 5–6, 12) and raises the topic of the worship conducted here (v. 20).

That is when the light bulb flickers on. Old Testament Shechem and New Testament Sychar occupied the same mountain pass. It was here Abraham learned that Canaan was the Promised Land, the very place that his family would grow into a great nation and in which the Messiah would save the world from sin (Gen. 12:1–7). Abraham and Sarah immediately built an altar and worshipped here. That makes Shechem/ Sychar the location that had waited longer than any other in the Promised Land for the promise of the Savior to be realized. No wonder Jesus "had to" come here.

The woman got it, shared it, and then the village of Sychar got it: "We know that this man really is the Savior of the world" (John 4:42).

For Further Reference: **Genesis 12:1–7; Isaiah 12:3; Jeremiah 2:13; Matthew 1:16; 16:16; Revelation 7:17; 21:6**

JESUS'S FIRST TRIP TO THE DECAPOLIS

Matthew 8:23–34; Mark 4:35–5:20; Luke 8:22–39

"So the man went away and began to tell in the Decapolis how much Jesus had done for him." (Mark 5:20)

▶ WHO & WHERE
Jesus, demon-possessed man, Decapolis

▶ WHAT IS THIS TEXT TALKING ABOUT?
Jesus's relationship with Gentiles

▶ WHAT DOES THIS TEXT TEACH?
Jesus is also the Savior of the Gentiles.

Just how large and diverse was the kingdom of God? Jesus enacts the answer during his first trip to the Decapolis.

The gospel writers use a variety of labels for the setting. Here, I will focus on two. The Greek label Decapolis ("ten cities") represents the European view. Decapolis cities were large urban centers imposed upon the land by European powers. The pagan temples and high culture within them were designed to persuade the locals that the Greco-Roman world was superior to their own. The territory ruled by each of these cities overlapped to become the region of the Decapolis that included much of the eastern shoreline of the Sea of Galilee. The other label represents the perspective of the observant Jewish culture living on the northwest shore of the Sea of Galilee. For them, this was "the other side" (Mark 4:35; Luke 8:22)—a devilish place to be avoided at all costs.

Many of the story's details reinforce this negative view of the Decapolis. As Jesus and the disciples crossed the lake, a surreal and unexpected windstorm threatened to swamp the boat. Surely a sign that they were headed in the wrong direction! When they touched the eastern shore, the uncleanness of the place is highlighted by the welcoming committee. (Matthew says there were two men, Mark and Luke focus on the spokesman who was most changed by the experience.) For observant Jewish men, this story is filled with cultural taboos such as naked men living in tombs with a herd of pigs nearby. Had Jesus brought the disciples here to demonstrate the ritually unclean, depraved nature of the Gentile world? Would they quickly turn around and head for home?

Jesus had come to teach a lesson, but not the one the disciples expected. Upon arrival, Jesus got out of the boat. I am not sure the disciples followed! In short order, the demon-possessed man was

Ruins of the Decapolis city of Hippos, the "other side" of the lake Jesus sought to reach with the gospel.

clothed and in his right mind (Mark 5:15; Luke 8:35). The demons and their new host, a herd of pigs, had run to the lake and drowned. And the man who had been healed received a commission. He begged Jesus to take him with him. Instead, Jesus instructed this Gentile believer to tell the people on his side of the lake "how much the Lord has done for you, and how he has had mercy on you" (Mark 5:19). He became the evangelist of the Decapolis. Jesus had come to seek and save all who were lost no matter which side of the lake they lived on.

For Further Reference: **Genesis 12:3; Isaiah 9:1–3; 58:6; 60:3; Matthew 4:12–17; Luke 4:18; John 3:16; Acts 2:39; Ephesians 3:1–6**

JESUS CELEBRATES THE EXEMPLARY FAITH OF A PHOENICIAN WOMAN

Matthew 15:21–28; Mark 7:24–30

"Woman, you have great faith!" (Matthew 15:28)

▶ **WHO & WHERE**

Jesus, Phoenician woman, region of Tyre and Sidon

▶ **WHAT IS THIS TEXT TALKING ABOUT?**

Gentile faith

▶ **WHAT DOES THIS TEXT TEACH?**

Gentiles are capable of exemplary faith.

Jesus had walked for two days and was now far north of his home base along the Sea of Galilee. He'd come to the region of Tyre and Sidon, a place associated with derogatory labels like "Canaanite" and "Phoenicia" (Matt. 15:22; Mark 7:26), to teach a lesson on Gentile faith.

This demonstration involves a local Phoenician woman. At first, we are suspicious of her because the most iconic female figure from this region in the Old Testament was Jezebel. This Phoenician princess entered the story of Israel as part of an economic development plan hatched by King Omri and his son Ahab. After Israel gained control of the overland trade routes east of the Jordan River, they struck a deal with Phoenicia to use their ships and trading centers around the Mediterranean Sea for distribution. To seal the deal, Jezebel became the bride of the Israelite prince Ahab. She immediately made her mark on her new home. She joined with Ahab in setting up a temple for the worship of Baal in the capital city (1 Kings 16:32). She executed the Lord's prophets and put pagan religious leaders on the royal payroll (1 Kings 18:4, 19). And she acquired the vineyard her husband wanted from Naboth by having this innocent man executed (1 Kings 21:11–14). In the end, Jezebel came to define the worst era in Israel's history (1 Kings 16:29–33).

But we quickly find that the woman Jesus met is no Jezebel. Her demon-possessed daughter desperately needed help. Nevertheless, she did not go to the pagan deities of her region but to the Jewish Messiah whom she addressed as "Lord, Son of David" (Matt. 15:22). This was a woman of faith. She humbly approached Jesus on her knees. When Jesus likened her posture to that of a dog (a feral scavenger, Ps. 59:14–15), she changed the image only slightly, likening herself to the household dogs begging under the table. And despite being initially ignored and addressed disparagingly, she boldly persisted with her request.

This was not just faith, but exemplary faith. And what made it more striking is that this Gentile woman from the home region of Jezebel demonstrated a faith unlike the kind of faith Jesus had seen in Israel. And that is why Jesus came all the way to the region of Tyre and Sidon. He wanted to show the disciples and us that Gentiles were capable not only of faith but of exemplary faith.

For Further Reference: **1 Kings 16:30–33; 18:4, 19; Matthew 8:10; Romans 1:16; 15:8–9, 18**

JESUS FEEDS FOUR THOUSAND HOUSEHOLDS

Matthew 15:29–39; Mark 7:31–8:10

"I have compassion for these people." (Matthew 15:32)

▶ WHO & WHERE
Jesus, Gentiles, Decapolis

▶ WHAT IS THIS TEXT TALKING ABOUT?
A dramatic change in the Decapolis

▶ WHAT DOES THIS TEXT TEACH?
Jesus changed the life of one man who changed the fate of the Decapolis.

What happened to this place?! We have all had the experience of visiting a hometown or favorite getaway only to find it different than we remembered. This story is about that kind of change.

Let's start with location. Jesus had left the region of Tyre and Sidon and traveled into the Decapolis on his way back to his home base on the northwest shore of the Sea of Galilee. The Decapolis on the east side of the

Sea of Galilee stood in dramatic contrast with the observant Jewish world on the northwest side of the lake. This was Gentile country—a place in which people ate pork and did not observe the Sabbath. Lacking meaningful contact with the Hebrew Scriptures, they did not know who God was nor did they expect a Messiah.

It is also a place we have been before with Jesus (Mark 5:1–20). But the change! The hillsides full of pigs are now filled with people, four thousand households totaling well over ten thousand people. The place where Jesus healed one demon-possessed man now witnessed hundreds of healing miracles. The place filled with pagan temples now heard people singing the praises of "the God of Israel" (Matt. 15:31). And the people who once pleaded with Jesus to leave their land now cannot get enough of him. In fact, they were so passionate about being with him that they outstayed

The traditional location of the tomb lived in by the demon-possessed man at Kursi. After Jesus healed him, his witness changed the Decapolis.

the small amount of food they brought with them. Rather than send them away, Jesus had compassion on them and turned a small number of fish and modest amount of bread into a feast that satisfied everyone there and showed Jesus's love and concern for the Gentile world.

What caused this place to look so different? Jesus changed one man. And the Holy Spirit worked through that one man to change the Decapolis. The horrible, hopeless life of the demon-possessed man changed when Jesus's boat touched his side of the lake. After being healed, this man begged Jesus to get in the boat and go with him. Jesus refused and instead said, "Go home to your own people and tell them how much the Lord has done for you, and how he has had mercy on you" (Mark 5:19). He did. And when he did, the Decapolis changed.

For Further Reference: **Mark 5:1–20; Romans 1:5; 15:7–12; Ephesians 3:6**

THE DEEPER MEANING OF THE TWO FEEDING MIRACLES

Matthew 16:5–12; Mark 8:14–21

"Then they understood that he was not telling them to guard against the yeast used in bread, but against the teaching of the Pharisees and Sadducees." (Matthew 16:12)

▶ WHO & WHERE
Jesus, the disciples, Sea of Galilee

▶ WHAT IS THIS TEXT TALKING ABOUT?
The geography of forgiveness

▶ WHAT DOES THIS TEXT TEACH?

Jesus offered forgiveness to everyone, no matter which side of the lake they lived on.

Taken separately, each of the two feeding miracles teaches that Jesus is compassionate and powerful. Taken together, they teach a profound lesson on the geography of forgiveness.

The key phrase in these verses can be as confusing to us as it was to the disciples: "Be on your guard against the yeast of the Pharisees and Sadducees" (Matt. 16:6). Jesus is using yeast as a metaphor for the teaching of the Jewish religious teachers that threatened to permeate and disable the future work of the disciples. That "yeast" assumed that the forgiveness of sins and membership in the kingdom was ethnically limited. This mistaken notion shows up in another food metaphor. Within Judaism, many visualized the coming kingdom as a great feast enjoyed with the founders of the Jewish faith (Matt. 8:11), but they presumed Gentiles were not on the guest list. This limiting of the kingdom is the "yeast" addressed by the two feeding miracles.

At first glance, the similarities between the feeding of the four and five thousand stand out. Thousands flocked to Jesus in remote locations, received his teaching, and were then fed by the miraculous multiplication of a small amount of food. These similarities make it clear that Jesus treated those present at both miracles in precisely the same way.

But who was present? That is where the miracles differ. We sense it first in the location of the miracles. Jesus fed the five thousand on the northwest side of the Sea of Galilee near Bethsaida. The four thousand were fed on the east side of the Sea of Galilee in the Decapolis. Generally speaking, these locations were home to different ethnic groups—northwest was Jewish and east was Gentile. The second difference is the number of basketfuls of leftovers collected. In the case of the five thousand, there were twelve—an ethnic marker for Jews (Josh. 3:12; Matt. 19:28). In the case of the four thousand, the number was seven—an ethnic marker for Gentiles (Deut. 7:1). This means the feeding of the five thousand was done for Jews and the feeding of the four thousand for Gentiles.

And that is why Jesus revisited both events in this narrative. He wants to be sure that the Twelve get the point. The "yeast" of the Pharisees and Sadducees limited the kingdom and forgiveness to the Jews. But Jesus used the two feeding miracles to show that the geography of forgiveness extended to all shores of the lake and so included all ethnic groups—for the Jews as well as for the Gentiles.

For Further Reference: Matthew 14:13–21; 15:29–39; Mark 6:30–44; 8:1–13, John 3:16

PETER'S FAITH DECLARATION

Matthew 16:13–20; Mark 8:27–30; Luke 9:18–20

"You are the Messiah, the Son of the living God."
(Matthew 16:16)

▶ WHO & WHERE
Jesus, Peter, region of Caesarea Philippi

▶ WHAT IS THIS TEXT TALKING ABOUT?
The identity of Jesus

▶ WHAT DOES THIS TEXT TEACH?
Jesus is the Messiah, the Son of the living God.

The stories of the Promised Land are meant to clarify who God is. One part of this land didn't get it, the region of Caesarea Philippi. This is where Jesus took the disciples for a conversation about divine identity.

Pick a story, any Old Testament story from the region of Caesarea Philippi, and you will be disappointed. This region's stories persistently present a confusing picture of who God is. In the Old Testament, King Jeroboam built a temple at Dan with golden calves (1 Kings 12:26–31). Jeroboam intentionally blended and confused worship of the Lord and Baal to achieve his political legacy. In the third century BC, the Greco-Roman world established a worship site for the half-goat, half-man deity, Pan. And by the time Jesus arrived, Herod the Great had built a temple dedicated to the Roman emperor. In all eras, the region of Caesarea Philippi got God wrong.

It is in this context that Jesus asked the disciples this question: "Who do you say I am?" Guided by the Spirit, Peter gave the prize answer: "You are the Messiah, the Son of the living God" (Matt. 16:15–16). Finally, the region heard an unambiguous and accurate description of the divine.

Jesus was not about to let the moment pass, and he used place to make it memorable. The pagan sanctuaries at Caesarea Philippi were built into a 131-foot (40-meter), multicolored cliff face, the southern toe of the sprawling Mount Hermon. This "rock" had been the foundation for so many mis-

representations of the one true God. Jesus said that it was not on *this* rocky outcropping, but on *this rock* of Peter's confession his church would be built. A correct understanding of God's identity was the foundation for everything else the church would say and do. They would get nothing else right if they got this wrong.

This cave at the base of Mount Hermon was connected with Hades and worship of the pagan deity Pan.

And when they got it right, the church's power was stunning. The beautiful rock wall at Caesarea is interrupted by a massive cave (66 feet wide and 49 feet tall [20 meters wide and 15 meters tall]). Eusebius tells us that the Romans thought this otherworldly looking place was the entry into the afterlife—the gate of Hades. It became a symbol of death. Jesus seized on the image, declaring that the well-founded church will be so powerful that death itself will yield before it: "The gates of Hades will not overcome it" (Matt. 16:18).

For Further Reference: 1 Kings 12:26–31; Psalms 2:7; 42:2; Romans 8:37–39; Hebrews 1:1–4

JESUS ANNOUNCES HIS IMPENDING DEATH IN JERUSALEM

Matthew 16:21–28; Mark 8:31–9:1; Luke 9:21–27

"Whoever wants to be my disciple must deny themselves and take up their cross and follow me. For whoever wants to save their life will lose it, but whoever loses their life for me will find it."
(Matthew 16:24–25)

▶ WHO & WHERE
Jesus, disciples, region of Caesarea Philippi

▶ WHAT IS THIS TEXT TALKING ABOUT?
The implications of Jesus's coming death and resurrection

The impending death and resurrection of Jesus provoked an increase in Satan's efforts, which meant that Jesus's followers would bear the cross.

Big changes were in the works. Jesus was about to trade his ministry in the north for mistreatment in Jerusalem. As they began the trip south, Jesus explained more fully what this meant for him and for the disciples.

For Jesus, the trip south signaled an increase in tensions with the Jewish leadership of Jerusalem that would culminate in his arrest, trials, abuse, and execution. He would rise from the dead, but that detail seems to have gotten lost amid the horror of the others.

For both Jesus and the disciples, this meant an increase in Satan's activity as he sought to upend the rescue plan. He was desperate to stop it, because this trip to Jerusalem spelled final defeat for this fallen angel. At the start of Jesus's public ministry, the Devil had used the flanks of Mount Hermon to offer Jesus a path to the kingdoms of the world without the cross (Matt. 4:8–11). Now in this same region, using the voice of Jesus's trusted follower Peter, this maniacal spirit sought to interfere with his trip south. The voice was Peter's, but Jesus quickly identified the one behind it: "Get behind me, Satan!" (Matt. 16:23). One thing was now certain. Satan's efforts to prevent the trip to Jerusalem had begun.

For the disciples and other followers of Jesus, this meant reframing their view of what it meant to be a believer. They also would bear the cross. The Romans often had the criminals and slaves facing execution carry part of the cross to the execution site. Here, Jesus is using that image as a metaphor. He is not talking about the hardships and difficulties that are generally part of the human experience. He is speaking of the consequences of being a follower of Jesus. Not all believers face the same kind or degree of challenge, but all believers of Jesus are challenged to demonstrate self-denial, putting the Lord and his church ahead of their own interests, even if that means surrendering life itself. "For whoever wants to save their life will lose it," Jesus explained, "but whoever loses their life for me will find it" (Matt. 16:25).

For Further Reference: Isaiah 52:13–53:12; Daniel 7:13–14; Matthew 4:8–11; Hebrews 11:1–12:3

JESUS'S TRANSFIGURATION

Matthew 17:1–13; Mark 9:2–13; Luke 9:28–36

"This is my Son, whom I love; with him I am well pleased. Listen to him!" (Matthew 17:5)

▶ WHO & WHERE
Jesus, Peter, James, John, Mount Hermon

▶ WHAT IS THIS TEXT TALKING ABOUT?
Resistance to Jesus's final trip to Jerusalem

▶ WHAT DOES THIS TEXT TEACH?
The transfiguration called for the disciples to support and encourage Jesus on his final trip to Jerusalem.

The problem is understandable. Jesus had just given details about his final trip to Jerusalem. There he faced arrest, trial, torture, and execution. While Peter verbally and vehemently objected, I suspect others felt the same way. The decision to go to Jerusalem under these circumstances was out of the question. The resistance had begun, and Jesus could not afford to expend time and energy fighting his students' objections all the way to Jerusalem.

The transfiguration was meant to defeat this resistance through four interacting components. First, Jesus led Peter, James, and John onto a "high mountain" (Matt. 17:1; Mark 9:2). Given the fact that they were still in the region of Caesarea Philippi with a return to Galilee still in the future (Matt. 16:13; 17:22; Mark 8:27; 9:30), this high mountain had to be near Caesarea Philippi. And given the adjective "high," there is only one mountain that fits. At 9,232 feet (2,814 meters), Mount Hermon is 2.3 times taller than its nearest competitor. Why would Jesus take the disciples onto the slopes of this mountain? Because mountains were the usual setting for the sharing of divine insights, like Mount Sinai or Mount Zion. When Peter recalls the experience, he puts the geography in that category, calling it "the sacred mountain" (2 Peter 1:18).

The second element was the physical change in Jesus's appearance: "As he was praying, the appearance of his face changed, and his clothes became as bright as a flash of lightning" (Luke 9:29). This powerful visual brought the disciples to a new level of attentiveness.

The third element was the appearance of Moses and Elijah. These were the two Old Testament prophets who played a significant role in advancing the plan of salvation. Note they were not merely present but were talking with Jesus about the next step of that plan, his trip to Jerusalem (Luke 9:31). If these noteworthy figures did not object, why should the disciples?

And finally, we have the voice booming from the heavens that offered this clear directive: "Listen to him!" (Matt. 17:5). All four elements combined to achieve one important purpose. The disciples had to stop resisting and instead support Jesus on this final trip to Jerusalem.

For Further Reference: Exodus 34:29–35; Psalm 2:6; Isaiah 42:1; John 1:14; 2 Peter 1:16–18

JESUS HEALS A DEMON-POSSESSED BOY

Matthew 17:14–21; Mark 9:14–29; Luke 9:37–43

"Why couldn't we drive it out?" (Matthew 17:19)

▶ **WHO & WHERE**

Jesus, disciples, Mount Hermon

▶ **WHAT IS THIS TEXT TALKING ABOUT?**

The ability to defeat evil spirits

▶ **WHAT DOES THIS TEXT TEACH?**

Jesus provides the knowledge and faith needed to defeat evil spirits.

We are not alone. We spend our weeks walking not only among people whom we can see but among spirits we can't. Some are evil and intend to harm us. This story demonstrates that Jesus is the key to their defeat.

The day after Jesus's transfiguration, the disciples were engaged in a heated discussion. A man whose son exhibited symptoms of epilepsy was pleading for their help. In this case, the cause of the severe illness was an evil spirit. Although the disciples had been given authority to drive out such spirits and had been successful before (Matt. 10:8; Mark 6:13), this time they failed. Jesus stepped in, healed the boy, and then dealt with the disciples' question, "Why couldn't we drive it out?" (Matt. 17:19).

Jesus points to two problems. The first is their lack of knowledge. They had found success against other fallen spirits and so presumed that

A field of white mustard whose tiny seeds Jesus used in a lesson on mountain-moving faith.

whatever they had done before would work in this case. Clearly, the spirit world is more complex than they realized. Jesus explained, "This kind can come out only by prayer" (Mark 9:29). Their lack of knowledge was compounded by their lack of faith. When the father approached Jesus, his own faith was shaken by the disciples' inability to help his son. Now, he wondered if Jesus could help. To which Jesus replied, "Everything is possible for one who believes" (v. 23).

But how much faith was needed? The answer comes from the natural world. Jesus points to two objects that differ dramatically in size. The first one you could not miss, Mount Hermon. It dominated the horizon soaring to 9,232 feet (2,814 meters) in elevation. The other was all around but largely unnoticed because it was so small, the seed of the mustard plant. This may have been white mustard (*Sinapis alba*), one of the dominant species in the northern part of Israel. The smallest imaginable amount of faith, like that of a mustard seed, combined with knowledge could do the unimaginable—move the likes of Mount Hermon.

For Further Reference: **Exodus 4:11; Proverbs 1:7; Isaiah 58:6; Matthew 10:8; Mark 6:13; Luke 4:18; Philippians 4:12–13; Hebrews 11:1–2**

JESUS ON DIVORCE

Matthew 19:1–12; Mark 10:1–12

"Is it lawful for a man to divorce his wife for any and every reason?" (Matthew 19:3)

▶ WHO & WHERE
Jesus, Perea

▶ WHAT IS THIS TEXT TALKING ABOUT?
Divorce

▶ WHAT DOES THIS TEXT TEACH?
Divorce is a deviation from God's original plan and should be pursued only under extreme circumstances.

Divorce was a risky topic for Jesus. But when the Pharisees tried to entrap him with their question, he turned the trap into an opportunity to clarify our thinking on the topic.

Let's begin by putting this conversation into its religious and political contexts. "Is it lawful for a man to divorce his wife for any and every reason?" (Matt. 19:3). The religious world of Judaism was debating how to understand the language of Deuteronomy 24:1. In this verse, Moses outlined the process of providing a certificate of divorce for the wife in this unfortunate situation. This process was initiated when her husband found "something indecent about her." What did this enigmatic phrase mean? Those who followed Rabbi Shammai said "indecent" suggested sexual infidelity. Those who followed Rabbi Hillel said that the "something" could be "anything," including a poorly prepared meal or even the finding of a more attractive marriage partner. The Pharisees wanted to know where Jesus stood on the continuum between these two answers.

Their apparent scholarly interest also had a political side. Jesus was traveling to Jerusalem through Perea. During the time he was in Perea and until he crossed into Judea, he was traveling in the area ruled by Herod Antipas. This ruler had recently executed John the Baptist for his criticism of Antipas's divorce and remarriage (Matt. 14:3–12). How Jesus answered carried the same risk for him.

Swayed neither by politics nor by religious agenda, Jesus gave his answer. The original plan of the Creator was still the best plan. He redirected his listeners from Deuteronomy to Genesis to establish the baseline. Genesis 2:24 defined marriage as a permanent relationship between husband and wife. This was still the Creator's intention. Marriage partners should maintain that as the goal, even in a sin-ruined world.

Moses had offered a concession to this principle because some marriages would not endure in a post-fall world. Jesus acknowledged this reality. And given the debate between the schools of Shammai and Hillel, Jesus was much closer to Shammai. He illustrates the kind of circumstances in which a marriage might become irretrievably broken, one plagued by sexual immorality. But he does not insist on divorce even in such circumstances nor does this illustration necessarily limit divorce to circumstances involving sexual immorality. His point? Divorce should be pursued only as a last resort and only when extreme circumstances have shattered the bond.

For Further Reference: Genesis 1:26–28; 2:18–25; Malachi 2:10–16; Matthew 5:31–32; 14:3–12

JESUS ON THE VALUE OF CHILDREN

Matthew 19:13–15; Mark 10:13–16; Luke 18:15–17

"Let the little children come to me, and do not hinder them,
for the kingdom of heaven belongs to such as these."
(Matthew 19:14)

▶ WHO & WHERE
Jesus, children, Perea

▶ WHAT IS THIS TEXT TALKING ABOUT?
The value of children

▶ WHAT DOES THIS TEXT TEACH?
Jesus valued children both as people and as examples to follow.

Our children can make us crazy, make us proud, and fill our lives with love. This brief story provides one of the most endearing pictures of Jesus. As he gathers kids into his arms, he shows just how much he values our children.

The way the culture of Jesus's time saw children is betrayed by the disciples' efforts to keep kids away from Jesus. To be sure, we have plenty of examples in the Bible that show parents doting on their children and verses that celebrate sons and daughters. But generally, society in Bible times regarded children as second-rate. There are a couple of related reasons for that. First, young children were consumers rather than contributors. Families tended to grow their own food, raise their own livestock, and in the absence of a police force, provided for their own protection. While

The author's wife playing with young children in Israel, like the kids Jesus valued in his day.

children benefited, they did little to contribute toward these basic family needs. Second, the promise that children would one day become contributors was tempered by the sad reality that many children died before reaching adulthood. So, while children were loved by their parents, society did not regard them with much esteem.

Jesus saw value where society did not. He clashed with his disciples when they blocked the path of parents bringing their young children to Jesus. He was not just miffed but indignant (Mark 10:14). After quickly removing the barrier, Jesus placed his hands on the children to bless them, prayed for them, and gathered them in his arms. All of this showed that Jesus valued children for who they were not just who they might become.

He also valued them as examples to follow. Jesus had interacted with many people who thought they deserved to be in the kingdom whether due to social status, family pedigree, wealth, or wisdom. The children, who appeared to offer so little, offered the best picture. The unpretentious child was the model for the one best suited for kingdom membership. Jesus stated this in no uncertain terms: "Truly I tell you, anyone who will not receive the kingdom of God like a little child will never enter it" (Luke 18:17).

For Further Reference: Psalm 127:3–4; Proverbs 17:6; Acts 2:39; Romans 8:17; Ephesians 6:4

JESUS ON WEALTH

Matthew 19:16–30; Mark 10:17–31; Luke 18:18–30

"Truly I tell you, it is hard for someone who is rich to enter the kingdom of heaven." (Matthew 19:23)

▶ WHO & WHERE
Jesus, rich man, Perea

▶ WHAT IS THIS TEXT TALKING ABOUT?
The relationship between wealth and eternal life

▶ WHAT DOES THIS TEXT TEACH?
Wealth can inhibit a healthy relationship with the Lord and impair the quest for eternal life.

M ost people among whom Jesus walked did not have the wealth of this man. So, his conversation with Jesus provides a unique opportunity for us to hear Jesus speak on the topic of wealth. This exchange yields three important insights.

First, wealth does not automatically exclude someone from heaven. We might get the impression Jesus is saying just the opposite. The wealthy man centers the conversation on the topic of eternal life, and Jesus tells him to sell all he has in order to obtain treasure in heaven (Matt. 19:16, 21). But if Jesus were insisting that wealthy people were automatically excluded, it would put him at odds with the fact that wealthy people like Abraham and Sarah, Job, and Zacchaeus developed a saving relationship with the Lord. So why does Jesus speak like this? He is challenging the man's overconfidence by asking him to engage in a thought experiment. Would he be willing to go so far as to abandon the trust he had in his wealth? This is not the same as asserting that wealth is automatically disqualifying. Rather, it is "*hard* for someone who is rich to enter the kingdom of heaven" (Matt. 19:23, emphasis added), not impossible.

Second, wealth can nevertheless inhibit a healthy relationship with the Lord and so impair the quest for eternal life. Wealth can impart a false sense of prestige, power, and security that makes it difficult to fully trust the Lord. The story illustrates this in two ways. The first is with the hubris of the wealthy man who boasted that he had kept the law perfectly. The second is with an illustration. Getting a wealthy person into heaven is as hard as getting the largest animal in the region through the smallest domestic opening. Who then can be saved? "With man this is impossible, but not with God; all things are possible with God" (Mark 10:27).

Third and finally, Jesus asserts that earthly wealth has no direct relationship to eternal well-being. Peter wondered about this: "We have left everything to follow you! What then will there be for us?" (Matt. 19:27). Like most others in the crowd, Peter was not wealthy. Would the advantages of wealth on earth transfer to well-being in heaven? No! Heaven is a place where the first will be last and the last first.

For Further Reference: **Psalms 52:7–9; 62:10; Proverbs 11:28; 23:4–5; 1 Corinthians 13:3; 1 Timothy 6:9–10; James 5:1–6**

THE PARABLE OF THE WORKERS IN THE VINEYARD

Matthew 20:1–16

"Don't I have the right to do what I want with my own money? Or are you envious because I am generous?" (Matthew 20:15)

▶ **WHO & WHERE**

Jesus, Perea

▶ **WHAT IS THIS TEXT TALKING ABOUT?**

Fairness in the kingdom

▶ **WHAT DOES THIS TEXT TEACH?**

The kingdom of God graciously distributes blessings based on need rather than the demand for fair and equal treatment.

"That is not fair!" You have heard it. You have said it. We live in a world that presumes everyone will get one cupcake at the birthday party and equal work will be honored with equal pay. Does the kingdom of God operate on the same principle? This parable teaches it does not.

In this story-illustration, the owner of a vineyard is searching aggressively for as many day laborers as he can hire to harvest his grapes. In first-century Israel, there was no shortage of those needing work. The landless poor and tenant farmers who needed to supplement their income would wait in the town square hoping for just such an opportunity. Fair labor practices of the day were well established. You would work a twelve-hour day from six in the morning to six at night in exchange for one denarius. In this story, workers are hired throughout the day, which means some worked a full twelve hours and others worked only one hour before being paid. The gracious landowner gave everyone the same wage no matter how long they worked. Those who worked less than twelve hours were stunned and grateful. Those who had worked all day and endured the heat of the

Jesus's parable of the workers in the vineyard illustrates that the Lord sees "fairness" very differently than the world does.

day cried foul. The landowner responded, "Don't I have the right to do what I want with my own money? Or are you envious because I am generous?" (Matt. 20:15).

The story illustrates that the kingdom of God operates on a different principle than the world—grace rather than perceived fairness. And that is a good thing. According to the world's standards, it is not fair that our sins be transferred to Jesus for punishment. It's not fair that some receive a greater share of forgiveness than others because they have sinned more. Yet the kingdom of God graciously distributes blessings based on need rather than following the world's demand for fair and equal treatment. And given that standard of fairness means I would spend eternity enduring punishment. But instead, I am eternally grateful that in God's kingdom, fair and equal gives way to grace.

For Further Reference: **2 Samuel 9; Proverbs 14:30; 1 Corinthians 13:4; Ephesians 2:8–9; Titus 3:5–7; James 3:16**

JESUS REPEATEDLY ANTICIPATES PASSION WEEK

Matthew 20:17–19; Mark 10:32–34; Luke 18:31–33

"Again he took the Twelve aside and told them what was going to happen to him." (Mark 10:32)

▶ WHO & WHERE

Jesus, the Twelve, Perea

▶ WHAT IS THIS TEXT TALKING ABOUT?

Passion Week, the events of Jesus's last week on earth

▶ WHAT DOES THIS TEXT TEACH?

As Jesus moved closer to Jerusalem and unveiled more details
about Passion Week, the disciples reveal how unprepared they
were for it.

Third time is the charm. But not in this case. This is the third time Jesus
spoke to the Twelve about the events of Passion Week, the last week of
his life. They did not find the idea appealing the first two times they heard
it. The third rendition did not change their perception. Let's take a look at
the evolving lesson Jesus taught and the way the disciples reacted to it.

First, note that each conversation on Passion Week occurs in a different location. We have already encountered the first time Jesus spoke of his
impending suffering, death, and resurrection. This occurred at the base
of Mount Hermon just before his transfiguration (Matt. 16:21–26; Mark
8:31–9:1; Luke 9:22–27). He raised the topic again when they got to Galilee
(Matt. 17:22–23; Mark 9:30–32; Luke 9:43–45). And now he tries again
in Perea. If we put these three lessons on a map and timeline, we will see
that each successive lesson puts us another step closer to Jerusalem and the
moment of Jesus's crucifixion.

Second, each successive lesson adds different details. The core content
of the lesson remained the same. But the second and third lessons add information about the role of the Gentiles and how Jesus would be mocked,
insulted, spit on, flogged, and crucified. These graphic details horrified
Jesus's students and made them resist the notion even more.

And that leads to the third difference we see in these Gospel accounts—
the reaction of the disciples. The first time, Peter pulled Jesus aside and
rebuked him. Such resistance is not mentioned following the second and
third lessons. Instead, the Gospels tell us that the disciples were "filled
with grief" (Matt. 17:23), confused, and uncertain about what he meant
(Mark 9:32; Luke 9:45; 18:34). Jesus tried to help by validating the plan
using the Old Testament: "Everything that is written by the prophets

about the Son of Man will be fulfilled" (Luke 18:31). But the disciples were not buying it. That view did not fit the disciples' expectations about the Messiah. And so, despite Jesus's efforts to prepare them for the dramatic events of Passion Week, we find them increasingly unprepared for the monumental moments to come.

For Further Reference: **Psalm 22; Isaiah 52:13–53:12; Luke 24:25–27**

JESUS ON THE CHARACTER OF KINGDOM LEADERS

Matthew 20:20–28; Mark 10:35–45

"Instead, whoever wants to become great among you must be your servant, and whoever wants to be first must be slave of all."
(Mark 10:43–44)

▶ **WHO & WHERE**
Jesus, the Twelve, Perea

▶ **WHAT IS THIS TEXT TALKING ABOUT?**
The character of kingdom leaders

▶ **WHAT DOES THIS TEXT TEACH?**
Kingdom leaders will be servant-leaders like Jesus.

The words came from their mother, but the thoughts were those of James and John. They were anxious to climb the leadership ladder.

The request grew from three errant assumptions. First, they presumed the kingdom of God had positions of varying authority, just like secular governments, with the higher positions being those of greater prestige and influence. Second, they presumed that the goal was to outclimb others on this leadership ladder, just like secular leaders whose career aspirations were fueled by pride and hubris. And third, they presumed they were already on the rise since they were among the three members of Jesus's "inner circle" who were invited to participate in special-invitation events like the transfiguration. When the other ten disciples got wind of the brothers' career move, they were indignant. They too aspired to greatness.

This gave Jesus the opportunity to address the character of kingdom leaders. He destroys the analogy between secular kingdom leadership and leadership in the kingdom of God in two ways. First, he uses words, particularly the words "servant" and "slave." They are not synonymous. If kingdom leaders want to be "great," they need to become "servants." Servants were individuals who were hired to do a job for someone who held greater authority than they did. If they wanted to become "first," they had to become "slaves." Slaves belonged to an even lower class than servants. First-century slaves in Israel were often debt-slaves, individuals who had gotten into financial difficulty and had only one thing of value left, themselves. They escaped debt by selling themselves into slavery and so became fully obligated to their owner. Jesus's point? In the kingdom of God, leaders did not climb the social ladder but descended it!

The second way Jesus makes the point is with his own example of servant leadership. The King of this kingdom "did not come to be served, but to serve, and to give his life as a ransom for many" (Matt. 20:28). They were about to see what that looked like as this Servant went to the cross. The church will thrive under leaders like this, those whose lives are characterized by self-effacing humility and guided by service to others.

For Further Reference: **Psalm 10:4; Proverbs 8:13; John 13:13–16; 2 Corinthians 8:9; Philippians 2:6–8**

CHAPTER 5

Jesus's Ministry in Judea

JESUS ATTENDS THE FEAST OF TABERNACLES

John 7:1–52

"On the last and greatest day of the festival, Jesus stood and said in a loud voice, 'Let anyone who is thirsty come to me and drink. Whoever believes in me, as Scripture has said, rivers of living water will flow from within them.'" (John 7:37–38)

▶ WHO & WHERE

Jesus, Jerusalem

▶ WHAT IS THIS TEXT TALKING ABOUT?

The liability of Jesus's Galilean heritage

▶ WHAT DOES THIS TEXT TEACH?

Jesus's Galilean heritage generated both animosity and confusion in Jerusalem.

Galilee was getting it; Judea was not. Judea's struggle is highlighted by this trip to Jerusalem for the last high festival of the year.

The seven-day Feast of Tabernacles looked both backward and forward. During this festival, Israel remembered the time of their ancestors' extended stay in the wilderness by building and living in temporary shelters. It was also a week to remember and give thanks for the harvest season. By this time, it had not rained in Israel for months. The cisterns in Jerusalem were nearly empty and the farm fields baked hard by the summer sun. So, this festival also looked ahead as people prayed for the timely arrival of the first rains of the next agricultural season.

Jesus picked up on the latter theme by inviting all who were thirsty to come *to him* for water. In doing so, he associated himself with the divine water giver—the one who had provided Israel with water in the wilderness (Ex. 17:6; Pss. 78:15–16; 105:40–41) and promised to provide "water from the wells of salvation" (Isa. 12:3; see also Isa. 55:1; Zech. 13:1).

But the Judeans of Jerusalem responded to this declaration of Jesus's divine identity with animosity and confusion. The animosity of the Jewish leaders in Jerusalem was fueled by their general distrust of all Galileans whom they viewed as uneducated and spiritually compromised. Even though Jonah also came from Galilee, they dismissed the plea of Nicodemus to give Jesus a hearing by saying, "Are you from Galilee, too? Look into it, and you will find that a prophet does not come out of Galilee" (John 7:52). Their animosity is noted at the start and close of the chapter. Four times within it we read of their intentions to have Jesus killed.

During the Feast of Tabernacles, water was taken from this reservoir, the Siloam Pool, and poured out at the Temple altar with prayers for rain.

N
W ⹄ E
S

Gordon's Calvary /
Garden Tomb ◇

Fish
Gate

*Sheep's Pools /
Pools of Bethesda*

*Struthion
Pool*

Israel's Pool

Sheep
Gate

Kidron Valley

Antonia
Fortress

Gethsemane

Court of the
Israelites

Calvary ◇

Temple

Eastern
Gate

*Tower's
Pool*

Court of the
Women

Court of the
Gentiles

Gennath
Gate

Palace of
Herod Antipas

Royal Stoa

Palace
of
Herod
the
Great

Huldah
Gates

UPPER
CITY

*Gihon
Spring*

Mansion of the
High Priest

LOWER
CITY

*Serpent's
Pool*

Upper Room

*Mount of
Olives*

Essene
Gate

Water Gate

*Siloam
Pool*

Hinnom Valley

0 ____ 500 ft
0 ____ 150 m

—— Wall of Herod the Great
—— Wall added by Agrippa, after AD 41
—— Wall built by Suleiman, 16th century AD

Another product of Jesus's Galilean heritage was confusion (John 7:41–43). Judeans knew the Messiah was to come from their district (Mic. 5:2). Although Jesus had been born in Bethlehem of Judea, he had spent most of his life in Galilee. This led many to conclude that he was born in Nazareth. Although his words and actions showed otherwise, many in Jerusalem dismissed Jesus's eligibility for the role of Messiah based on his Galilean heritage.

Within just a few pages, John invites us to follow Jesus as he returns to Jerusalem for his last week on earth. This story prepares us for the animosity and confusion that await him there.

For Further Reference: **Leviticus 23:33–44; Psalm 105:40–41; Isaiah 55:1; John 4:14; Revelation 21:6**

JESUS AND THE WOMAN CAUGHT IN ADULTERY

John 8:1–11

"Let any one of you who is without sin be the
first to throw a stone at her." (John 8:7)

▶ **WHO & WHERE**

Jesus, Jerusalem's Temple complex

▶ **WHAT IS THIS TEXT TALKING ABOUT?**

The application of justice and mercy

▶ **WHAT DOES THIS TEXT TEACH?**

Divine justice and mercy can be applied simultaneously.

W hether this story was originally found in the gospel of John is debated. But either way, this compelling story is likely authentic and provides an invaluable insight into a thorny question.

It takes place in the Temple complex within Jerusalem. Jesus had entered the more contentious home turf of the Jewish teachers of Jerusalem who persistently questioned his authority. They tried to arrest him without success and now try to entrap him with a question. The question fits the place. The Temple was not only a place to worship but also a place to discuss theology and the application of that theology to life. One of the hottest questions was and is how to understand the relationship between the mercy of God and the justice of God (Ex. 34:6–8).

The question of Jesus's detractors centered around the case of a woman caught in adultery. At face value, there were problems with the case. Where was the man? Her partner in the alleged sin was to face punishment as well (Lev. 20:10). And where were the witnesses? The law insisted that no one be put to death without the testimony of two or three witnesses (Deut. 17:6). And there was a third problem with their question. It presumed Jesus had to make an either-or choice. Either he would direct the execution, erring on the side of divine justice, or he would encourage forgiveness, erring on the side of divine mercy. Jesus's detractors cared less about his answer than the outcome. The answer he gave would alienate at least half of his audience.

Jesus delayed, bending over to write in the soil. Waiting until everyone was leaning in to hear the answer, Jesus addressed the accusers. The law said the first stone was to be thrown by a witness. Since there were none, Jesus said, "Let any one of you who is without sin be the first to throw a stone at her" (John 8:7). Their resolve dissolved. And one by one, they began to slink away. Then Jesus spoke to the woman. His words neither condemn nor sanction her sin, showing that justice and mercy can be applied simultaneously.

For Further Reference: Exodus 34:6–8; Leviticus 20:10; Deuteronomy 17:7; 22:22; Luke 6:37; John 3:16; Romans 2:1

JESUS AFFIRMS HIS IDENTITY

John 8:12–59

"'Very truly I tell you,' Jesus answered,
'before Abraham was born, I am!'" (John 8:58)

▶ **WHO & WHERE**

Jesus, Jewish religious leaders, Jerusalem

▶ **WHAT IS THIS TEXT TALKING ABOUT?**

Jesus's identity

▶ **WHAT DOES THIS TEXT TEACH?**

Jesus is the great "I am" who came from beyond this world to
bring us light, truth, and freedom.

"Who are you?" The Jewish religious leaders in Jerusalem repeatedly approached Jesus with this question (John 8:25, 53). In these verses, Jesus peppers us with powerful answers.

The first answer to the question comes in the simple phrase "I am." It appears in the first and last verses of this section and twice in between (vv. 12, 24, 28, 58). Jesus repeatedly employs this phrase because it captures the powerful revelation that followed when Moses asked God to identify himself. He said, "I AM WHO I AM. This is what you are to say to the Israelites: 'I AM has sent me to you'" (Ex. 3:14). Jesus was the Lord!

This stunning statement is followed by four others that expand on it. First, all of Jesus's listeners were products of the biological processes of this world. Jesus was not. He said, "You are from below; I am from above. You are of this world; I am not of this world" (John 8:23). It would take someone from outside the problem-filled world to solve its problems. Jesus was

At Mount Sinai, in response to Moses's question about the Lord's name, God called himself "I Am."

the one. Second, Jesus identifies himself as "the light of the world" (v. 12). Sin cloaked the world in a deep darkness. During the Feast of Tabernacles, special lighting of the Temple complex recalled the Lord's promise to return light to the world (Isa. 60:1–3). Jerusalem could now arise and shine for their "light" had come (John 8:12). Third, Jesus calls himself the truth-bringer (vv. 31–32). The Devil used a lie to cause the fall into sin and so is characterized as "a murderer from the beginning, not holding to the truth, for there is no truth in him. When he lies, he speaks his native language, for he is a liar and the father of lies" (v. 44). Jesus has come to dispel the lies the Devil spreads. And finally, Jesus is a freedom-giver (v. 32). Those who sin become slaves to sin. Jesus explained, "If the Son sets you free, you will be free indeed" (v. 36).

The Jewish religious leaders rejected Jesus's words and tried to kill him. We welcome these words that further affirm and clarify who Jesus is—the great "I am" who came from beyond this world to bring our world light, truth, and freedom.

For Further Reference: Exodus 3:14; Psalm 27:1; Isaiah 43:10–13; 60:1–3; John 1:1–5, 14–18; Romans 8:2

JESUS HEALS A MAN BORN BLIND

John 9:1–41

"I am the light of the world." (John 9:5)

▶ WHO & WHERE

Jesus, man born blind, Pool of Siloam in Jerusalem

▶ WHAT IS THIS TEXT TALKING ABOUT?

Jerusalem's fateful choice

▶ WHAT DOES THIS TEXT TEACH?

Although Jesus demonstrated that he is the "light of the world," many in Jerusalem chose to live in darkness.

Jerusalem, the city of learning, had much to learn from Jesus. But the lively dialogue within this story demonstrates that many in Jerusalem failed to take the lesson seriously.

Jerusalem was not only a place to worship but also a place to learn—the city in which the finest Jewish educators resided. But the story illustrates that Jerusalem's teachers were getting two things wrong. First, they saw Jesus as an imposter, putting anyone who said Jesus was the Messiah out of the synagogue (John 9:22). And second, they believed a person's physical disability was linked to a specific sin (vv. 1, 34).

This Jerusalem story addresses both mistakes, starting with Jesus's identity. It attaches a variety of telling labels to Jesus—prophet, Messiah, Son of Man, and light of the world (vv. 5, 17, 22, 35). And second, it centers on a well-investigated miracle, the restoring of the blind man's sight—the kind of miracle expected when the Messiah came (Isa. 29:18; 35:5). Any one of these elements in the story marks Jesus as the divinely sent Savior of the world; combined they leave no doubt.

Jesus also addressed the spiritual status of those with disabilities. First, he flat-out rejected the notion that a specific sin caused the man's blindness (John 9:3). Then, he sent him to the Pool of Siloam for healing. This pool was part of Jerusalem's water collection system. But its design also made it a large ritual bath that worshippers could use prior to worshipping at the Temple. Jesus likely used the pool to further confirm the man's spiritual well-being and signal that those with disabilities are not to be shunned in worship.

Clearly, Jerusalem's religious teachers had much to learn from Jesus. But sadly, they rejected this lesson. They rejected the healed man's invitation to become a disciple of Jesus (vv. 27–29). They attacked the man's credibility (v. 34). And they rejected Jesus's own invitation to believe in the Son of Man: "Some Pharisees who were with him heard him say this [to the healed man about the blind seeing and the sighted becoming blind] and asked, 'What? Are we blind too?' Jesus said, 'If you were blind, you would not be guilty of sin; but now that you claim you can see, your guilt remains'" (vv. 40–41).

The city of learning still had much to learn.

For Further Reference: **Deuteronomy 18:15; Psalm 27:1; Isaiah 9:2; 60:1–3; Daniel 7:13; Acts 3:17; 2 Corinthians 3:12–18; Ephesians 4:18; 1 Timothy 1:13**

JESUS THE GOOD SHEPHERD

John 10:1–21

"I am the good shepherd." (John 10:11)

▶ WHO & WHERE
Jesus, Pharisees, Jerusalem

▶ WHAT IS THIS TEXT TALKING ABOUT?
Jesus is the good shepherd

▶ WHAT DOES THIS TEXT TEACH?
Jesus is the good shepherd who provides superior leadership of God's flock.

This heartwarming, pastoral picture of Jesus erupted out of a heated exchange between Jesus and the Pharisees who claimed pride of place as the leaders of God's people. Jesus paints a picture that says otherwise.

The words Jesus used to paint this picture come to life in rural areas of Israel to this day. In the morning, the shepherd calls to the family flock and leads them into open country where the sheep and goats enjoy access to food and water. Because the pasturelands increase the risk posed by

Today in Israel the picture of the good shepherd still plays out every day as the family flock is moved between pen and pasture.

predators, the shepherd keeps a watchful eye out for trouble. And at the close of the day when darkness further advantages those predators, the shepherd leads the livestock into a secure sheepfold—a modified Judean cave or pen constructed of fieldstone walls.

In his conversation with the Pharisees, Jesus contrasts his style of shepherding with those who have a different relationship to the flock: thieves, strangers, and unmotivated hired hands. Jesus approaches the flock like a good shepherd who always uses the expected entry to the sheepfold—the gate. Only those with improper motives tried to enter "by some other way."

The second difference had to do with recognition. The flock recognized and responded to the voice of the shepherd because its tone and timbre were familiar. The shepherd knew the personality quirks of each member of the flock and gave each of them names. Strangers and thieves did not have this kind of intimate relationship with the flock.

The third area had to do with protection. The good shepherd would recline in the entry of the sheepfold until it was time to travel to the food and water sources that sustained the life of the flock. He or she was the "gate" that secured access and offered protection. When in open country, the shepherd was quick to put her or his life on the line when a wolf attacked. The hired hand ran the other way when danger threatened.

And finally, the good shepherd had a vision for expanding the size of the flock. For the hired worker, more sheep meant more work so there was no passion to expand the flock. But Jesus was anxious for the flock to grow. "I have other sheep that are not of this sheep pen. I must bring them also" (John 10:16).

In many ways, the Pharisees had failed in their role as leaders. Jesus bested them all because he offered superior leadership. That makes him the good shepherd.

For Further Reference: **Psalm 23; Isaiah 40:11; Jeremiah 23:1–2; Ezekiel 34:11–16, 23; Hebrews 13:20; 1 Peter 5:4; Revelation 7:17**

JESUS ON HIS RELATIONSHIP TO THE FATHER

John 10:22–42

"I and the Father are one." (John 10:30)

> ▶ **WHO & WHERE**

Jesus, Jewish religious leaders, Temple in Jerusalem

> ▶ **WHAT IS THIS TEXT TALKING ABOUT?**

The relationship of Jesus to the Father

> ▶ **WHAT DOES THIS TEXT TEACH?**

Jesus and the Father are one.

The growing acrimony between Jesus and the Jewish religious leaders is plain to see in this story. These men asked Jesus to speak more plainly about his identity. What Jesus said, where he said it, and when he said it struck at the very foundation of what these religious leaders believed.

Jesus asserted, "I and the Father are one" (John 10:30). Jesus's statement is hard to reconcile with the core Old Testament declaration in Deuteronomy 6:4: "Hear, O Israel: The LORD our God, the LORD is one." This language from Moses pushed back against the persistent, pagan misunderstanding that the ancient world was filled with many gods who lived in extended family relationships. Now, centuries later, Jesus said he and the Father are one. To these Old Testament teachers, this sounded like a slide back into an ancient pagan worldview.

The place where Jesus revealed this truth increased the apparent tension. Jesus's declaration echoed through the covered corridor called

Solomon's Colonnade. Although it carried Solomon's name, it was built much later than the First Temple built by Solomon. But the label puts us on the campus of the Temple in Jerusalem. Unlike pagan religious compounds, Jerusalem had just one temple and so asserted that God is one. The setting increases the tension between Jesus's statement and listeners' expectations.

Added to that, Jesus's words land on his listeners' ears during the Festival of Dedication. This is not a festival mandated in the Old Testament but one that Judaism adopted. You may know it as Hanukkah. It commemorates the liberation of the Temple in the second century BC from pagan hands by the freedom fighter Judas Maccabaeus. This festival championed the victory of the *one* true God over his pagan competitors.

At every level, Jesus's statement on his relationship with the Father stood out and challenged the religious leaders. It sounded like blasphemy. But here, Jesus offers a more complete explanation of who God is. I may not be able to fully understand how God is one at the same time Jesus and the Father are one. But the Holy Spirit caused me to believe it, similar to how the sheep who listen to Jesus's voice follow him. Why didn't the Jewish leaders at the Jerusalem Temple do the same? The answer is simple and tragic: "You do not believe because you are not my sheep" (John 10:26).

For Further Reference: **Deuteronomy 6:4; Psalms 2:7; 82:6; 110:1; Romans 15:6; 1 Corinthians 8:6; 1 John 2:23**

JESUS AND THE GOOD SAMARITAN

Luke 10:25–37

"Go and do likewise." (Luke 10:37)

> ## ▶ WHO & WHERE
Jesus, Samaritan, Judean Wilderness

> ## ▶ WHAT IS THIS TEXT TALKING ABOUT?
Neighborliness

> ## ▶ WHAT DOES THIS TEXT TEACH?
Treat everyone in need as a neighbor, offering selfless and
extravagant kindness.

Jesus's testy exchange with a Judean expert in the law birthed one of our
most treasured stories—a story that teaches both *whom* we are to help
and *how* we are to help.

This story is a wilderness travel story. It takes place on the road between Jerusalem and Jericho that navigates the dry, rugged, and forbidding landscape of the Judean Wilderness. The road climbs and descends
like a roller coaster. Throughout the trip, resources were all but absent, as
were towns or villages where supplies could be refreshed. Thieves, apex
predators, and terrain hazards haunted every turn, making this one of the
most dangerous roads to travel in ancient Israel. And if you were injured
along the way, help was far away.

The story opens as we meet a Jewish man traveling this road who has
been critically injured by robbers. Given his location, he has little hope of
survival. Fortunately, two fellow Jews who are also religious leaders happened upon him. Stunningly, they passed by the man lying on the narrow
path, ignoring his pain-filled pleas. The third man on the scene is the one
we least expect to render aid. But this Samaritan set aside the social
and religious differences between himself and the injured man to offer
assistance. In doing so, the Samaritan shows us that our neighbor is
anyone we meet who needs our help.

This story also highlights not just whom but how we are to help. The
Samaritan man showed extravagant love for his neighbor. Think of all

The wilderness road between Jerusalem and Jericho is the setting for the story of the good Samaritan.

the ways he disadvantaged himself. The Samaritan stopped to render aid while thieves were still in the area. His delay threatened to push his travel into the evening hours when the wilderness became even more risky. He used the personal items he had packed for the trip to render aid, knowing they could not be replaced. He used his donkey to transport the injured man through the rolling terrain. And when he arrived at a place where further aid could be rendered, the Samaritan gave the innkeeper money to continue his care. At every turn, the Samaritan man's unselfish, extravagant love demonstrates how to love our neighbor in need.

Jesus combines place with story to teach a powerful lesson in neighborliness, a story that ends with this powerful call to action: "Go and do likewise" (Luke 10:37).

For Further Reference: Leviticus 19:18; 2 Kings 17:24–41; Matthew 5:7; John 4:9, 39–42; James 2:13

JESUS ON SETTING PRIORITIES

Luke 10:38–42

"'Martha, Martha,' the Lord answered, 'you are worried and upset about many things, but few things are needed—or indeed only one. Mary has chosen what is better, and it will not be taken away from her.'" (Luke 10:41–42)

▶ WHO & WHERE

Jesus, Mary, Martha, Bethany

▶ WHAT IS THIS TEXT TALKING ABOUT?

Setting priorities

▶ WHAT DOES THIS TEXT TEACH?

Nothing is more important than giving Jesus our undivided attention.

Life is full—wall-to-wall full—of things we need to do. This story is about how we choose to use our time and the consequences of those choices.

Jesus entered the small Judean village of Bethany with an entourage of students. Bethany was too small to have public lodging or dining establishments, so this group lands at the home of Jesus's friends—Mary, Martha, and Lazarus. Their arrival triggers a set of social expectations that fall on the shoulders of the senior female member of the household. Martha knew what hospitality was expected and how to get it done.

But this cultural expectation required a choice. It was not whether she would listen to Jesus, but how she would listen. The typical home in Bethany was only about four hundred square feet (thirty-seven square meters).

And since most of her hospitality duties would take place either in the house or adjacent to it, she calculated that she could listen to Jesus and work at the same time. Mary made a different choice. She deferred on the work and chose to sit at Jesus's feet in the posture of a student, single-tasking rather than multitasking.

The Church of Lazarus in Bethany marks the town in which Jesus visited the home of Mary, Martha, and Lazarus.

Martha was indignant with her sister and sought Jesus's help: "Tell her to help me!" (Luke 10:40). Jesus's response provides powerful insight on setting priorities. He did not diminish the importance of showing hospitality but observed how Martha's multitasking left her worried, upset, and distracted by things that were of less importance. Mary had made the better choice.

And he adds that the choice had consequences: "it will not be taken away from her" (v. 42). What did he mean? Time with Jesus on earth was now calculated in weeks rather than years. If they did not seize this moment to listen to Jesus, they would lose it. In addition, life was about to take a hard turn for the sisters. Their brother, Lazarus, would soon die. And Martha's choice left her less prepared to meet this moment. Later, when Jesus spoke to her about his ability to restore Lazarus to life, Martha heard what Jesus said but struggled to believe (John 11:40). Her choice, like ours, has consequences.

For Further Reference: **Psalm 27:4; Luke 9:51; John 11:21–40; Acts 17:25; Hebrews 13:2; 1 Peter 4:9**

JESUS ON PRAYER

Matthew 6:9–13; Luke 11:1–13

"Lord, teach us to pray." (Luke 11:1)

> ## WHO
Jesus, disciples

> ## WHAT IS THIS TEXT TALKING ABOUT?
Prayer

> ## WHAT DOES THIS TEXT TEACH?
Strive for a mature prayer life that is persistent, confident, and Spirit-enabled.

Prayer is a fundamental exercise of the Christian faith that is well known but often poorly practiced. The disciples felt the shortcomings in their own prayer life. They had watched Jesus pray and now asked him to teach them how they could do it better. He did. And we are blessed with insights that can mature our own prayer life.

First, Jesus urges persistence. Note his repetition of the threefold ask, seek, and knock—each word is more intense than the last. Jesus urges us to pray like the host faced by unannounced, late-night guests. Culturally it was the host's obligation to provide a meal, but the host lacked even the most fundamental element of the meal, bread. So, he went to his neighbor's home in search of it. The host was so persistent that he caused a sleepy father to risk waking his sleeping children in their one-room home to fulfill the request.

Second, Jesus invites us to pray confidently. Each mention of asking, seeking, and knocking is followed by a statement that affirms the success of the effort: "So I say to you: Ask and it will be given to you; seek and you will find; knock and the door will be opened to you" (Luke 11:9). We can be confident that the Lord hears and answers prayer. This again is followed by an illustration. Human fathers know how to give good gifts to their children. How much more confident can we be in our heavenly Father to give us just what we need.

Third, Jesus speaks to the topic of content. What should we ask for most often? What becomes known as the Lord's Prayer lays out the categories: a life that causes the Lord's name to be honored, the advance of God's kingdom and will, gratefulness for the Lord's provision, readiness to seek forgiveness from the Lord and to give that forgiveness to others, strength in temptation, and deliverance from evil.

But there is a surprise that is kept until the very end. Jesus suggests that the most important thing we can prayer for is the giving of the Holy Spirit (Luke 11:13). The Holy Spirit creates, sustains, and matures faith. And it is precisely that faith which we need to live out every other petition in the Lord's Prayer.

For Further Reference: 1 Kings 8:22–61; Psalms 4; 86; 143; Romans 8:26; Philippians 4:6; James 5:16

BRING IN THE LIGHT

Luke 11:33–36

"Your eye is the lamp of your body. When your eyes are healthy, your whole body also is full of light. But when they are unhealthy, your body also is full of darkness." (Luke 11:34)

▶ WHO & WHERE
Jesus, Judea

▶ WHAT IS THIS TEXT TALKING ABOUT?
Receiving the revelation of Jesus

▶ WHAT DOES THIS TEXT TEACH?
A healthy faith is the key to receiving the revelation of Jesus.

Jesus offers the most profound insights with the simplest words. This is a classic case. He speaks about the revelation he brings and the reception of it using three analogies: light, lamp, and eye.

The first time Luke uses the term "light" in his gospel informs our understanding of how Jesus uses it in the rest of the book. In Luke 2:32, Luke describes how Simeon holds Jesus in his arms at the Temple in Jerusalem and identifies the infant as the long-awaited light (Isa. 60:1–3). For Luke, light is revelation from God.

In the time of Jesus, one source of light was the household lamp. Every home had this simple device. In an era before electricity, it provided light so that household activities could continue after the sun set. The first-century lamp was a small clay vessel that held olive oil. A wick was draped into the fuel and ignited to provide modest but effective illumination. Effective, that is, so long as it was set in a prominent place in the home where its light was unobstructed. The light of Jesus's revelation is like the well-placed lamp, providing light for the entire room.

But revelation did not guarantee reception. Here is where the analogy of the eye comes in. In Jesus's day, the world did not yet understand how the eye worked with its cornea, lens, and optic nerve. People of antiquity who subscribed to the science of the ancient Greek world believed that light worked somewhat like modern radar works today. They thought light exited the eye, contacted an object, and then returned to the eye. Jesus employs this understanding of the eye when he likens it to the lamp of the body.

But will the light bounce back and reenter the body? If the eye were diseased, damaged, or willfully closed, then the answer is no. In this analogy, the eye receiving light is faith. Even though the "lamp" is delivering unobstructed "light," a person can willfully prevent that "light" from entering their body and so defeat the change that light can bring. Jesus's encouragement here is to make sure that the "eye" or faith is healthy and wide open. Then our "whole body is full of light" (Luke 11:36).

For Further Reference: Psalm 119:105; Isaiah 60:1–3; Luke 2:32; 2 Corinthians 4:6; 1 Peter 2:9; 2 Peter 1:19; 1 John 1:7

LIVE LIKE THE PEOPLE OF GOD

Luke 11:37–12:12

"Be on your guard against the yeast of the Pharisees, which is hypocrisy." (Luke 12:1)

▶ WHO & WHERE
Jesus, Pharisees, Judea

▶ WHAT IS THIS TEXT TALKING ABOUT?
The lifestyle of the believer

▶ WHAT DOES THIS TEXT TEACH?
The lifestyle of the believer is marked by generosity, a concern for social justice, and confident witness.

We all have role models. And in Judea, many viewed the Pharisees as setting the bar for righteous living. Here in Luke 11–12 we hear Jesus boldly attack these paragons of virtue, calling out their

This Palestine sunbird is much more ornate than the unassuming brown sparrows of Israel, yet God cares for them all.

shortcomings, and interweaving a description of what it means to live like the people of God.

The sharply worded criticism began even before dinner was served. A Pharisee had invited Jesus to dine in his home and then criticized him for not washing his hands using a ritual practiced by the Pharisees. I suspect this Pharisee wished he had kept quiet, because this initiated a long and pointed critique. Jesus called out the false piety of these religious teachers reflected in the ritual washing of vessels and tithing of herbs. He came down on their self-aggrandizing behaviors like choosing the seats of honor in the synagogue and basking in respectful greetings in the marketplace. He highlighted their complicity in the shameful treatment of God's messengers, noting murders that span Old Testament history—from the murder of Abel (Gen. 4:8) to the murder of Zechariah the priest (2 Chron. 24:20–21). But even more stunning was their failure to properly employ "the key to knowledge" (Luke 11:52). That key is the core message of forgiveness that opens the door to the rest of God's revelation.

Within this critical review of the Pharisees, Jesus highlighted the behaviors that marked authentic believers. He begins with generosity to the poor and champions social justice fueled by love for God. But Jesus lingers most on confident witness. This witness naturally flows from two realities. First, the Lord is constantly aware of our circumstances. Jesus illustrates this awareness by pointing to the sparrows sold in the market. A denarius was a day's wage for a common laborer. Five sparrows were sold for one-sixteenth of a denarius, "yet not one of them is forgotten by God" (Luke 12:6). The Lord even knows the exact number of hairs on our head! We can be confident in our witness because we live under God's watchful eye. And lest we be concerned that we will be embarrassed by not having the right words, Jesus says that the Holy Spirit will provide the very words that are right for that moment and place (vv. 11–12). Generosity, social justice, and confident witness—this is what it means to live like the people of God.

For Further Reference: Micah 6:8; Romans 10:9; Colossians 2:2–3; 2 Timothy 2:11–13; 1 Peter 5:6–9

THE PARABLE
OF THE RICH FOOL

Luke 12:13–21

"Watch out! Be on your guard against all kinds of greed; life does not consist in an abundance of possessions." (Luke 12:15)

▶ **WHO & WHERE**

Jesus, Judea

▶ **WHAT IS THIS TEXT TALKING ABOUT?**

Greed

▶ **WHAT DOES THIS TEXT TEACH?**

Guard against greed for money that cannot provide the certain future
enjoyed by those who have a rich relationship with the Lord.

As the noisy crowd pressed in around Jesus, one voice stood out.
Someone in the crowd wanted Jesus's help with an inheritance issue.
Following the death of their father, his brother had not divided and shared
the estate to his satisfaction. Jesus quickly saw that it was not the transfer
of property that was the problem. The problem was greed, giving Jesus the
opportunity to take up the topic. "Watch out!" Jesus warned. "Be on your
guard against all kinds of greed; life does not consist in an abundance of
possessions" (Luke 12:15). At base, greed is fueled by the mistaken notion
that possessions have the power to provide personal well-being and a secure future. They cannot. And Jesus drives the point home with a parable.

A well-to-do man had a windfall. His agricultural fields produced a
bumper crop of grain. He carefully mulled his options. He could give the
surplus back to the Lord as a freewill offering. He could use the surplus to
help the many families living in poverty. But instead, he decided to keep it
for himself. This meant he had to renovate his grain storage facilities. The
barns that are mentioned here are not the equivalent of my grandparents'
barn. Their red, wooden structure so iconic of rural American landscapes
was large enough to house livestock as well as grain. The "barn" of the
ancient world was an underground silo, a pit dug and lined with stones just
for the storage of grain. A dome made of bricks covered this kind of barn to
keep the elements and animals away, securing the grain for years of future
use. By renovating his storage structures, the rich man presumed that his
future well-being was guaranteed.

But that very night, his future took a different turn. He died and all the
grain went to others. As the man stood in that judgment before the Lord,
all the possessions now left behind did him no good. Greed had misled
him. His possessions could not guarantee an eternal future. Only a strong,

personal relationship with the Lord does that. And in that respect, this parable remains a cautionary tale for us: "This is how it will be with whoever stores up things for themselves but is not rich toward God" (Luke 12:21).

For Further Reference: Job 20:20–21; 31:24–28; Proverbs 11:4; 15:27; Ecclesiastes 5:10, 13–15; 6:1–2; 9:11–12; Ephesians 5:3; 1 Timothy 6:10, 17

JESUS BRINGS BOTH PEACE AND DIVISION

Luke 12:49–53

"Do you think I came to bring peace on earth? No, I tell you, but division." (Luke 12:51)

▶ **WHO & WHERE**
Jesus, Judea

▶ **WHAT IS THIS TEXT TALKING ABOUT?**
Impact of Jesus's mission

▶ **WHAT DOES THIS TEXT TEACH?**
The mission of Jesus designed to bring peace will also result in division.

What? That does not sound right. Perhaps Jesus misspoke. He is clearly upset, anxious to get on with the more difficult parts of his mission in Jerusalem involving the abuse he will receive from his captors, the suffering and death on the cross. But did he mean to say that he had not come to bring peace but division?

The Soreg warning inscription and associated wall restricted Gentile access to certain portions of the Temple campus. Jesus's message removed such cultural barriers.

We feel the tension because the Old Testament, Luke, and Paul all say that Jesus's mission on earth is intimately tied to peace. Jesus is called the "Prince of Peace" (Isa. 9:6), the one tasked with bringing peace on earth (Luke 2:14), and "our peace" who makes the two one (Eph. 2:14). How do we square what Jesus just said with Bible passages like these? To be sure, Jesus's mission was designed to bring peace between the Creator and the people of this world. But in accomplishing that mission, the world would experience significant disruption realized in the most basic social unit, the family.

We can hear the longing in Jesus's words. He yearns for the difficult part of his mission to be over, speaking of it as a fiery baptism. We are about to see it as Luke takes us to the cross where we see Jesus absorb the anger of the Father at sin so that sinners would be exempted from divine punishment. His pain would bring the world peace.

But the mission to bring peace would also bring division, causing households to fracture. People in Bible times typically lived in family compounds together with members of their extended family. The unity of such households was championed because a large, harmonious household assured the production of adequate food and provided the personal security we find in other social institutions like the police force. But these households became battlegrounds because the Devil sought to destroy our relationship with Jesus, the bridge to God that brings peace. When our enemy is successful, households suffer and fracture. It is not Jesus's intention to bring division, but it is a consequence of the battle for souls that rages in every family.

For Further Reference: Isaiah 9:6; Jeremiah 21:12; Malachi 4:1; Luke 2:14; Ephesians 2:14; Colossians 1:20

FOCUS ON JESUS, NOW!

Luke 12:54–59

"Hypocrites! You know how to interpret the appearance of the earth and the sky. How is it that you don't know how to interpret this present time?" (Luke 12:56)

▶ WHO & WHERE
Jesus, Judea

▶ WHAT IS THIS TEXT TALKING ABOUT?
Focus of attention

▶ WHAT DOES THIS TEXT TEACH?
Focus your attention on the opportunity to be with Jesus before it is gone.

Urgent! Some things are and some things aren't. Developing a meaningful relationship with Jesus is. And for those living when Jesus walked the earth, it was particularly urgent that they take advantage of his three-year ministry because it would end more quickly than they realized.

Three years is not a long time. But it was long enough for people to lose interest and become distracted by other things. Jesus was deeply concerned that people living in his time were missing the unique opportunity they had to meet God face-to-face, hear him speak, and ask him questions. They had lost their sense of urgency. So, Jesus used strong language and two illustrations that called for people to pay closer attention to what he was saying and doing.

The first illustration has to do with the weather. For five months of the year, it does not rain in Israel. Even the appearance of a single cloud is rare. That changes in October. Cumulus clouds build and darken over the Mediterranean Sea, signaling the start of the rainy months. People urgently looked for this sign of seasonal change because it meant their water collection systems would recharge and signaled the start of the grain-growing season. The winds that brought the rain came from the west-northwest. When the wind started to blow from the south-southeast, people in the Promised Land noticed, because that signaled a vastly different meteorologic experience. These unwelcome sirocco winds brought in the dust, low humidity, and the extreme heat of the desert. People paid attention to the weather because it was important. In the same way, people needed to attend to Jesus so they could see that he was fulfilling the Old Testament expectations that marked him as the Messiah.

Jesus used a second illustration to address the negligence. Poverty was rampant in first-century Israel. Everyone knew someone who had the experience of falling behind in their loans and being called to account by their creditor. The best one could hope for was to settle with the creditor prior to arriving in court. Wait too long and the judge would control the outcome, which typically led to prison time. In the same way, it was urgent for people to give Jesus their attention now before the opportunity was gone.

For Further Reference: **Matthew 16:2–3; Luke 24:25–27; John 5:39–40; Acts 3:18; 13:27**

JESUS ON MINIMIZING THE IMPACT OF OUR SIN

Luke 13:1–9

"But unless you repent, you too will all perish." (Luke 13:5)

▶ **WHO & WHERE**

Jesus, Judea

▶ **WHAT IS THIS TEXT TALKING ABOUT?**

The impact of personal sins

▶ **WHAT DOES THIS TEXT TEACH?**

Do not minimize the impact of personal sins by either comparing your level of sin with others or finding comfort in the absence of immediate consequences.

If there is something more dangerous than sin, it is minimizing the impact of sin. Jesus raises two mistaken assumptions that put us in peril.

The first is minimizing sin by comparing our level of sinfulness with others'. Jesus comments on two tragic stories about which we know nothing more than what is reported in Luke. In the first, the Roman governor executed Galileans who were worshipping at the Temple in Jerusalem. This story sounds all too familiar. Galileans were prone to protest, and Pilate was prone to respond violently to dissent. The second tragedy involved the collapse of a tower near a water-collection reservoir in southeastern Jerusalem called the Pool of Siloam. Given the fact that this pool was often used for ritual washing before worship, the eighteen who died in this accidental collapse may also have been in Jerusalem to worship. Why would pious people like these die in such violent fashion? Some perceived them to be "worse sinners" and "more guilty than all the others living in Jerusalem" (Luke 13:2, 4), thus excusing their own behavior as less heinous.

The second way people underplayed the impact of their sin was by finding respite in the absence of immediate consequences. In response, Jesus told the parable of the barren fig tree. The scene is typical of any Judean farm field in which the owner grew grapevines, olive trees, and fig trees. Jesus directs our attention to a fig tree that is at least three years old. By this time, it was mature enough to produce fruit but was not. The owner wanted this problem tree destroyed immediately, but the caretaker asked for one more year in which he would lavish the tree with extra care. If the tree did not bear fruit within the year, it would be cut down. Jesus likens this to the patience of the Father. But we dare not misinterpret his patience. A delay in consequences does not mean our sin is inconsequential. Rather, the Lord "is patient with you, not wanting anyone to perish, but everyone to come to repentance" (2 Peter 3:9).

For Further Reference: **Numbers 14:18; Lamentations 3:19–42; Ezekiel 18; Joel 2:13; Acts 2:38; Romans 6:23; 2 Peter 3:9**

JESUS HEALED A DISABLED WOMAN ON THE SABBATH

Luke 13:10–17

"Then should not this woman, a daughter of Abraham, whom Satan has kept bound for eighteen long years, be set free on the Sabbath day from what bound her?" (Luke 13:16)

▶ WHO & WHERE
Jesus, synagogue leader, disabled woman, synagogue

▶ WHAT IS THIS TEXT TALKING ABOUT?
The value of those who are undervalued by society

▶ WHAT DOES THIS TEXT TEACH?
Jesus demonstrates that everyone in our society is a person of value, deserving of our attention and compassion.

She struggled to find a seat in the synagogue. Her spine was bent and fused in a way that made it impossible for her to stand upright. But as difficult as movement was, she came to hear Jesus speak. She did not expect to be healed or to become the center of attention. But Jesus had other plans.

The synagogue leader did not see the same woman Jesus saw. The synagogue community chose him for his job because of his attention to detail. He was good at what he did, organizing the worship service and monitoring its progress for any kind of disruption. As he watched people arrive, he gave little attention to the disabled woman. First, she was a woman—tolerated but not celebrated in the male-dominated world of the synagogue. And second, in this case a cloud of suspicion hung over her. Within first-century Judaism, many thought a disability was the sign of a moral failing (John 9:1–2). So despite her quiet piety and physical challenges, this synagogue leader felt less compassion for her than he would for his draft animals needing water on the Sabbath.

Jesus saw someone different. Her bent frame, the difficulty with which she walked, and the pain she experienced in sitting immediately filled him with compassion. Jesus did not see her as a woman of lesser value than the men in the room but as a "daughter of Abraham" (Luke 13:16)—valued as a child of God and as a member of God's chosen people. Her disability was not punishment for a specific sin but part of a cosmic struggle between his Father and Satan (v. 16).

And because Jesus saw her differently, he treated her differently. Although it was the day of rest, a day when healing miracles caused controversy, Jesus invited her to rise and spoke words of release from her infirmity. "Then he put his hands on her, and immediately she straightened up and praised God" (v. 13). And as she stands, we are challenged to inspect not only how we see her but how we see others who walk into our places of worship, lest we see them differently than Jesus does. All are people of value who deserve our attention and compassion.

For Further Reference: **Deuteronomy 5:12–15; 22:1–4; Micah 6:8; Luke 14:1–6; Ephesians 4:32–5:2; Colossians 3:12–14**

LESSONS ON PRIDE FROM THE BANQUET

Luke 14:1–14

"For all those who exalt themselves will be humbled, and those who humble themselves will be exalted." (Luke 14:11)

▶ **WHO & WHERE**

Jesus, Pharisees, banquet

▶ **WHAT IS THIS TEXT TALKING ABOUT?**

Honor and humility

▶ **WHAT DOES THIS TEXT TEACH?**

Honor will find and favor the humble heart.

Sprawling and ornate homes like this one in Jerusalem allow us to picture the lavish banquets given by the wealthy and influential citizens of Jesus's day.

Jesus often matched his lesson to the moment. In this case, he used two banquet illustrations while attending a fancy meal at the home of a prominent Pharisee to address what most threatened a Pharisee's eternity—pride.

Hubris was so intimately bound to the culture of these religious leaders that it became an unnoticed extension of their personality. Jesus puts this flaw front and center by telling two banquet stories that highlight the kinds of decisions Pharisees made. In the first case, Jesus portrays the Pharisees as guests invited to a wedding feast who are deciding where to sit. These are not the kind of seats reserved for guests at a modern wedding ceremony but seats associated with the feast that followed. Such seats were assigned varying levels of honor. This means that Pharisees had to carefully weigh who else was invited to be sure that they chose the right seat. In the story, pride gets the man in trouble who selects a seat for which he is not qualified and finds himself demoted by the host.

In the second illustration, Jesus pictures a Pharisee as the host of the banquet. This is not the feast associated with a wedding but a social gathering for lunch or dinner. Here, Jesus puts our attention on the guest list. It was the habit of Pharisees to invite only those who could return the invitation, excluding the disadvantaged members of society. In other words, the usual guests were friends, family members, and wealthy neighbors rather than the poor, crippled, lame, and blind. The disadvantaged members of society did not have the means to reciprocate. But inviting such guests signaled progress against personal pride: "Although they cannot repay you, you will be repaid at the resurrection of the righteous" (Luke 14:14).

Jesus often battled with the Pharisees, but he loved them too. He knew that their pride was so knit into their professional lives that it went unnoticed. That is why he called it out and warned them of its grave consequences: "I tell you, not one of those who were invited will get a taste of my banquet" (v. 24). Honor will find and favor the humble heart.

For Further Reference: **Proverbs 8:13; 25:6–7; Isaiah 25:6; James 1:10; 1 John 2:16; Revelation 19:9**

CHAPTER 6

Jesus En Route to Jerusalem

JESUS SET HIS FACE ON JERUSALEM

Luke 9:51–56

"As the time approached for him to be taken up to heaven, Jesus resolutely set out for Jerusalem." (Luke 9:51)

▶ **WHO & WHERE**

Jesus, northern Samaria

▶ **WHAT IS THIS TEXT TALKING ABOUT?**

Jesus's mindset and demeanor on the way to Jerusalem

▶ **WHAT DOES THIS TEXT TEACH?**

Jesus resolutely set out for Jerusalem with mercy on his mind.

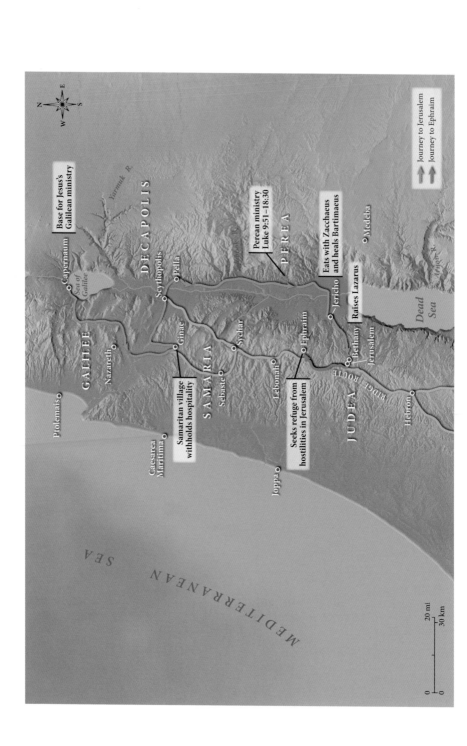

There was something different about Jesus. He had recently told the disciples he was on the way to Jerusalem (Luke 9:22). Now there was a distinct look in his eyes, a different pace to his stride. His body language joined with his words to reveal his determination. He resolutely set his sights on Jerusalem. The story that follows offers two insights into the journey.

First, Jesus was intentionally putting himself in harm's way. No one tricked him into going to Jerusalem. This trip was not a mistake that accidently put Jesus in the wrong place at the wrong time. Jesus made a conscious, voluntary decision to do exactly what he had come to earth to do. And that had to be done in Jerusalem.

Second, Jesus was on a mission of mercy not judgment. This becomes clear as Jesus meets opposition from Samaritans. The Roman district of Samaria lay between Galilee and Judea. When Galileans traveled to Jerusalem, they typically traveled through the heart of Samaria on the Ridge Route. This was the shortest and fastest path that avoided the Gentile-pagan world of the Decapolis to the east. But it was not always trouble free. The Samaritans were an ethnically blended people whose theology resembled but did not match the Jewish theology in Jerusalem (2 Kings 17:40–41; John 4:20). And while the Gospels provide striking examples of Samaritan compassion and excitement over Jesus (Luke 10:25–37; John 4:39–43), bad blood periodically surfaced, as it does in this story.

Jesus sent messengers ahead to secure lodging in a Samaritan village, but they refused to show the expected Middle Eastern hospitality because "he was heading for Jerusalem" (Luke 9:53). Perhaps this snub was linked to the memory of the Jewish king, John Hyrcanus, who destroyed the Samarian temple in 128 BC or to the fact that Jesus was not going to stay long enough to benefit them with his stories and miracles. Whatever it was, James and John took offense. They wanted to call down fire like Elijah had done in Samaria (2 Kings 1:10, 12). But judgment was not Jesus's first thought. And after a quick rebuke, Jesus resolutely set out again for Jerusalem with mercy on his mind.

For Further Reference: 2 Kings 1:10, 12; Isaiah 50:7; Romans 9:15; Hebrews 12:2; James 2:13

JESUS SENDS OUT THE SEVENTY-TWO

Luke 10:1–24

"He told them, 'The harvest is plentiful, but the workers are few. Ask the Lord of the harvest, therefore, to send out workers into his harvest field.'" (Luke 10:2)

▶ WHO & WHERE
Jesus, Perea

▶ WHAT IS THIS TEXT TALKING ABOUT?
The nature of Christian mission

▶ WHAT DOES THIS TEXT TEACH?
Christian mission is urgent, dangerous, discouraging, and joy-filled.

Time's up. Jesus was en route to Jerusalem for the last time. As he walked, his heart turned to those places he would not personally visit to announce, "The kingdom of God has come near to you" (Luke 10:9). In response, Jesus sent seventy-two gifted people in his place. And in their commissioning, we learn more about the nature of our mission.

First, the believer's mission is urgent. Jesus used the metaphor of the ripe grainfield (v. 2). Hurry-up-and-wait aptly describes the farmer's life in Jesus's day. With the first rains of fall, the farmer rushed to plow and plant. Then the waiting began over the months it took for the grain to grow and mature. And when it ripened, the rush was on again to harvest. Delay would mean loss to hungry wildlife or would find the plant naturally dropping its seed from the stalk. In the same way, our mission is urgent. Death waits for no one. And those who are dying need to know how God thinks about them. This mission cannot wait.

Second, Christian mission is dangerous. The Lord is asking his representatives to take on Satan himself (vv. 17–19). This fallen angel will fight to keep the fallen souls in his possession. So, the danger to those who oppose his mission is real. Jesus likened the mismatch to that of an inexperienced lamb against the Iranian wolf packs that threatened the Middle Eastern flock. Our mission is rife with danger.

Third, the believer's mission can be discouraging. Before sending them, Jesus told the seventy-two that they would be rejected (vv. 10–15). He assured them that this was not a failing on their own parts since Jesus himself had been rejected by many in Chorazin, Bethsaida, and Capernaum—the very places he had spent most of his ministry days (Matt. 11:20–24). Our mission will know the discouragement Jesus knew when people reject the message.

Fourth and finally, Christian mission is joy-filled. Certainly, there is joy in seeing the way people's lives are changed. But Jesus urges the seventy-two to find joy in the unique privilege they enjoy. The Old Testament is filled with people who longed to see the

Jesus used the image of a grainfield ready for harvest to illustrate the urgency of the gospel mission efforts.

moment in which Jesus's disciples are living (Luke 10:24). And he urges them to find joy in the daily reminder that their "names are written in heaven" (v. 20). In this way, our mission can also be filled with joy.

For Further Reference: Psalm 91:13; Isaiah 14:12–15; Jeremiah 9:23–24; 1 Corinthians 1:26–31; 2:8; 1 Peter 1:10–12; Revelation 20:12

PARABLES OF THE MUSTARD SEED AND YEAST

Luke 13:18–21

"What is the kingdom of God like? What shall I compare it to?"
(Luke 13:18)

▶ **WHO & WHERE**
Jesus, Perea

▶ **WHAT IS THIS TEXT TALKING ABOUT?**
The nature of God's kingdom

▶ **WHAT DOES THIS TEXT TEACH?**
The size and impact of God's kingdom will be greater than expected.

The kingdom of God was not just something Jesus spoke about. It was something he *always* spoke about. And in this case, he used two parables to defeat low expectations about it.

First, Jesus compared the kingdom of God to a mustard seed. The species identification of the plant in the parable is challenging. In the parable, it was a local plant. It was something a farmer planted, making it culturally valuable. It had a proverbial small seed. And it grew to be treelike in size. The closest we come to a species that matches this description is black mustard (*Brassica nigra*). This plant has seeds which are about one millimeter in length. When given the necessary space and ideal growing conditions, it can become a large bush from 6 to 8 feet (1.8 to 2.4 meters) tall. This substantial "tree" produces a black seed that people in Bible times used to make condiments. If Jesus is using the word "tree" with a measure of hyperbole, this identification fits. His point? We don't expect something so big to grow from something so small.

Second, Jesus compared the kingdom of God to the effect of yeast in a batch of dough. Bread was baked every day by families in Bible times, in most cases with yeast. For Jesus's listeners, "yeast" was a bit of bread dough saved from the last batch of bread making and allowed to ferment. When this yeast mixed with the other ingredients in the bread dough, it generated carbon dioxide, a gas that caused the dough to rise. Here in the parable, Jesus highlights the way a small amount of yeast can impact sixty pounds (twenty-seven kilograms) of dough.

As people walked with Jesus toward Jerusalem knowing he would die when he arrived, some wondered what the legacy of his movement would be. It all seemed to be going so well. But they had seen this before—a Galilean reform movement that started with great promise and fizzled. Jesus used these two parables about God's kingdom to defeat those low expectations. The kingdom of God would grow much larger than most expected. And it would have an impact on the world that far outstripped its modest start in Galilee.

For Further Reference: Ezekiel 17:22–23; Matthew 13:31–33; Mark 4:30–32; Hebrews 1:8; Revelation 5:8–10; 12:10

THE NARROW DOOR

Luke 13:22–30

"Make every effort to enter through the narrow door, because
many, I tell you, will try to enter and will not be able to."
(Luke 13:24)

> **WHO & WHERE**

Jesus, Perea

> **WHAT IS THIS TEXT TALKING ABOUT?**

The door to eternal life in heaven

> **WHAT DOES THIS TEXT TEACH?**

Give time and attention to entering the door that leads to eternal
life before it closes.

"Lord, are only a few people going to be saved?" (Luke 13:23). The person who asked the question was doing what I should do more—think about where I will spend my eternity. Jesus did not answer the question directly, but he did address two mistaken impressions about the eternal "feast in the kingdom of God" (v. 29) by using the metaphor of a household doorway.

The first mistaken notion is that the door to heaven is wide. In Bible times, people included doorways in the design of their homes, but they were much lower and narrower entries than we find in homes today. The doorway that leads into heaven is like that—smaller and more restricted than many people think. It was a popular notion in first-century Judaism that all descendants of Abraham and Sarah would be saved. Others following Jesus assumed that mere familiarity with him was enough.

The doorways of homes in Jesus's day were much smaller and more restricting than those of today.

Some today presume that the Lord will let everyone in. But Jesus reminds them and us that it takes effort to get through the narrow door. The Gospels define that effort when they speak of repentance and faith in Jesus as the Savior from sin (Luke 13:3; John 3:16). That is the passageway that leads to eternal joy.

The second mistaken impression is that the doorway will always be open. Again, this contradicts the experience Jesus's listeners had with home entries. The typical entry to a home had a swinging door that remained open during the daytime to allow light and fresh air into the home. But at night, that door was closed. In the same way, the opportunity to get through the doorway to heaven is time-limited. The Lord gives every person a time of grace in which to develop the personal relationship with Jesus that leads into heaven. But that doorway is not permanently open. And once it closes, no amount of knocking or pleading will lead to its reopening.

Jesus thus urges us as he did his first listeners, "Make every effort to enter through the narrow door, because many, I tell you, will try to enter and will not be able to" (Luke 13:24).

For Further Reference: Psalm 6:8; Isaiah 25:6; Acts 3:19; Romans 10:9; 2 Corinthians 6:1–2; 2 Timothy 2:19

THE JERUSALEM IMPERATIVE

Luke 13:31–35

"In any case, I must press on today and tomorrow and the next day—for surely no prophet can die outside Jerusalem!"
(Luke 13:33)

▶ WHO & WHERE
Jesus, Perea

▶ WHAT IS THIS TEXT TALKING ABOUT?
The reasons Jesus had to go to Jerusalem

▶ WHAT DOES THIS TEXT TEACH?
Jesus had to go to Jerusalem because he loved the people of that city and because the people of that city would carry Jesus to the cross.

There were places Jesus chose to go in order to teach a lesson. And there were places Jesus *had to go* to complete his mission. Jerusalem was a place he had to go. These verses speak about the Jerusalem imperative.

This portion of Luke begins with something that *did not* motivate Jesus's final trip to Jerusalem. He was not yielding to the pressure of the Pharisees. These religious leaders dogged Jesus throughout Galilee, challenging his authority and teaching wherever he went. Their harassing voices continued as Jesus entered Perea: "Leave this place and go somewhere else" (Luke 13:31). Like Galilee, Perea was ruled by Herod Antipas. The Pharisees played up the risk by suggesting that Jesus would face the same fate as John the Baptist, whom Herod executed (Luke 9:7–9). But Jesus's travel plans would not be influenced by this ruler. The Pharisees suggested that Herod was like one of the predators that threatened ancient travelers—the lion, bear, or wolf. Jesus countered by saying Herod was more like a fox, more nuisance than threat (Song 2:15). Jesus would continue his trip to Jerusalem but at the pace he intended without fear of Herod's shadow.

So what motivated his trip? Jesus was compelled by love. Using an illustration from the natural world, Jesus likens his feelings for the people of Jerusalem to the maternal instincts of a hen who places herself between the chicks and danger. Jesus knew the risk that sin imposed on the people of Jerusalem. He would go to Jerusalem to protect them from themselves.

And ironically, it would be the people of Jerusalem who would bring about his death. Jesus observed that Jerusalem had a history of threatening God's messengers with death whether that was Zechariah, Uriah, or Jeremiah (2 Chron. 24:20–21; Jer. 26:20–23; 38:4–6). Now the hostility of Jerusalem would turn against God's Son. The Jerusalem imperative was set. "In any case," Jesus explained, "I must press on today and tomorrow and the next day—for surely no prophet can die outside Jerusalem!" (Luke 13:33). The story to come had to be a Jerusalem story.

For Further Reference: **2 Chronicles 11:16; Psalms 118:26; 122:1–9; Luke 11:47; Hebrews 10:1–14; 13:11–12**

THE COST OF COMMITMENT

Luke 14:25–35

"In the same way, those of you who do not give up everything you have cannot be my disciples." (Luke 14:33)

▶ **WHO & WHERE**

Jesus, Perea

▶ **WHAT IS THIS TEXT TALKING ABOUT?**

The cost of commitment to Jesus

▶ **WHAT DOES THIS TEXT TEACH?**

Disciples of Jesus must consider the cost of discipleship and be ready to give up everything in order to hold on to him.

Try as I might, I cannot find a way to soften the challenge in these words. It is easy to follow Jesus. But it is hard to commit to the cost because discipleship costs us everything.

The salt that builds naturally on the shores of the Dead Sea provided the sodium chloride used in every Jewish home.

There was an air of casualness in the crowd impulsively pressing in around Jesus. This prompted Jesus to comment on their commitment. He urged those within earshot to consider the cost of following him before taking another step. Failure to do so would be akin to a builder who failed to consider the cost of an entire project prior to laying the foundation. It would be like a king who set off for war without doing proper force assessment.

But true disciples do more than consider the cost; they commit to the cost. Lest anyone misunderstand, Jesus made it clear: "Those of you who do not give up everything you have cannot be my disciples" (Luke 14:33). Everything? Did he mean everything? Jesus illustrates how serious he is by saying that "everything" includes the things that are most precious to his listeners—their families and their own lives. This is not the cost of admission into the kingdom. We are given forgiveness as a free gift. But being a follower of Jesus can come with a price. That price is the product of living in a sin-ruined world.

And partial commitment will not do. You are either in or out. Jesus highlights this with the mention of salt. The Dead Sea provided the people of Israel with sodium chloride (table salt). It came to their homes not in the refined grains we know today but as a chunk of stone that included both salt and other impurities. You would tap the chunk on a hard surface to liberate some of the salt. But in time, the chunk would "[lose] its saltiness" and become so dominated by impurities that it was not good for anything, not even the manure pile. Dried manure was often used as a fuel source for cooking in Jesus's day. And people believed that this fuel was enhanced by adding salt to it. Chunks that had lost most of their salt were not even useful for this lowly task. Jesus's point? Partial commitment is no commitment. And the cost of commitment is everything.

For Further Reference: 2 Samuel 24:24; Proverbs 4:7; John 12:25; Philippians 3:7–9

PARABLES OF THE LOST COIN
AND LOST SON

Luke 15:8–32

"In the same way, I tell you, there is rejoicing in the presence of the angels of God over one sinner who repents." (Luke 15:10)

▶ WHO & WHERE

Jesus, Perea

▶ WHAT IS THIS TEXT TALKING ABOUT?

The undisputed value of those who see themselves as lacking value

▶ WHAT DOES THIS TEXT TEACH?

The Lord vigorously pursues, restores, and celebrates the recovery of the lost who see themselves as lacking value.

Not everything we lose demands an aggressive search, particularly items of modest value. These two parables show that God thinks differently about individuals who are lost.

Both parables revolve around the loss of something of little apparent value. In the first parable, a woman has lost a coin. It is just one of ten that she has. And the coin she has lost is worth about a day's labor. It is worth looking for, but not worth looking for all day. In the second parable, the lost son also lacks value. He insults his family by demanding his share of the inheritance prior to his father's passing. He moves out of the Promised Land into a place where Gentiles lived. He uses his inheritance irresponsibly and lives immorally. In the end, he becomes the victim of his own poor choices, tending pigs and longing to eat the carob pods they were eating.

Both parables come with a twist. In the first, the woman enacts an aggressive search for the lost coin that seems incompatible with the coin's value. And when she finds it, she calls her friends and neighbors together for a celebration that seems a bit over the top for the coin's value.

When the prodigal son comes to his senses and returns home hoping for nothing more than servant status in his father's household, his father reacts in a way that must have shocked Jesus's listen-

In Jesus's parable of the lost coin, the woman diligently swept her home's floors with a broom like this during the search.

ers. Senior members of households did not run, but this father ran to meet his son. Rather than upbraid him for his mistakes, this father embraced and kissed him. Instead of demoting him to the hoped-for role of household servant, the father dresses him in the garments worn by a full-status family member, even giving him the kind of ring used to authorize agreements on behalf of the family, a signet ring. In contrast to the older brother who is embarrassed by his wayward brother's return and indignant at all the fuss, the father calls for a family-wide feast.

Jesus tells these stories to highlight how God thinks about those who think less of themselves. The Lord vigorously pursues, restores, and celebrates the recovery of the lost, those who see themselves as lacking value.

For Further Reference: **Deuteronomy 21:17; Psalm 51:1–12; Luke 19:10; 1 Corinthians 6:10–11; Ephesians 2:1–5; Titus 3:3–7**

PARABLE OF
THE SHREWD MANAGER

Luke 16:1–15

"I tell you, use worldly wealth to gain friends for yourselves,
so that when it is gone, you will be welcomed into eternal
dwellings." (Luke 16:9)

▶ WHO & WHERE

Jesus, Pharisees, Perea

▶ WHAT IS THIS TEXT TALKING ABOUT?

The use of worldly wealth

▶ WHAT DOES THIS TEXT TEACH?

Use worldly wealth that fades for eternal purposes that do not.

Funeral coaches do not come with trailer hitches—and with good reason. Our personal possessions do not transition with us from this life to the next. So how can we best use worldly wealth here?

Jesus begins to answer that question by pointing to the Pharisees who "loved money" (Luke 16:14). The Lord intends for us to love people and use money. The Pharisees had it backwards. They loved money and used people. What caused their thinking to go awry? Love of money displaced God as the master who controlled their thoughts and actions. They were thinking badly because they had loved badly. Jesus diagnosed their dilemma: "You cannot serve both God and money" (v. 13).

Jesus addressed the proper use of money by telling the parable of the shrewd manager. In Jesus's day, wealthy individuals were either purchasing or seizing family farms that they then amassed into large estates. Managers ran these estates for the owners, renting land to those who paid their rent with produce like olive oil and wheat. The manager in the parable was terrible at his job. He allowed the renters to get so far behind in their payments that they were unable to catch up. When this came to the attention of the owner, he intended to fire the inept manager. In a burst of panic, the manager summoned those who owed his master money and reduced their debt substantially. He did not do it for his master's benefit or in a bid to save his job. His dishonest plan was meant to secure his future. "When I lose my job here," he reasoned, "people will welcome me into their houses" (v. 4). Although the inept manager was still going to be terminated, the owner of the land paid homage to the shrewdness of this tactical and financial move.

Jesus did not tell this parable to encourage lazy or dishonest management of personal wealth. But he urges us to replicate the manager's shrewdness in our efforts at handling our own personal wealth. We, like the Pharisees, are tempted to love money and make it our master, expecting it to be with us longer than it is and do more for us than it can. Here Jesus urges us to use worldly wealth that fades for eternal purposes that do not.

For Further Reference: **Deuteronomy 8:18; Proverbs 23:5; Ecclesiastes 5:10; Isaiah 10:3; 1 Timothy 3:3; Hebrews 13:5**

THE RICH MAN
AND POOR LAZARUS

Luke 16:19–31

"Abraham replied, 'They have Moses and the Prophets;
let them listen to them.'" (Luke 16:29)

▶ WHO & WHERE
Jesus, Perea

▶ WHAT IS THIS TEXT TALKING ABOUT?
Eternal destiny

▶ WHAT DOES THIS TEXT TEACH?
Our eternal destiny is not causally linked to our economic status but hinges on our response to the message of the Bible and is fixed upon death.

The best use of our time in this life is to prepare for the one to come. This story invites us to reflect on our eternal destiny.

The story of the rich man and Lazarus is a story steeped in contrasts. The only thing the rich man lacks is a name. His undergarments are made from the softest Egyptian linen. His outer garments are dyed Phoenician purple. This dye is acquired from a small, Mediterranean Sea mollusk called the murex. Each creature offers just one drop of color, making a pound of purple wool worth fifty thousand days' wages! This is how the rich man dressed "every day." He lived a self-absorbed, self-indulgent life of luxury.

By contrast, the only thing Lazarus had was a name. He was not covered in fine clothing but sores. His daily diet consisted of food scraps from the rich man's feasts. His only friends were the feral dogs that joined him for the meal. The one thing both men have in common is that they die. That is when their experiences again diverge. Lazarus went to be where Abraham was, which is the equivalent of going to be where the Lord is. The rich man went to the place of the unrighteous dead—a place of eternal torment.

What follows offers three powerful insights into our eternity. First, our eternal destiny is not based on or necessarily predicted by our socioeconomic circumstances in this life. This is a comfort for the impoverished and a warning to those who presume their life of luxury is a sign of divine favor. Second, our final destiny hinges on only one thing: our response to the words God speaks to us. The rich man presumed a dramatic appearance of the deceased Lazarus would help his brothers avoid his fate. But no, only belief in the revealed word, the Law and the Prophets, could change eternal destiny (Luke 16:31). Third and finally, our eternal destiny is fixed at the time of our death. The rich man requested that Lazarus come to him and bring a drop of water. Abraham refused his request because "a great chasm has been set in place, so that those who want to go from here to you cannot, nor can anyone cross over from there to us" (v. 26).

For Further Reference: **Deuteronomy 18:15; Mark 16:16; John 5:45–47; Acts 16:29–31; Hebrews 9:27**

JESUS RAISED LAZARUS FROM THE DEAD

John 11:1–57

"I am the resurrection and the life. The one who believes in me will live, even though they die; and whoever lives by believing in me will never die." (John 11:25–26)

▶ WHO & WHERE

Jesus, Martha, Mary, Lazarus, Bethany, Jerusalem

▶ WHAT IS THIS TEXT TALKING ABOUT?

Jesus's power over death

▶ WHAT DOES THIS TEXT TEACH?

Jesus's power over death affirms that he is the Messiah and animates reactions in Jerusalem.

The traditional tomb of Lazarus in Bethany hosted the dramatic miracle that changed Jerusalem's response to Jesus.

The always-unwelcome visitor paid a visit to the household of Lazarus. When Jesus arrived, his first words to Martha were filled with the compassionate and comforting language that any of us would offer a family who had lost a loved one (John 11:23). But Jesus could say and do more.

Jesus then said to Martha, "I am the resurrection and the life" (v. 25). Death always seemed to win in the end. But not this time. Jesus's thundering declaration asserted that he had power over death that no mortal had ever demonstrated. Jesus asked Martha if she believed it. Her reply? She affirmed that she believed in him, in essence saying, "I will know I have met the Messiah when I meet the man who raises the dead" (v. 27). There is the insight that helps us appreciate the Jerusalem responses. When Jesus summoned Lazarus from his cold stone tomb, his actions asserted he was the Messiah.

The timing of the miracle is also emphasized and critical to the responses produced in Jerusalem. Jesus raised Lazarus four days after his death (vv. 17, 39). To appreciate that detail, consider that Jesus had raised the dead before but always on the same day as death—Jairus's daughter and the widow's son at Nain. This was different. The fourth day is important because of a folk belief that circulated in first-century Judaism. It assumed that the life force of a person remained near the body for three days. On the fourth day, all hope of restoration expired. Jesus raised Lazarus on the very day it was no longer expected.

Then there is the location. John emphasizes that this took place in Bethany, adding that the village was about 1.75 miles (2.8 kilometers) from Jerusalem (vv. 1, 18). This miracle is also different than the two other resurrection miracles that took place in Galilee far from Jerusalem. By putting this miracle at Jerusalem's doorstep, Jesus guaranteed that those living in the holy city would hear it and could investigate its authenticity by taking the short walk to Bethany.

Assemble all the parts and you will appreciate the response of Jerusalem to the story. Many who saw what he did, believed Jesus was the Savior from sin (v. 45). This became the moment that the believing community in Jerusalem swelled in size. Others saw it differently. For members of the Jewish Sanhedrin, this was the last straw: "If we let him go on like this, everyone will believe in him" (v. 48). They were right and yet put themselves on the wrong side of history: "So from that day on they plotted to take his life" (v. 53).

For Further Reference: **Daniel 12:2; Mark 5:21–43; Luke 7:11–17; Acts 23:6–8; 1 Corinthians 15:26, 50–57**

THE GRATEFUL SAMARITAN

Luke 17:11–19

"Were not all ten cleansed? Where are the other nine?
Has no one returned to give praise to God except this foreigner?"
(Luke 17:17–18)

▶ WHO & WHERE
Jesus, Samaritan, border between Galilee and Samaria

▶ WHAT IS THIS TEXT TALKING ABOUT?
The socially marginalized

▶ WHAT DOES THIS TEXT TEACH?
Those who are socially displaced have a place with Jesus.

If you have felt out of place or unwelcomed in society, you know how the Samaritan man felt. His story teaches us that the socially displaced have a place with Jesus.

JESUS EN ROUTE TO JERUSALEM

The social dislocation of this man is, in part, revealed by the geography. Jesus was traveling through the southern portion of the Jezreel Valley on the border between the Roman districts of Galilee and Samaria. Eight hundred years earlier, the Assyrians had invaded this region. They brought in Gentiles who commingled with local Jews to form a new people group, the Samaritans. Cultural and religious differences between Jews and Samaritans birthed a legacy of tension that was alive and well at the time of this story (2 Kings 17:24–41; John 4:9). All ten men in the story knew that tension well because they lived on the border between the districts—the place in which people were most prone to question to whom you were loyal.

A second dimension of social marginalization is linked with their disease. Modern leprosy (Hansen's disease) is not the same as the "leprosy" mentioned in the Bible. This leprosy witnessed in the first century encompassed a variety of skin disorders that ranged from psoriasis to ring worm. The Old Testament law code called for those with such leprosy to remain socially isolated from others. That coupled with public fear of the unknown left lepers displaced from society and bonded to one another. Consequently, here was one place Jews and Samaritans found common cause.

As Jesus approached these ten lepers living on the border, they cried out for his help. He sent them to the priests in Jerusalem, who doubled as the public health officers. For those in the Jewish world, the priests could offer the bill of good health that allowed for a full return to Jewish society. The Samaritan man went along with his friends as instructed, although the declaration of the Jewish priest would have had little consequence for him.

On the way, all were healed. Imagine the joy of all ten! And imagine the quandary of the Samaritan. He no longer shared a disease with the other nine. He did not share their Jewish faith. And he had spent so much time with Jewish lepers that the prospect of a return to Samaritan culture was uncertain. He was displaced from every place, except one. So, he rushed back, fell at Jesus's feet, and gave thanks. And as he does, he leaves us with this lesson. The socially displaced have a place with Jesus.

For Further Reference: **Leviticus 13:38–46; 14:1–20; Numbers 5:2–3; 2 Kings 5:1–15; Galatians 3:28; Colossians 3:11**

PARABLE OF
THE PERSISTENT WIDOW

Luke 18:1–8

"And will not God bring about justice for his chosen ones, who cry out to him day and night? Will he keep putting them off?"
(Luke 18:7)

▶ WHO & WHERE
Jesus, disciples, Perea

▶ WHAT IS THIS TEXT TALKING ABOUT?
Prayers that appear unanswered

▶ WHAT DOES THIS TEXT TEACH?
Persist in prayer, particularly when you feel your prayer is unanswered.

Deflated, discouraged, and ready to give up. If you have felt this way about an unanswered prayer, if you are there right now, this parable is for you.

The parable Jesus told is about a widow with a grievance that went unaddressed through the expected channels. People in Bible times

What is the best response to seemingly unanswered prayers? More prayer!

anticipated that their disputes would be dealt with and settled within the extended family unit. That worked well in most instances but not always for those who had lost their husband. The problem for widows had to do with their more ambiguous connection to the extended family. Was she part of her childhood family unit or did she still belong to the family of her deceased husband? The ambiguity often put widows in financial jeopardy and left them vulnerable to injustice (Ex. 22:22–23). That was the case here. So, she took her case to a village elder who served as the arbiter in legal disputes that could not be settled at the family level (Deut. 16:18).

Such judges were governed by a code of conduct (Deut. 25:1). But the judge who heard the widow's case lacked spiritual and ethical integrity.

He "neither feared God nor cared what people thought" (Luke 18:2). This man was the widow's only option. So, she badgered him relentlessly until he finally yielded and provided justice.

This parable offers two insights that help me when I feel my prayers have gone unanswered. First, God remains my only option. The widow did not go to another person for justice because the judge, although incompetent, was the only person who could deliver what she needed. Of course, God is not incompetent or unethical. But like the judge in the parable, he is my ultimate source of help and my best option. Second, Jesus teaches that the sole response to unanswered prayer is more prayer. Like the judge in the parable, the Lord will yield to our persistence. That is Jesus's message in the parable. We "should always pray and not give up" (Luke 18:1).

For Further Reference: **Exodus 22:22–23; Deuteronomy 10:17–18; Psalm 146; Lamentations 3:21–26, 31–36; Isaiah 40:31; Acts 1:14; Romans 12:12; Ephesians 6:18; 1 Thessalonians 5:17**

PARABLE OF THE PHARISEE AND THE TAX COLLECTOR

Luke 18:9–14

"I tell you that this man, rather than the other, went home justified before God. For all those who exalt themselves will be humbled, and those who humble themselves will be exalted."
(Luke 18:14)

▶ WHO & WHERE

Jesus, Perea

▶ WHAT IS THIS TEXT TALKING ABOUT?

Self-righteousness

▶ WHAT DOES THIS TEXT TEACH?

God sees the self-righteous differently than they see themselves.

What does God see when he looks at us? That depends a great deal on what we see when we look at ourselves.

In this parable, we meet two men who are going to the same place, the Temple in Jerusalem. Here, the Lord made his presence known in a unique way. That made it the most desirable place for people to pray, and that is what we find the two men doing in this parable. But the fact that they prayed is the only thing they have in common.

Society regarded them very differently. Pharisees were the careful students of God's Word who championed pious living. They were the role models to whom you pointed your children. Tax collectors were despised because they took the hard-earned wages of ordinary people and sent it to Rome. Cheating and overcharging were just part of the job. In the popular mind, they belonged in the same category as robbers, prostitutes, and adulterers.

The differences play out in the parable. The Pharisee stood by himself because he was too good to stand with others. The tax collector stood at a distance because he felt unworthy of standing with others. The Pharisee confidently looked up into the face of God. The tax collector looked down, uncomfortable with God's gaze. The Pharisee saw himself as the star of the show. He tallied his long list of accomplishments, confirming for himself and God that no one in view was more deserving of divine approval than he. While the Pharisee was busy patting himself on the back, the tax collector beat his breast. He had not come to parade his accomplishments but to penitently seek mercy from the Almighty. These two men saw themselves very differently.

And here is the point: the Lord saw them differently than they saw themselves. The Pharisee went home convinced of his right standing before the Lord. But his self-righteousness had displaced the righteousness that God offered. This pious-appearing man lacked what he thought he had. And that is the word of caution found in this parable—a word addressed to those who are "confident of their own righteousness" (Luke 18:9). God sees the self-righteous differently than they see themselves.

For Further Reference: Numbers 12:3; Proverbs 15:8, 29; Isaiah 66:2; Jeremiah 9:23–24; Micah 6:8; 1 Corinthians 1:31; 1 Timothy 1:15–16; 1 Peter 5:5–6

HEALING OF BARTIMAEUS

Matthew 20:29–34; Mark 10:46–52; Luke 18:35–43

"When he heard that it was Jesus of Nazareth, he began to shout, 'Jesus, Son of David, have mercy on me!'" (Mark 10:47)

▶ WHO & WHERE
Jesus, Bartimaeus, Jericho

▶ WHAT IS THIS TEXT TALKING ABOUT?
Jesus's identity

▶ WHAT DOES THIS TEXT TEACH?
Jesus is the Son of David poised to enter Jerusalem the way the prophets foretold the Messiah would as he completed his mission on earth.

This story gives us something even more precious than it gave Bartimaeus. While the blind man received sight, we receive insight into Jesus's identity.

The first of two ways the story clarifies Jesus's identity is through the title "Son of David." All three gospel accounts of this healing mention this title, and all three signal its importance by repeating the title twice in the storytelling (Matt. 20:30–31; Mark 10:47–48; Luke 18:38–39). To be sure, Jesus was a biological descendant of David, but it goes beyond that. King David was promised that the Messiah would descend from his bloodline (2 Sam. 7:12–16) and so the label, Son of David, became a title for the Messiah (Matt. 1:1). Before Jesus takes another step toward Jerusalem, these gospel writers emphasize that this is not just another pious pilgrim on the way to the Holy City for Passover. This is not just another biological descendant of David headed for the nation's capital. They tag Jesus as the Messiah.

The second detail common to all three gospels is the geography. This is a Jericho story (Matt. 20:29; Mark 10:46; Luke 18:35), and that says something about Jesus's route. Jericho in the first century was situated a full day of walking northeast of Jerusalem in the Jordan River valley near the place where Jesus was baptized. The road that led from Jericho to Jerusalem involved a grueling climb through the difficult and dangerous Judean Wilderness. This geography is important because the Old Testament prophets announced that the Messiah would culminate his mission on earth by entering Jerusalem like the rising sun, from the east, through the Judean Wilderness (Isa. 40:3–5; 60:1–3;

The healing of the blind man in Jericho prepares us for what follows in Jerusalem by marking Jesus as the promised Messiah.

63:1; Mal. 4:2). So while the route was not a matter of consequence in Jesus's other trips to Jerusalem, this one was.

Up to this point, we had known Jesus was headed for Jerusalem, but there was some ambiguity about the route he was traveling to get there. The fog dissipates with the mention of Jericho. Jesus had left Galilee and traveled down the Jordan River valley to Jericho. Now we know he is poised to approach Jerusalem from the east by transiting the Judean Wilderness in the very way the prophets foretold the Messiah would as he completed his mission on earth.

For Further Reference: 2 Samuel 7:12–16; Isaiah 40:1–5; Jeremiah 23:5–6; Ezekiel 37:24–25

JESUS AND ZACCHAEUS

Luke 19:1–10

"For the Son of Man came to seek and to save the lost."
(Luke 19:10)

▷ WHO & WHERE
Jesus, Zacchaeus, Jericho

▷ WHAT IS THIS TEXT TALKING ABOUT?
The lost whom Jesus came to save

▷ WHAT DOES THIS TEXT TEACH?
The lost whom Jesus came to save reside at every level of society.

Zacchaeus was a tax collector. That takes some explaining because we are accustomed to thinking of tax collection in connection with a detailed tax code. Rome's tax collection in the various provinces of the empire was guided by one principle. Funnel as much money as possible, in any way possible, from the local economies into Europe. Toward that end, local businessmen bid on tax collection contracts. Rome awarded the contract to the highest bidder who, in turn, hired subordinates to harvest the cash. Overcharging, fraud, and extortion were the tools used to collect more than contracted. That became the profit harvested at every level of this tax collection pyramid.

Zacchaeus became wealthy not only because he was good at defrauding others but also because he had contracted to collect taxes at a particularly profitable location, Jericho. Here, the geography limited travel options, funneling commerce into a narrow corridor between Perea and Judea. As the traffic bottlenecked in Jericho, the chief tax collector became one of the wealthiest residents in the city.

But this is not a story about what Zacchaeus had but what he lacked. This man, who appeared to have it all, lacked the most important thing of all—eternal security. That is why we see him doing the comical, undignified thing that has come to characterize him. This short man climbed a sycamore-fig tree so that he could see Jesus. It worked better than he could have hoped. Jesus called him from the tree, invited himself to dinner, and brought with him the gift of salvation. Zacchaeus finally had what he most lacked. The change in his soul quickly changed his attitude toward both his money and others. This man whose life centered on gathering money was now obsessed with giving it away, righting wrongs that had littered his life.

The story of Zacchaeus offers a striking counterpoint to the story that precedes it—the story of the blind beggar. These men who came from opposite ends of the economic spectrum had the same need. Jesus addressed it. Salvation came to Zacchaeus's regal estate as it had to the homeless man on the roadside. "For the Son of Man came to seek and to save the lost" at every level of society.

For Further Reference: **Leviticus 6:4–5; Numbers 5:5–7; Ezekiel 34:16; John 3:17; Romans 4:16**

PARABLE OF THE TEN MINAS

Luke 19:11–27

"He went on to tell them a parable, because he was near Jerusalem and the people thought that the kingdom of God was going to appear at once." (Luke 19:11)

▶ **WHO & WHERE**

Jesus, road between Jericho and Jerusalem

▶ **WHAT IS THIS TEXT TALKING ABOUT?**

Expectations about the coming kingdom of God

▶ **WHAT DOES THIS TEXT TEACH?**

The ultimate realization of the kingdom of God will be delayed, opposed, and preceded by a time of social injustice and violence.

It was time for a reality check. Many of those traveling with Jesus to Jerusalem for Passover thought that the grand finale was imminent. Jesus used this parable to correct misunderstandings they had about the kingdom's arrival.

On his way out of Jericho, Jesus walked past a sprawling palace complex built and renovated by the Herodian family. This likely prompted him to tell the parable of the ten minas, which echoed a story about one of Herod the Great's sons. Following his father's death, Archelaus went to Rome to convince the senate they should make him king in place of his father. According to the first-century historian Josephus, fifty Judeans followed him to this distant country to oppose the coronation. This local opposition coupled with other misgivings that Rome had about him meant that Archelaus was given the lesser role of ethnarch rather than king until he could prove himself, which was prudent because he didn't and eventually lost the position. However, when Archelaus returned to Jerusalem as ethnarch, he unleashed a violent response against those who opposed him.

The lessons in the parable are related to this story. First, like Archelaus, Jesus would be leaving for a while, going to a distant place. The full onset of the kingdom of God would have to wait for his second coming.

As Jesus walked past the ornate Herodian palace in Jericho, he used the story of Archelaus to teach a lesson on the world's response to God's kingdom.

This is contrary to what many expected who thought that Jesus's arrival in Jerusalem would usher in the end of time (Luke 19:11).

Second, like Archelaus, Jesus's quest would be opposed. To be sure, the excited wavers of palm branches and people spreading their cloaks on the road called for Jesus's coronation as he rode the young donkey down the Mount of Olives approaching Jerusalem (Luke 19:28–40). But the sign posted above Jesus's head on the cross told a different story (Luke 23:38). This "king of the Jews" ran into strong opposition. His quest to become king had apparently failed, just like that of Archelaus.

And third, the time of Archelaus was shrouded in social injustice and violence. The social injustice in the parable is evident in the amount of money two of the servants made. The servants given three months' wages (a mina) to superintend could not have multiplied them five or tenfold without doing so on the backs of the poor. Finally, the man of noble birth in the parable had the same fiery temperament as Archelaus: "Bring them here and kill them in front of me" (Luke 19:27).

Between the parable's details and the real-life story of Archelaus mirrored in it, Jesus had this to say: the ultimate realization of the kingdom of God will be delayed, opposed, and preceded by a time of social injustice and violence.

For Further Reference: **Psalm 2; Daniel 7:13–14; Luke 12:49–53; Acts 1:6–8; 2 Peter 3:4–10**

CHAPTER 7

Jesus's Final Days in Jerusalem

TRIUMPHAL ENTRY

Matthew 21:1–11; Mark 11:1–11; Luke 19:28–44; John 12:12–19
"Blessed is the coming kingdom of our father David!"
(Mark 11:10)

▶ WHO & WHERE

Jesus, Mount of Olives, Bethphage, Jerusalem

▶ WHAT IS THIS TEXT TALKING ABOUT?

Jesus's final entry into Jerusalem

▶ WHAT DOES THIS TEXT TEACH?

Jesus's final entry into Jerusalem marked him as the long-awaited King.

Jesus had entered Jerusalem many times before, but never like this—the donkey, the waving palm branches, the ecstatic crowd. What we may miss is the vital role geography plays in this familiar story.

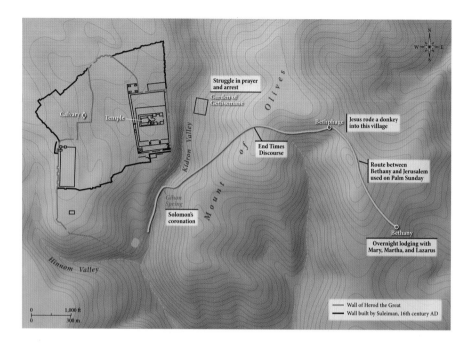

Jesus rode a donkey into Bethphage. This small village, that lies just east of the summit on the Mount of Olives, is mentioned only here in the entire Bible. Matthew, Mark, and Luke mention it for two reasons. First, Bethphage is the village from which Jesus got the donkey for this historic entry into the Holy City—a necessary tool for fulfilling the prophecy of Zechariah 9:9. Luke shines a spotlight on the animal by twice saying, "The Lord needs it" (Luke 19:31, 34). And Jesus "needed it" prior to his arrival in Bethphage. That is the second reason the Gospels mention it. Although this village was up the ridge and across the valley from down-town Jerusalem, well outside the defensive walls of the city, it was widely regarded as the city limits of Jerusalem. When Jesus rode the donkey *into* Bethphage, he was riding the donkey *into* the city of Jerusalem, fulfilling the geographic dimension of the prophecy in Zechariah 9:9.

Jesus's arrival animated the crowd on the Mount of Olives who call for his coronation. Again, it is geography that influences their language and exclamations: "Hosanna to the Son of David!" "Blessed is the coming kingdom of our father David!" "Blessed is the king who comes in the name of the Lord!" "Blessed is the king of Israel!" (Matt. 21:9; Mark 11:10; Luke 19:38; John 12:13). From their vantage point on the west slope of the Mount of Olives, they saw history repeating itself. Just across the valley, King David put his son Solomon on a mule. He sent him riding downslope into the Kidron Valley and toward the Gihon Spring. That is where King Solomon's coronation took place (1 Kings 1:38–48). Centuries later, on the first Palm Sunday, the crowd saw the same story unfolding. The Son was riding on a donkey provided by his Father downslope toward the very place that Solomon was crowned as Israel's king. What Jesus was doing joined together with where he was doing it to animate these familiar exclamations of Palm Sunday. The triumphal entry of the Messiah King had begun.

For Further Reference: 1 Kings 1:38–48; 2 Kings 9:13; Psalm 118:25–26; Isaiah 62:11; Zechariah 9:9

JESUS'S ACTION-PACKED TEMPLE SERMON

Matthew 21:12–17; Mark 11:15–19; Luke 19:45–48; John 2:13–17

"It is written, . . . 'My house will be called a house of prayer,' but you are making it 'a den of robbers.'" (Matthew 21:13)

▶ WHO & WHERE
Jesus, Temple in Jerusalem

▶ WHAT IS THIS TEXT TALKING ABOUT?
Misuse of sacred space

▶ WHAT DOES THIS TEXT TEACH?
Misused sacred space is destined to face divine judgment.

It is a Temple story we have heard before, a story with roots in the time of Jeremiah. When it starts, we know how it will end.

The Temple in Jerusalem was unique. It was where God's people came to worship him and to present their prayers before him (Isa. 56:7). This was the most sacred space on earth because the Lord was present here in a special way.

But at the time of Jeremiah and later Jesus, this sacred space had been corrupted through misuse. The Lord sent Jeremiah to preach a powerful sermon that detailed the abuses (Jer. 7:6–10) and led to this stirring question: "Has this house, which bears my Name, become a den of robbers to you?" (v. 11). Jesus quoted these words because the same place had become corrupted again. The problem was not with providing sacrificial animals for those who traveled long distances (Deut. 14:24–26) or even exchanging money for payment of the Temple tax. The problem was that the aristocratic priests had set up a market between the Temple entrance and Temple proper. It filled the view of those coming to worship. At best it was a distraction, at worst it became the purpose of the space—a profit-making business rather than a place of worship.

Jesus and Jeremiah both called for a change—Jeremiah at the entrance of the Lord's house and Jesus in the Temple courtyards. While Jesus quoted Jeremiah's sermon, his actions speak as loudly as his words. Jesus

The Temple complex in Jerusalem was the most sacred space on earth. But it had been misused and corrupted by the Sadducees.

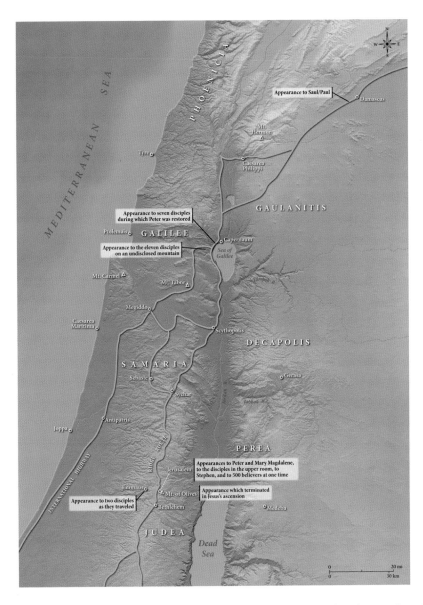

overturned tables and sent the livestock scrambling with whip in hand. Both Jesus and Jeremiah sought cleansing of this sacred space.

The reaction to both was also the same. The Temple leadership plotted against Jeremiah (Jer. 11:18), called for his execution (26:11), and arrested him (37:16). But none of that muted the outcome. As promised (7:14), the Lord permitted the unthinkable. In 586 BC, Jerusalem and its Temple were destroyed by the Babylonians. Jesus stood in the rebuilt Temple complex where the Sadducees and teachers of the law responded to him in similar fashion. They were indignant when the children sang, "Hosanna to the Son of David" (Matt. 21:15). They plotted Jesus's execution (Mark 11:18; Luke 19:47). And in the end because they failed to heed Jesus's words, the Temple faced destruction again—this time by the Romans in AD 70.

The Lord takes misuse of his sacred space very seriously.

For Further Reference: **Deuteronomy 14:23–26; 2 Chronicles 6:18–42; Psalm 69:9; Isaiah 56:7; Jeremiah 7:1–20; Matthew 24:1–2; Luke 2:49**

A LESSON ON PRAYER FROM THE LANDSCAPE

Matthew 21:18–22; Mark 11:12–14, 20–24

"If you believe, you will receive whatever you ask for in prayer."
(Matthew 21:22)

▶ WHO & WHERE
Jesus, disciples, Herodium, Dead Sea

▶ WHAT IS THIS TEXT TALKING ABOUT?
Prayer

▶ WHAT DOES THIS TEXT TEACH?
Be confident in the power of your prayers.

Prayer is more than a wish list. It is more than a pious, spiritual exercise. Prayer is a powerful tool.

The palace-fortress called the Herodium provided Jesus with the visual he used to teach a powerful lesson on prayer.

This is the second lesson Jesus taught from the landscape that day because the disciples missed the first. A hungry Jesus spied a distant fig tree that had sprouted leaves. In spring, this meant it should also have produced early-season figs. It hadn't. When Jesus was close enough to see the "hypocrisy" of the tree that mirrored the hypocrisy he had seen in Jerusalem, he caused it to wither. The disciples missed the connection, however, because they were "amazed" at how quickly the tree withered (Matt. 21:20). Their amazement signaled a lack of confidence in their own prayer life, so Jesus quickly pivoted to a new lesson, lifting their eyes from the fig tree to the horizon.

The next lesson for that day was linked to a specific mountain and sea, likely the Herodium and the Dead Sea (Matt. 21:21). The Herodium was a palace-fortress built by Herod the Great, perched on rising terrain. As Jesus and the disciples crossed the Mount of Olives on their way back to

Jerusalem from Bethany, it was hard to miss. Even though it was 7.5 miles (12 kilometers) away, "this mountain" soared above other terrain features. It grabbed the disciples' attention for several reasons. It was tall. The palace included a five-story hall and an eight-story tower. It was round, unlike other buildings of this era or most things in nature. And it had a history of being moved. Herod draped the circular foundations of the upper palace with a thirty-two-degree slope of soil and rock. To get those materials, Herod cut off the top of the adjacent mountain and moved it to the Herodium. It was an amazing feat of engineering and stunning piece of architecture, but "this" mountain symbolized something more sinister. For peasants, it embodied the Roman occupation and all the social injustices that attended it.

But what could they do? They were powerless peasants. Jesus's response? "Pray!" They had a powerful tool they were underestimating. They could do so much more than Jesus had done to the fig tree. They could say to "this" mountain, go throw yourself into the Dead Sea, the place Jewish tradition said was the proper place for all pagan items, and it would happen.

That is the power of prayer.

For Further Reference: Psalm 88:1–2; Hosea 9:10; Acts 2:42; 4:23–31; Romans 12:12; 2 Corinthians 10:3–5; Ephesians 6:18; Philippians 4:6; James 5:16; 1 Peter 3:12

A LESSON ON AUTHORITY

Matthew 21:23–27; Mark 11:27–33; Luke 20:1–8

"'By what authority are you doing these things?' they asked. 'And who gave you this authority?'" (Matthew 21:23)

▶ **WHO & WHERE**

Jesus, Jewish leaders in Jerusalem, Temple courts

▶ WHAT IS THIS TEXT TALKING ABOUT?
True authority

▶ WHAT DOES THIS TEXT TEACH?
Jesus exposed the weakness of those who presumed they had power over him.

It had to stop. The whispered stories about Jesus's miracles, the crowds calling for Jesus's coronation, the disruption of the Temple markets . . . it all had to stop. So, a self-important group approached Jesus as he taught in the Temple courts. They were on a power trip and presumed Jesus would be cowed by their presence and intimidated by their authority.

The group consisted of aristocratic priests or Sadducees, the senior scholars of the Pharisees called the teachers of the law, and other well-to-do, influential leaders within the Sanhedrin. This pretentious group confronted Jesus with a pair of questions. They cared little about the answers. Their goal was to intimidate Jesus, bullying him into backing down. They got something quite different than they expected.

Jesus went on the offensive. He replied to their questions with one of his own—a question that put the spotlight on how these esteemed elite dealt with John the Baptist. Like Jesus, John presented as a teacher who was uncredentialed by the Jerusalem school system. Did they regard John as an authorized teacher of the faith?

The Jewish leaders stepped to the side, wringing their hands over the dilemma. John had been executed by Herod years earlier. Yet his case remained a hot topic these Jewish leaders deftly avoided because though uncredentialed, John was extremely popular. Fearing an uprising against them, the pious elite returned to Jesus without an answer. And their nonanswer accomplished exactly what Jesus intended. It exposed that their bravado was a sham.

True to the agreement, Jesus refused to answer their initial set of questions. That is not because he lacked an answer. Ironically, Jesus could have pointed them to the moment John baptized him in the Jordan River—a moment when his authority from heaven was on full display (Matt. 3:16–17). But Jesus's refusal to answer spoke more directly to the point he was making. Their intimidation had failed. Jesus gave them no answer because none was owed. And in doing so, he exposed the weakness of those who claimed to have authority over him.

For Further Reference: Isaiah 40:1–5; Matthew 3:16–17; Mark 1:22, 27; Acts 4:7; 7:27

PARABLE OF THE TWO SONS

Matthew 21:28–32

"Truly I tell you, the tax collectors and the prostitutes are entering the kingdom of God ahead of you." (Matthew 21:31)

▶ **WHO & WHERE**
Jesus, Jewish leaders in Jerusalem, Temple courts

▶ **WHAT IS THIS TEXT TALKING ABOUT?**
Repentance that leads to kingdom membership

▶ **WHAT DOES THIS TEXT TEACH?**
Repentance that leads to kingdom membership penetrates past the surface.

Things are not always as they appear, particularly when we look in the mirror. In this parable, Jesus calls for us to examine our lives for a change that is more than skin-deep.

The parable introduces us to a father who makes the same request of two sons. He asks both to work in the family vineyard. This is not an exotic request. It is what sons did to preserve the well-being of the extended family. Yet these two sons respond in opposite ways, leading Jesus to ask the question, which of these two really did what the father wanted?

Jesus addressed the question to the chief priests and Sanhedrin elders standing nearby (Matt. 21:23). When they looked in the spiritual mirror, they liked what they saw. Within the stratified society of first-century Jerusalem, they were at the top of the ladder—the religious elite, distinguished by their knowledge and piety. By contrast, the low rung on the ladder was reserved for tax collectors and prostitutes. Tax collectors sold out to the Romans and made their living on the backs of common people. Prostitutes also serviced the Romans but in a different fashion. Although Jewish society saw those on the top and bottom of the social ladder differently, God did not. All were sinners who needed to change how they were thinking and living. The Old Testament prophets, John the Baptist, and Jesus called for such repentance.

The real difference comes in how these groups responded. The chief priests and elders changed on the surface. They looked good in their own eyes and in the eyes of others. But that change never made it into the core of their being and living as it had with some of the tax collectors and prostitutes. That is why Jesus's words to them landed with a loud thud: "Truly I tell you, the tax collectors and the prostitutes are entering the kingdom of God ahead of you" (Matt. 21:31). Only repentance that is more than skin-deep opens the door for membership in the kingdom of God.

For Further Reference: Psalms 32:5; 51:4–10; Isaiah 5:1–7; Ezekiel 18:21–24; Joel 2:12–13; Luke 7:29–50; Acts 2:38; Romans 2:28–29; 2 Corinthians 7:10; 2 Timothy 2:19–22

PARABLE OF THE TENANTS

Matthew 21:33–46; Mark 12:1–12; Luke 20:9–19

"The stone the builders rejected has become the cornerstone;
the Lord has done this, and it is marvelous in our eyes."
(Matthew 21:42)

▶ **WHO & WHERE**

Jesus, Jewish leaders, Jerusalem

▶ **WHAT IS THIS TEXT TALKING ABOUT?**

Rejection of Jesus by the Jewish leaders in Jerusalem

▶ **WHAT DOES THIS TEXT TEACH?**

The rejection of Jesus by the Jewish leaders was unwarranted and
must be ignored.

Something had to be said lest the mistaken views of the Jewish leaders
in Jerusalem infect the common people. Jesus takes us to the vineyard
and construction site to highlight their failures.

The parable leans into a cultural picture that was well known by those
living in the Judean hill country. This was prime grape-growing land, so
the people of Jerusalem knew how much work it took to establish a vineyard. Because the terrain was steep, a landowner had to build a farm field
using terraces. A single acre could take a decade or more to build. Prom-
ising grape shoots were acquired, planted, and cultivated for four to five
years before the vineyard began to produce. In the meantime, the farmer
put infrastructure in place—a wall, a winepress, and a watchtower. This
image captures the long and difficult process the landowner or Lord used
to establish his vineyard, his chosen people (Isa. 5:1–4).

The landowner then turned the care and keeping of the vineyard over to others. The others are the Jewish leaders in Jerusalem who do the unthinkable. When it was time for the tenants to pay the rent, they refused. When he sent servants to collect, the tenants mistreated them. And when he sent his son, they killed him. Outrageous! Yet it illustrates the way Israel's authority figures had treated the prophets (Jer. 7:25–26) and were treating Jesus. The views of the religious elite were flawed.

To drive the point home, Jesus takes us to the construction site. There amidst the quarry rubble, we look at a carefully cut stone. It was unique and necessary—either the cornerstone of the building that guided the walls' symmetry or the wedge-shaped capstone of an arch. Only a foolish builder would reject this kind of stone. Yet, that's exactly what Psalm 118:22–23 speaks about. In its Old Testament context, the foolish builders are the nations who underestimate how the Lord will use the nation of Israel. In Jesus's use of the image, the foolish builders are the Jewish leaders that reject him as the Messiah.

Both illustrations carry the same message. The Jewish leaders in Jerusalem were making unwarranted assumptions about Jesus and had to be ignored.

For Further Reference: **Psalms 2; 118:22–23; Isaiah 5:1–7; Jeremiah 7:25–26; Acts 4:8–12; Hebrews 1:1–2; 1 Peter 2:4–7**

THE TIME HAD COME

John 12:20–36

"The hour has come for the Son of Man to be glorified." (John 12:23)

▶ **WHO & WHERE**

Jesus, Jerusalem

▶ WHAT IS THIS TEXT TALKING ABOUT?
Jesus's impending death

▶ WHAT DOES THIS TEXT TEACH?
Jesus chose to die on the cross because it was a necessary part of
his mission that would bring glory to the Father.

This moment marks a turning point in Jesus's life. John repeatedly reports that Jesus's time or hour had not yet come (John 2:4; 4:23; 7:8,
30; 8:20). Now Jesus said, "The hour has come" (12:23). It was time for
Jesus to enter a new phase of his work. These verses explore what it will be
like and how Jesus thinks about it.

First, note that Jesus uses three figures of speech to say he is going to
die. This was important enough to say more than once and in more than
one way to correct a popular misunderstanding. Because portions of the
Hebrew Bible spoke about the eternalness of the Messiah (Isa. 9:7; Dan.
7:14), many believed that the Messiah would not die. Jesus corrects the
view with three pictures. He likens himself to a kernel of wheat that falls
to the ground and "dies" (John 12:24). The language sounds strange to
us because we know that the seed
is part of the life cycle of a plant.
But because the seed appeared to
"die," those living in Jesus's day
associated the planting of a seed
with death. Second, Jesus said he
would be "lifted up" (12:32–33).
This of course is the elevation
associated with his crucifixion.
Third, he spoke of the sun going
down. John had introduced us to
Jesus as the "light" (1:4–5). Jesus

Jesus likened himself to a kernel of wheat that must
"die" in order to achieve the end of producing a new
plant with many seeds.

had reached the sunset of his life on earth. Light would give way to the darkness (12:35). These three figures of speech combine to affirm that in this new phase of his life, Jesus would die.

And what did Jesus think about that? It was necessary. Theoretically, Jesus could have gone to his Father and begged off the mission, avoiding the "very reason I came to this hour" (12:27). Death was a product of sin and the final enemy to be defeated. Jesus had to die to rise from the dead. That meant his death was necessary. But Jesus's death would do more than just defeat death on our behalf. Jesus's death would bring glory to the Father. In other words, the death of Jesus was an act of worship through which Jesus would glorify the Father's name (v. 28).

Things were about to change and Jesus was all in.

For Further Reference: **Genesis 3:15; Isaiah 52:13; Daniel 7:14; Luke 24:19–26; 1 Corinthians 15:26; Hebrews 12:2; 1 Peter 1:10–11**

DISAPPOINTMENT OVER JERUSALEM'S UNBELIEF

John 12:37–50

"Even after Jesus had performed so many signs in their presence, they still would not believe in him." (John 12:37)

▶ WHO & WHERE
Jesus, Jerusalem

▶ WHAT IS THIS TEXT TALKING ABOUT?
The reception of Jesus in Jerusalem

▶ WHAT DOES THIS TEXT TEACH?

The Lord was deeply disappointed by the reception he received in Jerusalem.

T he disappointment, sadness, and frustration are all keenly felt in these words of John concerning Jerusalem's failure to believe and receive Jesus.

Jerusalem, Jesus, and John shared the same goal. The Holy City was the urban center chosen by God. Here, he most clearly revealed who he was, how he thought about people, and how passionate he was to save them from their sin. When Jesus walked its streets and spoke in its courtyards, the invitation became even more personal and real. Note that Jesus did not whisper this invitation but shouted it aloud: "Whoever believes in me does not believe in me only, but in the one who sent me" (John 12:44). When the Spirit led John to write this story of Jesus in Jerusalem, he had the same goal in mind: "But these are written that you may believe that Jesus is the Messiah, the Son of God, and that by believing you may have life in his name" (20:31).

What an opportunity God gave the Holy City! There are two responses to this opportunity that fueled the Lord's disappointment. First, there were those who had crossed the threshold. For them, belief was no longer possible. When the Holy Spirit works on the heart soliciting faith, a clock begins to run. There is only so much time while the door remains open for a response before eyes can no longer see and hearts can no longer be changed. John quotes Isaiah to show that what had happened before in Israel was now happening in Jerusalem, even though Jesus was speaking in its streets. Second, the other response that also disappointed the Lord was that some of those who believed hid their faith. This was particularly true of influential Jewish leaders who came to believe that Jesus was the Messiah. But they hid their belief from others, fearing excommunication from the synagogue and being socially ostracized by their neighbors. They preferred the praise of their colleagues to the praise of God.

Jesus felt disappointment, frustration, and sadness over the people who walked the streets of Jerusalem but refused to believe in him.

These are some of the most troubling words in the gospel of John. They take us near to the heart of God to show how disappointed he was at the reception Jerusalem gave his Son.

For Further Reference: Psalm 132:13–18; Isaiah 6:9–10; 53:1; Acts 28:23–27; Romans 10:10–21; 2 Corinthians 3:14–16; Hebrews 1:1–2

PARABLE OF THE WEDDING BANQUET

Matthew 22:1–14; Luke 14:15–24

"For many are invited, but few are chosen." (Matthew 22:14)

▶ WHO & WHERE
Jesus, Temple courts in Jerusalem

▶ WHAT IS THIS TEXT TALKING ABOUT?
Invitation to join the kingdom of heaven

▶ WHAT DOES THIS TEXT TEACH?
God's invitation to the kingdom is broad and persistent, yet resistible.

W hom should we invite? Are we going to go? These questions still swirl around the wedding invitations we send and receive. This parable revolves around the same questions.

Matthew and Luke each tell a version of this parable. If you read them closely, you will see that they differ from one another in a few details though their point is the same. Here, we will focus on the more detailed parable recounted by Matthew.

As soon as Jesus said the word "banquet," everyone within earshot knew the topic. Within the Jewish orbit, the banquet or feast was the way they pictured life with the Lord in eternity (Isa. 25:6; Luke 14:15). They expected Jesus to weigh in on the ongoing debate among the teachers in Jerusalem over just who would be invited to the heavenly banquet. Some thought the invitation was extended only to the rabbis, others only to descendants of Abraham, and still others to Jews and a handful of worthy Gentiles. All were surprised by what followed.

The first thing that stands out is the king's persistence in growing the guest list. There are four separate invitations in all. The first is unmentioned here but presumed. It was customary in Jesus's day to send an initial invitation or "save the date" notification. The second invitation announced that food preparation was underway (Matt. 22:3). The third came after the second invitation was ignored. It was particularly enticing because it included mention of beef, something rarely on the average family's menu (v. 4). And the fourth invitation broadened the guest list to include anyone the messengers could find no matter what their social status or character (v. 9). This part of the parable highlights the Lord's nondiscriminatory persistence in calling people into the kingdom.

The second thing that stands out are the refusals. Despite the honor of being invited to a royal wedding, many trashed the opportunity. The first group refused to come when they received the second invitation despite having accepted the first. Shocking! Then, these same invitees either ignored, mistreated, or executed the messengers carrying the third invitation. Unthinkable! And finally, there is the man who came but dressed improperly for the event. Because most common people like those who received the fourth invitation did not have a closet full of clothes, the king provided appropriate clothes for the wedding banquet. This man refused to wear the gifted garment. A total affront! The king's response to all these stunning miscues was swift and harsh.

All of us have received a persistent and gracious invitation to faith. This parable challenges us to ask an important question: have I been casual or incautious in responding to it?

For Further Reference: Isaiah 25:6–9; Romans 8:29–30; 2 Corinthians 6:1–2; Revelation 19:9

PAYMENT OF TAXES TO CAESAR

Matthew 22:15–22; Mark 12:13–17; Luke 20:20–26

"So give back to Caesar what is Caesar's, and to God
what is God's." (Matthew 22:21)

▶ WHO & WHERE

Jesus, Pharisees, Herodians, Temple courts in Jerusalem

▶ WHAT IS THIS TEXT TALKING ABOUT?

Loyalty to civil authority and God

▶ WHAT DOES THIS TEXT TEACH?

Loyalty to civil authority and God are not mutually exclusive.

An unlikely alliance had formed between the two groups pushing their way through the crowded Temple courts toward Jesus. The Pharisees and Herodians generally saw the world differently. But they had this in common—a distaste for the popularity of Jesus. So, they joined forces to bring an end to his teaching and influence.

They confronted Jesus with a question about the census, the annual poll tax of one denarius collected by Rome from men ages fourteen to sixty-five and women ages twelve to sixty-five. The census reminded them of the Roman occupation of their land and the way the poll tax was used to support the pagan ideology of Rome. If Jesus advocated payment of the tax, then the Pharisees had what they needed to discredit him among the common people.

If he spoke against the tax, the Herodians had what they needed. The Herodians were Jews loyal to the family of Herod and had cut a deal with Rome to secure political positions. They supported the tax system and were particularly suspicious of Galileans like Jesus since Galilee was where tax revolts typically originated. All they needed was for Jesus to speak one word against the tax and they would summon the Roman soldiers posted in the nearby Antonia Fortress. The trap was set. No matter which way Jesus answered, he was in trouble.

In reply, Jesus asked for a coin and held it up as a visual aid. He asked whose image and inscription were on it. Even those too far away to see knew the answer because they had personally handled such a coin. It was stamped with the bust of the emperor. The inscription included his name, Tiberius Caesar, and an allusion to his divine status. He paused and the crowd leaned in to see what Jesus would say next. His answer was brilliant.

Jesus did not give a comprehensive lecture on the relationship between his followers and the state. But in a single sentence he turned an either-or question into a both-and answer: "So give back to Caesar what is Caesar's, and to God what is God's" (Matt. 22:21).

His followers owed ultimate loyalty to the God who is sovereign over all. But because God used agents like government, loyalty to civil authority and God are not mutually exclusive.

For Further Reference: **Deuteronomy 10:12; Ecclesiastes 8:2; Romans 13:1–7; 1 Timothy 2:1–3; Titus 3:1–2; 1 Peter 2:13–14**

MARRIAGE AT THE RESURRECTION

Matthew 22:23–33; Mark 12:18–27; Luke 20:27–40

"At the resurrection people will neither marry nor be given in marriage; they will be like the angels in heaven."
(Matthew 22:30)

▶ WHO & WHERE
Jesus, Sadducees, Temple courts in Jerusalem

▶ WHAT IS THIS TEXT TALKING ABOUT?
Jesus's divine nature

▶ WHAT DOES THIS TEXT TEACH?
Jesus demonstrated his divine nature by providing a previously unknown insight into the realities of life after death.

It was a setup from the start. The aristocratic priests (the Sadducees) sought to discredit Jesus with a question he could not possibly answer. But Jesus used this opportunity to demonstrate there was much more to him than they realized.

The Sadducees used the Torah (Genesis through Deuteronomy) as the source for their theology. Because they found no evidence of an after-life in these books, they did not believe in resurrection or life after death. So, they used a passage from Deuteronomy to set up a scenario that would force Jesus to admit they were correct. They picked the wrong guy with whom to play Bible trivia!

Jesus would get to the verses in Deuteronomy but starts with Exodus 3:6. While meeting with Moses at the burning bush, the Lord offered this description of himself: "I am the God of your father, the God of Abraham, the God of Isaac and the God of Jacob." While the Sadducees' attention went to the proper names, Jesus pointed to the verb, "I am." Although these notable Old Testament believers had died centuries earlier, God speaks of them as existing, "for to him all are alive" (Luke 20:38). Here is Torah evidence the Sadducees missed that spoke about life after death. When Jesus pointed it out, he signals just how unique he is.

Then Jesus moves to the Torah passage the Sadducees used to set up the challenge, Deuteronomy 25:5–6. In this law, the Lord directed a man to marry his deceased brother's widow and have a son. This levirate marriage provided the widow with economic security and clarified the path for inheritance. Jesus's discussion partners used this passage to create an unlikely situation in which a woman ended up married to seven brothers.

אֶֽהְיֶ֖ה אֲשֶׁ֣ר אֶֽהְיֶ֑ה

Hebrew for "I AM WHO I AM" (Ex. 3:14).

Then comes the question: whose wife will she be at the resurrection? In this case, Jesus did not point to a Bible verse because the Old Testament does not offer insights into marriage in the afterlife. But don't miss what he did instead. Jesus provided a new insight: resurrected believers in heaven do not marry. Jesus could know this only because he had been there. And only God had been there.

For Further Reference: Exodus 3:6; Deuteronomy 25:5–6; Acts 4:1–2; 23:6–8; 1 Corinthians 15:12

THE CRITICAL COMMANDMENTS

Matthew 22:34–40; Mark 12:28–34

"Of all the commandments, which is the most important?"
(Mark 12:28)

▶ **WHO & WHERE**

Jesus, teacher of the law, Temple courts in Jerusalem

▶ **WHAT IS THIS TEXT TALKING ABOUT?**

The essence of the law

▶ **WHAT DOES THIS TEXT TEACH?**

The essence of the law is realized in all-encompassing love for God and unselfish love for our neighbors.

A ll week, Jesus had fielded the same kinds of questions in the Temple courts. Given where he was, that makes perfect sense.

While we are prone to think of the Jerusalem Temple as a place to worship, it was also a place to learn. Remember that as a boy Jesus came to the Temple to get answers for the questions that had gone unanswered in Nazareth (Luke 2:46). Now, as an adult, Jesus may well have been interacting with some of the same teachers. These Pharisees identified 613 unique directives or prohibitions in the Torah (the first five books of the Old Testament). From the swirling details, they carried on a long-standing debate about which of the laws was most important—the single law that would help interpret all the others. It's no wonder that Jesus had been dealing with questions about the law all week when visiting the Temple courts.

But this interaction is different. Other Pharisees maliciously sought to entrap Jesus (Mark 12:15). This man approached him with a sincere question, giving the whole exchange a different tenor and feel. Jesus answered the man's question directly. This Pharisee valued the response. And in turn, Jesus complimented him (vv. 33–34).

The uniqueness of the exchange causes us to lean in for a closer look. How would Jesus respond? He observed that the most important law is captured by the language of Deuteronomy 6:4–5. Observant Jews knew the language well. It is called the Shema and was recited twice a day, morning and evening. The Shema declared the singularity of the Lord and confirmed one's all-encompassing love for him.

Honoring the sincerity of his student, Jesus then went on to answer the question that was unasked. What is the second most important commandment in Torah? Here, he quotes Leviticus 19:18, which uses the very same word "love" but directs it toward our neighbor. This love for others is not different in quality but extent. Love the Lord with all your heart, soul, mind, and strength becomes love your neighbor in the same way you love yourself.

For Further Reference: Leviticus 19:18; Deuteronomy 6:4–5; 1 Corinthians 8:3; Galatians 5:14; 1 John 4:20

WHOSE SON IS THE MESSIAH?

Matthew 22:41–46; Mark 12:35–37; Luke 20:41–44

"What do you think about the Messiah? Whose son is he?"
(Matthew 22:42)

▶ WHO & WHERE

Jesus, Pharisees, Temple courts in Jerusalem

▶ WHAT IS THIS TEXT TALKING ABOUT?

The Messiah's family heritage

▶ WHAT DOES THIS TEXT TEACH?

The Messiah is both the Son of David and the Son of God.

Being partially right can mean you are all wrong. That was the case with the Pharisees who gathered around Jesus.

They raised questions related to the family heritage of the Messiah, particularly his relationship to King David. This may have been motivated, in part, by the view. Just south of the southern entrance of the Temple we find the City of David. There, in the royal palace, just a ten-minute walk to the south of where Jesus was speaking, is the place the Lord promised King David that one of his descendants would be the Messiah (2 Sam. 7:12–16).

But what exactly did that mean? Many of the Pharisees presumed this messiah would be a mere mortal—a biological descendant of David but no more. They anticipated the coming of a warrior-king who would liberate

Jesus used Psalm 110, a psalm of David, to unveil his divine nature. This is the traditional tomb of David located in the City of David, not far from where Jesus offered this insight.

them from Roman occupation, but they weren't really expecting someone who could liberate them from the power of sin.

To correct their view, Jesus quoted Psalm 110—the most frequently cited portion of the Old Testament in the New Testament—and a psalm written by King David. In it, the Holy Spirit inspired David (Mark 12:36) to report on a conversation occurring in heaven between the Father and the Messiah: "The LORD says to my lord" (Ps. 110:1). Jesus calls attention to the personal pronoun. It would be socially inappropriate for a forebearer like David to use an honorary title like "lord" for one of his descendants. But when he does, it shows that the Messiah was no ordinary descendant of David. This Son of David was also the Son of God.

Jesus was not playing a Bible trivia game with the Pharisees. This was serious. The Pharisees saw Messiah as less than he was and thus was capable of delivering less than he would.

For Further Reference: **2 Samuel 7:12–16; Psalm 110:1–4; Proverbs 30:1–4; Isaiah 9:6–7; Matthew 1:1; Luke 3:21–38; John 1:1–2, 14, 18; 10:34–38; Acts 2:34–36; 1 Corinthians 15:25; Hebrews 1:13**

THE COLLAPSE OF THE JERUSALEM RELIGIOUS SYSTEM

Matthew 23:1–39; Mark 12:38–40; Luke 20:45–47

"The teachers of the law and the Pharisees . . . do not practice
what they preach." (Matthew 23:2–3)

▶ WHO & WHERE
Jesus, Temple courts in Jerusalem

▶ WHAT IS THIS TEXT TALKING ABOUT?
The system that produced Israel's religious teachers

▶ WHAT DOES THIS TEXT TEACH?
The system that produced Israel's religious teachers had failed.

Jesus had given incendiary talks before, but none like this. Standing in Jerusalem where Israel's religious teachers were trained and certified, Jesus declared that the system had failed.

Jesus points to the graduates, those who "sit in Moses' seat" (Matt. 23:2), and says they cannot be trusted. The seat of Moses is like the pulpit in some of our churches—the place from which the religious leader explains and applies God's Word. The problem with the ones sitting in those appointed seats was that their training had not changed their hearts. They did not practice what they preached.

Three pictures highlight the failure. First, Jesus points to *tefillin* and *tsitsith*, two worship aids. *Tefillin* are small leather boxes tied to the head and left arm that contained short quotes from the Old Testament. They are used to remind the worshipper to keep the Word of God on their mind and in their hearts (Ex. 13:9, 16; Deut. 6:8). The *tsitsith* were the tassels sown into the four corners of their garments (Num. 15:38). These tassels swept back and forth as a constant reminder to obey Torah. As devotional aids, there was nothing wrong with either. But Israel's teachers made them huge to draw people's attention—piety gave way to hypocrisy (Matt. 23:5).

The second picture is comical. The religious food laws of Leviticus 11 brand both gnats and camels as unclean and so not fit for consumption. Here Jesus pictures the teachers of Israel using a piece of cloth to strain their beverages, concerned about a *galma* (Aramaic for gnat), while swallowing a *gamla* (Aramaic for camel), a further illustration of their hypocrisy (Matt. 23:24).

The third picture turns our eyes east to the Mount of Olives, which served as a cemetery for the residents of Jerusalem. Contact with a grave made a person ritually unclean (Num. 19:16). During Passover, a fresh coat of chalk was used to mark gravesites so that visitors unfamiliar with the landscape did not inadvertently wander into a cemetery. The chalk made the graves look better than what they contained. Jesus said that the religious teachers trained in Jerusalem were like that (Matt. 23:27–28).

These pictures join with others in these verses to highlight the failed religious system in Jerusalem. Its graduates were about to do the unthinkable. The Old Testament from beginning to end told stories of unrighteous acts of murder from the first book in the Hebrew Bible to the last (Gen. 4:8; 2 Chron. 24:19–21). But all those murders paled in comparison to what these Pharisees and teachers of the law were about to do—agitate for the execution of God's Son.

For Further Reference: **Genesis 4:8; Exodus 13:9, 16; Numbers 15:38–39; Deuteronomy 6:6–8; 22:12; 2 Chronicles 24:19–21; Micah 6:8; Matthew 11:25–26; 1 Corinthians 2:8; Galatians 3:24–25**

THE POOR WIDOW'S GIFT

Mark 12:41–44; Luke 21:1–4

"Truly I tell you, this poor widow has put more into the treasury
than all the others. They all gave out of their wealth; but she,
out of her poverty, put in everything—all she had to live on."
(Mark 12:43–44)

▶ **WHO & WHERE**
Jesus, widow, Court of the Women in the Temple at Jerusalem

▶ **WHAT IS THIS TEXT TALKING ABOUT?**
Charitable giving

▶ **WHAT DOES THIS TEXT TEACH?**
The Lord values the faith of the giver more than the size of the
gift.

The world values wealth and people who have it. The Lord values faith
and people who show it. That is the lesson Jesus taught as he sat in the
Court of the Women and watched those making charitable donations, one
of whom was a poor widow.

In Bible times, women who lost their husbands were at risk. When a
young woman married, she left her parents' living compound and joined
her husband's. This meant connecting her economic and social well-being
to that of her husband's extended family. If her husband died, she could
be caught between her parents' and husband's households with neither
willing to provide her with food and shelter. That was the case with this
widow. We don't know her name, but we do know she was in desperate
financial straits.

Nevertheless, she has come to the Temple to give a gift. Jesus spots her entering the Court of the Women. According to later Jewish writings, thirteen shofar-shaped containers with wide mouths and narrow bodies stood around the perimeter of this courtyard—each labeled for a specific type of offering.

The widow is not alone. Many well-to-do people were also approaching these giving containers. We can imagine the scene as they slowly dropped one coin after the next into the horns, each coin clinking to the bottom and providing audible evidence of the size of their gift. When it was the poor widow's turn, it did not take long for her to drop in her two small copper coins, lacking the bright sound of the others' silver coins. She gave two lepta, each worth a fraction of a denarius, the amount of money a laborer made in one day.

The accounting of the world finds her gift to be of little consequence. What value were pennies in a world of hundred-dollar bills? But Jesus did not look at the size of the gift but the faith of the giver. In Jesus's accounting, the widow gave more than the others.

For Further Reference: **Luke 6:20; 12:21–34; 2 Corinthians 8:12; James 2:5**

END TIMES INSIGHTS

Matthew 24:1–51; Mark 13:1–37; Luke 12:35–48; 17:20–37; 21:5–38

"As Jesus was sitting on the Mount of Olives, the disciples came to him privately. 'Tell us,' they said, 'when will this happen, and what will be the sign of your coming and of the end of the age?'"

(Matthew 24:3)

> ▶ WHO & WHERE
Jesus, disciples, Mount of Olives

> ▶ WHAT IS THIS TEXT TALKING ABOUT?
The end of this present age

> ▶ WHAT DOES THIS TEXT TEACH?
The last days will be just as the Old Testament describes them. However, more precise information on the timing is not available.

Within minutes of placing an online order, I know what is coming and when to expect it. After listening in the Gospels to Jesus's extended discourse on the end times, I know what is coming. Can I know when?

The disciples had often seen Jesus link lesson and landscape. Now it was their turn. The disciples were sitting with Jesus on the western slope

This tumble of stones is what remains of the Jerusalem Temple complex after the Romans destroyed it in AD 70.

of the Mount of Olives overlooking the Kidron Valley and Temple complex of Jerusalem. When the Old Testament prophets spoke about judgment day, they used geographic language that included the ridge on which they sat and the valley below them (Joel 3:2, 12; Zech. 14:2–4). It was the perfect place to explore the topic of the last days.

Jesus follows the disciples' lead and delivers one of his longest lessons. What's particularly striking is that virtually all that he shares about the last days has already been revealed in the Old Testament. First, Jesus begins with the experiences that will lead up to that stunning day (Dan. 9:27; 12:1). It is a hard list to read, a checklist of items that attacks every dimension of well-being. The Temple in Jerusalem will be destroyed. War, famine, natural disasters, and persecution of Jesus's followers will break out. These days will be so bad that they will erode and exhaust people's ability to show love (Matt. 24:2–13, 15–28). Second, Jesus assures that this great social and economic disruption will not prevent the spread of the gospel (v. 14). The Old Testament anticipates that the forgiveness of sins will reach the world (Gen. 12:3; Isa. 60:1–3). The process now underway would continue. Third, Jesus echoes the Old Testament language that describes the unique nature of the last day (Isa. 13:9–10; 34:4; Dan. 7:13–14; Joel 2:31). Disruption in the heavenly bodies, the appearance of Jesus coming on the clouds, and the blast of the trumpet that gathers God's own to him will signal that the day has arrived (Matt. 24:29–35).

There is just one thing missing from that Old Testament discussion of judgment day—the date! Just when we think Jesus might tip his hand, he tells us that this information is not available to anyone—not even the angels or Jesus himself, only the Father knows (v. 36). That guarantees that this day, which will be like no other, will be a day like every other—a day just like the one that came before the horrific destruction of the world at the time of Noah (Genesis 6–7). People will be dining, getting married, doing fieldwork, and preparing food just like they do every other day. A day like today. "Therefore keep watch," Jesus warned, "because you do not know on what day your Lord will come" (Matt. 24:42).

For Further Reference: Matthew 28:18–28; Acts 1:6–8; 1 Corinthians 15:51–55; 1 Thessalonians 5:1–11; 2 Thessalonians 2:3–4; 1 Peter 1:3–5, 13; Revelation 1:7–8

THE PARABLE
OF THE TEN VIRGINS

Matthew 25:1–13

"Therefore keep watch, because you do not know the day or the hour." (Matthew 25:13)

▶ WHO & WHERE
Jesus, disciples, Mount of Olives

▶ WHAT IS THIS TEXT TALKING ABOUT?
Jesus's second coming

▶ WHAT DOES THIS TEXT TEACH?
Prepare thoughtfully for the second coming of Jesus.

The fact so easily slips to a remote corner of my mind, displaced by other priorities. Jesus is coming back. So, here it is. One more reminder to be prepared.

This parable takes us to a village wedding in first-century Israel. Two families had carefully weighed the proposed match and discussed the

relevant financial matters. A contract was signed, the engagement announced, and a wedding day set. The groom then went to work adding
a room to his family living compound where he and his bride would live.
The family prepared food and beverages for the weeklong celebration.
And the bride selected young, unmarried women who would attend her
on that day. They formed part of the wedding procession that escorted her
through the village to her new home. And in case the groom came to get
his bride after sunset, the attendants made sure that they each had their
lamps prepared.

Of course, these were not powered by batteries but generated light
by burning olive oil. The typical lamp of this era was a slipper-shaped ce-
ramic lamp that fit neatly in the palm of one's hand. It had a round opening on the top for adding fuel and a spout through which a wick could be
draped. These lamps were not high-powered flood lights but sufficed to
illuminate a portion of the home and were carried by young women if they
moved around the village after sunset. Even though the streets were familiar, it was a matter of cultural honor for them to carry a lamp so that
others would know who they were and that their nighttime movements
were honorable.

The parable divides the ten attendants into two groups of five—one
wise and one foolish. The wise attendants thought ahead. They allowed
for a possible delay in the arrival of the groom, calculated the amount of
additional oil needed for their lamps, and secured that additional fuel in a
flask. The foolish attendants did not. And therein lies the point of the illustration. The timing of Jesus's second coming, like the arrival of the groom
at the home of the bride, is unknowable (Matt. 24:36). It simply has not
been revealed. That leaves us with one option. Be thoughtfully prepared
every day.

For Further Reference: **Hosea 2:19; 1 Corinthians 15:52; 1 Thessalonians
4:16; 5:1–6; 2 Timothy 4:8; Hebrews 10:23–25, 36–39; 1 Peter 1:8–9; 2 Peter
3:3–13; Revelation 19:9**

THE PARABLE OF THE TALENTS

Matthew 25:14–30

"After a long time the master of those servants returned and settled accounts with them." (Matthew 25:19)

▶ **WHO & WHERE**

Jesus, disciples, Mount of Olives

▶ **WHAT IS THIS TEXT TALKING ABOUT?**

The use of our time between now and Jesus's second coming

▶ **WHAT DOES THIS TEXT TEACH?**

Jesus will critically review the way we use our gifts while he is away.

I am a list maker. I start every morning by making a list of things I plan to do. This parable has something important to say about what I put on that list.

The first part of it speaks to the time before Jesus's second coming. A wealthy man is preparing to leave on an extended trip. In advance of his departure, he entrusts his assets to servants so that they can manage them. The assets are significant. The value of a single "talent" was equivalent to approximately twenty years of a day-laborer's income! A tremendous amount of good could be accomplished even by the servant who received just one. Honoring the difference in native skills, the master distributed the assets unequally. Nevertheless, his expectation for each was the same. That they would put the money to work conscientiously, thoughtfully, and carefully.

The second part of the parable takes us to the time of Jesus's return when he will critically review the way believers have used their "talents" while he was away. In the parable, the first two servants did what the master expected and so doubled the value of the assets they were given. Even though the amount of profit varied between the two, the master commended both in the same way for the honorable and faithful way they acted. The same was not in store for the third servant. The value of his asset was frozen because he dug a hole in the ground and buried it. He had not even bothered to do with it what required the least effort—invested it with the money changers. When confronted by his failure, the servant pointed to the harsh and cruel reputation of the master—a characterization that is unsupported by the rest of the story. The master brushes aside his excuses and points instead to the servant's lack of engagement and laziness.

The gifts the Lord has given us are not the same or distributed in equal fashion. But Jesus expects us to use our intelligence, personality, mechanical skills, and wealth to enhance the well-being of his kingdom. And that challenges me to think carefully about what is on today's to-do list.

For Further Reference: **Proverbs 10:4; Luke 16:10; Romans 12:3–8; 1 Corinthians 15:58; 2 Thessalonians 3:7–13**

THE SHEEP AND GOATS OF JUDGMENT DAY

Matthew 25:31–46

"All the nations will be gathered before him, and he will separate the people one from another as a shepherd separates the sheep from the goats. He will put the sheep on his right and the goats on his left." (Matthew 25:32–33)

▶ WHO & WHERE
Jesus, disciples, Mount of Olives

▶ WHAT IS THIS TEXT TALKING ABOUT?
Judgment day

▶ WHAT DOES THIS TEXT TEACH?
The way we treat the socially disadvantaged indicates where we will be standing on judgment day.

The last event on the last day of this world's history will be the final judgment. In these verses, Jesus likens it to the management of a Middle Eastern flock.

In ancient Israel, sheep and goats were commingled for most of the year in the family flock. That is because both contributed to the well-being of the family in their own way. Sheep provided wool for clothing and better-tasting meat. Goats contributed high-quality milk and material for making tent panels and containers. Since both types of livestock required similar care and pasture, they were kept together in one flock. Jesus uses this image of the commingled flock to portray the commingled world in which believers and unbelievers live on the same neighborhood block, attend the same schools, shop at the same stores, and work in the same locations.

The Middle Eastern flock was separated when the family gave attention to tasks unique to either the sheep or goats—for example when they milked the goats or sheared the sheep. Jesus describes judgment day as a day for separating the people of the world because they will face different eternal fates. Believers will enjoy the inheritance prepared for them since the creation of the world (Matt. 25:34). Unbelievers will know the cursed eternity shared by the Devil and his angels (v. 41).

So how will that day turn out for you and me? The Lord has made a change in us that secures our eternity (Rom. 8:30). This internal change

The typical Middle Eastern flock consisted of both sheep and goats which were pastured together but separated for milking and shearing.

that is unseen produces external evidence that can be seen. Jesus points us to the love we lavish on those who are socially disadvantaged and in need—the hungry, thirsty, strangers, inadequately clothed, and in prison. We may not be able to physically see the changes the Lord has made in us that secure our eternal life. But we can see the difference it makes in our lives. Jesus sees it too: "Truly I tell you, whatever you did for one of the least of these brothers and sisters of mine, you did for me" (Matt. 25:40).

For Further Reference: Leviticus 19:9–10, 33–34; 25:35–43; Deuteronomy 15:7–11; Job 31:16–23, 32; Proverbs 19:17; Isaiah 58:6–10; Daniel 12:2–3; Romans 8:30; Hebrews 6:10; 13:1–2; James 2:15–17

THE PLOT TO EXECUTE JESUS

Matthew 26:1–5; Mark 14:1–2; Luke 22:1–2

"As you know, the Passover is two days away—and the Son of
Man will be handed over to be crucified." (Matthew 26:2)

➤ WHO & WHERE
Jesus, disciples, Mount of Olives

➤ WHAT IS THIS TEXT TALKING ABOUT?
The plot to execute Jesus

➤ WHAT DOES THIS TEXT TEACH?
Jesus knew that the plot to execute him was underway and yet did
nothing to prevent it.

If only I had known . . . If only I had known the car was going to break
down. If only I had known the food had spoiled. If only I had known the
power would go out. If we could know what was coming, we could avoid
many unpleasant experiences. What is so striking about this short paragraph
is that Jesus knew what was going to happen but did nothing to prevent it.

This is not the first time Jesus spoke of his impending death in Matthew.
He raised the topic on three prior occasions (Matt. 16:21; 17:22–23; 20:17–
19), telling the disciples in some detail what was going to happen to him, who
was responsible for it, and where it would happen. This information led Jesus
to avoid Jerusalem for months, after he raised Lazarus from the dead, in order
to prevent the Jewish religious leaders from acting against him (John 11:54).

Here, Jesus adds one more stunning detail to the list. He knew not
just what, who, and where his death would occur but when. It was just two
days away!

Ironically, Jesus knew more than those who plotted against him. We are given access to one of their secret meetings in which they decided *not* to arrest Jesus during the Passover festival (Matt. 26:5). This was one of the three high holy days on the Jewish calendar that brought tens of thousands to the Holy City. The size of the crowd, Jesus's growing popularity, and highly charged emotions of the festival could easily result in a riot. Their plan was to wait.

But Jesus knew they would change their minds and that he would be arrested within the week. He could have used that information to save himself. Jesus was already on the Mount of Olives, on the outskirts of the city. Had he chosen to do so, Jesus was poised to put even more distance between himself and the city.

He didn't because he had no intention of avoiding crucifixion. It was not inevitable, but enduring the cross was necessary for him to accomplish the mission on which he had come. And so, "he humbled himself by becoming obedient to death—even death on a cross!" (Phil. 2:8).

For Further Reference: **Psalm 2:2; Matthew 16:21; 17:22–23; 20:17–19; John 3:16; 11:47–53; Philippians 2:8; 1 John 3:16; 4:9–10**

THE ANOINTING OF JESUS

Matthew 26:6–13; Mark 14:3–9; John 12:1–11

"Why are you bothering this woman? She has done a beautiful
thing to me." (Matthew 26:10)

▶ WHO & WHERE

Jesus, disciples, Mary, Bethany

▶ WHAT IS THIS TEXT TALKING ABOUT?

The anointing of Jesus

▶ WHAT DOES THIS TEXT TEACH?

The anointing of Jesus marks him as the promised Savior from sin and anticipates his coming death.

The actions of Mary took everyone by surprise.

Jesus was the guest of honor at a banquet in Bethany during the final week of his life on earth. Although the meal was hosted by a man whom Jesus healed, Simon the Leper, it is Mary (the sister of Lazarus) who moves to the foreground. She poured expensive perfume on Jesus's head and feet. It was not unusual for the guest of honor to have a drop of fragrant oil daubed on his head during such a meal, surrounding him with a pleasing aroma. But everything Mary did was extravagant. The oil she used was pure nard. This is not locally produced but imported from India. The cost of its transportation coupled with modest supply made it extremely expensive. She poured the entire container, about a pint, onto Jesus—the cost equal to wages a laborer would earn in three hundred days! As Jesus reclined at the meal, she wiped his feet with her hair.

The significance of her actions was lost on the disciples but not on Jesus. With no little male hubris, the disciples criticized her actions. This expensive perfume could have been sold and the proceeds given to the poor (Matt. 26:8–9). Judas's objection was driven by more selfish motives. As the keeper of the cash, he had

Jesus was the guest of honor at a banquet in Bethany just days before his execution. Here, Mary anointed Jesus with the kind of perfume used during a burial.

been embezzling money (John 12:6). But Jesus called Mary's actions a "beautiful thing."

In a world where a woman's voice was often unwelcomed, Mary had something to say. The Old Testament described the coming Savior from sin as the Anointed One, the Messiah. By pouring fragrant oil on Jesus, she said all she needed to say without words. Her actions confessed her faith in Jesus as the promised Savior. Within her actions, Jesus saw something more: her recognition of what the disciples had vehemently resisted. Jesus would die and be buried—with the anointing oil serving as preparation of his body before death. The woody, spicy smell of so much oil would have lingered on Jesus for days, a constant reminder of what was to come.

As a result of Mary's actions, Jesus added a promise that is being fulfilled even as you read this: "Truly I tell you, wherever this gospel is preached throughout the world, what she has done will also be told, in memory of her" (Matt. 26:13).

For Further Reference: Psalm 2:2; Isaiah 61:1; Daniel 9:25–26; Romans 9:5; 1 Peter 1:10–11; Revelation 12:10

THE BETRAYAL OF JESUS

Matthew 26:14–16; Mark 14:10–11; Luke 22:3–6

"Then Satan entered Judas, called Iscariot, one of the Twelve.
And Judas went to the chief priests and the officers of the temple
guard and discussed with them how he might betray Jesus."
(Luke 22:3–4)

⟫ WHO & WHERE

Judas, the chief priests, Satan, Jerusalem

▶ WHAT IS THIS TEXT TALKING ABOUT?
The betrayal of Jesus

▶ WHAT DOES THIS TEXT TEACH?
The betrayal of Jesus was a carefully coordinated effort that involved Judas, the chief priests, and Satan.

What would it take to bring down Jesus? The answer comes in a handful of verses that speak about a malicious meeting.

The Temple authorities came to the meeting with motivation and power. Ever since Jesus had raised Lazarus from the dead in Bethany, they had looked for a way to end his life. They saw Jesus as a disruptive force that threatened their position, influence, and wealth (John 11:47–53). These Temple leaders also brought considerable power to the table. They had their own police force that could be used to arrest Jesus as well as a religious, judicial system to try him.

We don't know what motivated Judas to participate in this meeting, but he brought two important things the chief priests did not have. First, he was an insider who knew the rhythms of Jesus's movements. The chief priests feared an attempted arrest during the Passover in Jerusalem would provoke a riot. But Judas could provide the inside information that would help them locate and arrest Jesus when he was isolated from the throngs that followed him. Judas had one more thing to offer—trustworthiness. The other disciples of Jesus were from Galilee. As Judeans, the chief priests found these Galileans inherently untrustworthy. Judas Iscariot was different. His name suggests he was a Judean. "Iscariot" means "man from Kerioth." The Bible makes only one other reference to a town by that name in Israel. Joshua refers to a Kerioth in the southern reaches of the tribal inheritance of Judah. (He knows it as Kerioth Hezron; Josh. 15:25.) Judas, Jesus's disciple from Judah, traded his insider information and tribal heritage for thirty pieces of silver.

There was one more unseen member at this meeting—the Lord's arch-nemesis. Satan had entered Judas and so becomes a key player in what follows. This fallen angel was poised to lose everything. Jesus was the one who would crush his head (Gen. 3:15). Satan had tried and failed earlier to derail Jesus's mission. We are told that after tempting Jesus, the Devil went away quietly, waiting for the "opportune time" (Luke 4:13). It had arrived.

This is what it took to bring down Jesus—an unholy alliance between the chief priests, Judas, and Satan.

For Further Reference: Joshua 15:25; Zechariah 11:7–13; Matthew 10:2–4; 27:9–10; John 6:66–71; 11:47–53

PREPARATION FOR THE PASSOVER

Matthew 26:17–19; Mark 14:12–16; Luke 22:7–13

"Jesus sent Peter and John, saying, 'Go and make preparations for us to eat the Passover.'" (Luke 22:8)

▶ **WHO & WHERE**

Jesus, Peter, John, Jerusalem

▶ **WHAT IS THIS TEXT TALKING ABOUT?**

Preparation for the Passover

▶ **WHAT DOES THIS TEXT TEACH?**

Jesus becomes the Passover lamb who takes away the sins of the world.

In some stories, what is missing can be more important than what is present. This is one of those stories.

It was the day before Passover, a high festival whose history reaches back to the time of the Israelites' exodus from Egypt. It was the night of a terrible plague. The firstborn in each household would die unless that household slaughtered a lamb and painted its blood on the top and on both sides of the doorframe. The focal point of the festival was the sacrifice and eating of the Passover lamb (Ex. 12:2–23).

The Gospels mention two dimensions of the celebration we expect. First, Jesus and the disciples remained in Jerusalem. During this week, we have watched Jesus spend the evening and overnight in Bethany, returning each day to Jerusalem to teach. This day was different. Jesus stayed to eat the Passover meal within Jerusalem where it was supposed to be eaten (Deut. 16:2). Second, Jesus secured a room, fulfilling the requirement that Passover be eaten indoors. Apparently, Jesus had arranged the use of a guest room with a Jerusalem family that recognized him as the "Teacher"

The traditional location of the upper room in which Jesus celebrated his last Passover and established the first Lord's Supper.

(Luke 22:11). Peter and John were to look for something unusual, a man carrying a jar of water (unusual because this was typically a task assumed by female members of a household; Gen. 24:13; John 4:7). That person would lead them to the correct house. It had an upper room perfectly arranged for the Passover celebration.

But there is something missing—arguably the most important thing—the unblemished male lamb. Family representatives would take the lamb to the Temple where it was slaughtered. Its blood was poured at the base of the altar, and its fat portions burned on the altar. The priests returned the rest of the animal to the family representatives who took it to the place the family would eat the Passover meal. While Mark and Luke mention that this is the customary way to celebrate Passover, Jesus does not instruct Peter and John to secure a lamb nor is lamb mentioned as part of the meal (Mark 14:12–16; Luke 22:7–13). Why not? I believe the text speaks loudest where it goes silent. Jesus's "appointed time" had come (Matt. 26:18). Jesus was the lamb, the Lamb of God who had come to take away the sins of the world (John 1:29).

For Further Reference: **Exodus 12:21–23; Deuteronomy 16:1–8; 2 Chronicles 35:16–19; Isaiah 53:7, 10; John 1:29, 36; 1 Corinthians 5:7; Hebrews 4:15; 1 Peter 1:18–19; Revelation 5**

JESUS ANNOUNCES THE BETRAYAL

Matthew 26:20–25; Mark 14:17–21; Luke 22:21–23; John 13:18–30

"Jesus was troubled in spirit and testified, 'Very truly I tell you, one of you is going to betray me.'" (John 13:21)

▶ WHO & WHERE

Jesus, the Twelve, upper room in Jerusalem

▶ WHAT IS THIS TEXT TALKING ABOUT?

Jesus's betrayal

▶ WHAT DOES THIS TEXT TEACH?

Jesus announced his impending betrayal in a fashion that accomplished three goals.

Every step of this upper room story is carefully choreographed to achieve Jesus's goals.

First, Jesus preannounced that he would be betrayed to confirm his divine identity. As mortals, we can guess what the future might hold but cannot know for sure what will happen. When Jesus announced the betrayal before it happened, he revealed his divinity: "I am telling you now before it happens, so that when it does happen you will believe that I am who I am" (John 13:19; compare Ex. 3:14).

Second, Jesus used this announcement to animate Judas's actions. This disciple had already cut a deal with the Temple leaders and received payment for his services. But he apparently needed a push to animate the heinous plan. So Jesus said to Judas, "What you are about to do, do quickly" (John 13:27).

Third, Jesus made this announcement in a manner that prevented the other eleven disciples from stopping Judas. Jesus accomplished this by taking advantage of the seating arrangement around the triclinium table that allowed for both public and private conversations. The upper room likely

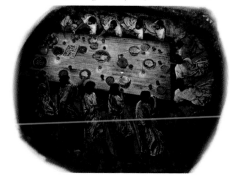

The upper room likely had a triclinium table. Those at the meal would recline around three sides of this low table, leaning on their left elbow.

had a triclinium table. This was a low, U-shaped table. The diners reclined around the three outside surfaces of the table, supporting themselves on their left elbow while eating with their right hand. Jesus begins by raising his voice to make a public announcement. Selecting words from Psalm 41, he announced the impending betrayal for all to hear (John 13:18–21). What follows is a series of private exchanges (vv. 22–27).

Within the upper room, Jesus was flanked by John who was reclining ahead of him and Judas behind him. Peter was across the table from the three. Peter signaled to John to get him to lean back on Jesus and privately ask whom Jesus meant. Jesus responded privately to John: "It is the one to whom I will give this piece of bread when I have dipped it in the dish" (v. 26). Jesus dipped the bread into a bowl and reached over his shoulder to give it to Judas. He then publicly urged Judas to get on with his task. It appears that only John knew that Judas was the one about to betray Jesus. The other disciples who were not aware of the private exchange between Jesus and John presumed Judas, the money manager, needed to purchase extra supplies for the festival. In the end, no one made an effort to stop him (vv. 27–28).

For Further Reference: Exodus 3:13–14; Psalm 41:9; Proverbs 6:16–19; Daniel 9:26; Acts 17:2–3

THE PERIL OF PURSUING SOCIAL STATUS

Luke 22:24–30; John 13:1–17

"Now that I, your Lord and Teacher, have washed your feet, you
also should wash one another's feet. I have set you an example
that you should do as I have done for you." (John 13:14–15)

▶ WHO & WHERE
Jesus, the disciples, upper room in Jerusalem

▶ WHAT IS THIS TEXT TALKING ABOUT?
Social status

▶ WHAT DOES THIS TEXT TEACH?
The demand for social recognition interferes with the acts of humility that mark the followers of Jesus.

The Roman world was very class-conscious. And the competitive interest in social rank had rubbed off on the disciples.

On a night when we expect the focus to be on Jesus, we find the disciples focused instead on themselves. Luke states it baldly: "A dispute also arose among them as to which of them was considered to be greatest" (Luke 22:24). This dispute was likely prompted by the table! Jesus and the disciples were reclining around a wooden triclinium. This was a low, U-shaped table around which the diners reclined with their feet extending away from the table. When it was time for the meal, the diners took positions around the three outside edges. So far, the table sounds unusual but benign. That is until we realize that in the Roman world, social status was tied to the wing at which one dined. One wing was reserved for the host family and special guests. The other two wings were for those of either higher or lower social status. Those on the lower-status side of the table were expected to serve (Luke 22:27). Such practical elements of the evening meal triggered the dispute over who would sit where and who would serve.

Jesus gently upbraids them for these Gentile-like attitudes and follows up with an enacted lesson. He speaks of the titles that the Gentile world used to designate social status. "Kings" demand honor through force. "Benefactors" garner public honor by providing support for those of lower social rank. "But you are not to be like that. Instead, the greatest among you should be like the youngest, and the one who rules like the one who serves" (Luke 22:26). Then, the disciples watched slack-jawed as Jesus enacted the lesson. He did exactly what a servant in the household would do—removed his outer garment, wrapped himself with a towel, and washed their feet. Jesus had the titles of "Lord" and "Teacher," but he never allowed those signs of social rank to impede the humble service that was the hallmark of his ministry and that are to be the hallmark of our own.

For Further Reference: **Mark 10:45; Luke 9:46–48; Galatians 5:13; Philippians 2:6–8; 1 Timothy 5:10; 1 Peter 5:5–6**

THE LORD'S SUPPER

Matthew 26:26–30; Mark 14:22–26; Luke 22:14–20
"And he took bread, gave thanks and broke it, and gave it to them, saying, 'This is my body given for you; do this in remembrance of me.' In the same way, after the supper he took the cup, saying, 'This cup is the new covenant in my blood, which is poured out for you.'" (Luke 22:19–20)

▶ WHO & WHERE
Jesus, the disciples, upper room in Jerusalem

▶ WHAT IS THIS TEXT TALKING ABOUT?
The Lord's Supper

▶ WHAT DOES THIS TEXT TEACH?
The Lord's Supper marks the transition between the Old and New Testaments and removes the geographic restriction placed on Passover.

This meal marks a change in time and place even as it makes a change in us.

First, it is a meal that marks a transition in time. The disciples prepared the upper room for a meal they had previously celebrated every year—the Passover. The food eaten and words recited joined to recall Israel's last night in Egypt before the dramatic exodus. This was as Old Testament as it gets. But this meal that starts in the Old Testament does not end there. Jesus's language creates the bridge to a new era: "This is my blood of the covenant" (Matt. 26:28) and "This cup is the new covenant in my blood" (Luke 22:20). Jeremiah anticipated a time when the Lord would establish a new or renewed covenant with Israel (Jer. 31:31–34). The language of Jesus signals that day had come. This was the night the world fully stepped over the threshold between the Old and New Testaments.

The transition from the Old Testament era to the New Testament era is marked by the first celebration of the Lord's Supper.

Second, there is a change in the spatial dimension of the meal. Jesus calls for all believers to do this in remembrance of him but does not say where. We "do this" when we do what the disciples did that evening. They ate bread and drank wine while listening to the words of Jesus. But is there a specific place we must do this? Passover had to be eaten in Jerusalem—the place of God's own choosing (Deut. 16:2). But this geographic limitation is not imposed on the New Testament meal. It can be and is celebrated throughout the world.

The restrictions are dropped so that this meal can be enjoyed more than once a year in more than one place. We are now free to enjoy this soul-stirring meal regularly so that we can hear Jesus speak these words to us: "This is my blood of the covenant, which is poured out for many for the forgiveness of sins" (Matt. 26:28).

For Further Reference: **Deuteronomy 16:1–8; Jeremiah 31:31–34; 1 Corinthians 10:16–17; 11:23–26; 2 Corinthians 3:6; Hebrews 8:6; 9:15**

MASS DEFECTION OF THE DISCIPLES

Matthew 26:31–35; Mark 14:27–31; Luke 22:31–38; John 13:31–38

"Then Jesus told them, 'This very night you will all fall away on account of me.'" (Matthew 26:31)

▶ **WHO & WHERE**

Jesus, the disciples, upper room in Jerusalem

▶ **WHAT IS THIS TEXT TALKING ABOUT?**

Spiritual defection

▶ WHAT DOES THIS TEXT TEACH?

Our spiritual defection is not fatal to our relationship with Jesus.

This story sounds uncomfortably familiar. In Jesus's final hours, he spoke of the disciples' coming spiritual defection in a way that looks hauntingly like our own.

Jesus announced that a mass defection was coming. Every one of the disciples was implicated (Matt. 26:31). When he the Shepherd was struck down, all the sheep would scatter just as pictured in Zechariah 13:7. The warning becomes more precise for Peter. He will deny Jesus before "rooster crow." While these words could point to the crowing of an animal and refer to some indefinite moment when Peter would deny Jesus, the phrase can also be understood metaphorically. The rationale for weighing alternatives comes, in part, from a prohibition on raising chickens in Jerusalem recorded in later rabbinic literature. This later prohibition may well have been part of the Jerusalem reality in Jesus's day. So what other options do we have for understanding the phrase? "Cock crow" has two metaphoric meanings. In the case of Luke who had a Gentile audience in view, he may be referring to the period between midnight and three o'clock in the morning. In the Roman camp, this was the third watch of the night called "cock crow." For Mark's audience a different metaphor may well have come to mind. A variety of events associated with the Temple in Jerusalem were marked by the sounding of the shofar. In the Jewish traditional writings, this blast on the trumpet was called "cock crow." In either of these cases, Jesus would be telling Peter not only how he would sin but when to expect it.

The warning to Peter also suggests what lies behind this mass defection of the disciples. Satan was asking for the opportunity to sift Peter like wheat (Luke 22:31). This is an agricultural metaphor associated with the processing of wheat. After the winnowing took place on the threshing floor, the final separation of wheat from inedible debris involved the violent shaking of the wheat in a sieve. Satan's sifting was complemented

Peter's denial of Jesus is portrayed in this piece of art found within the Church of Saint Peter in Gallicantu, in Jerusalem.

by the hubris of Peter. Despite knowing what sin was coming and when he would face the temptation to deny Jesus, Peter boldly claimed that he was above it all: "Even if I have to die with you, I will never disown you" (Matt. 26:35).

This story sounds all too familiar. And that is why I value the subtle reminder that our disloyal behavior is not fatal to our relationship with Jesus. Tucked into the warnings is this powerful reminder. Jesus would meet them in Galilee (Matt. 26:32; Mark 14:28). Although we abandon him, Jesus will never abandon us.

For Further Reference: Exodus 3:11–12; Deuteronomy 31:8; Joshua 1:5; Job 1:6–12; Psalm 23:4; Isaiah 53:12; Zechariah 13:7; Matthew 1:23; John 14:18; Romans 8:34; 2 Timothy 2:11–13; Hebrews 13:5

JESUS COMFORTS
THE DISCIPLES

John 14:1–16:33

"Do not let your hearts be troubled." (John 14:1)

▶ WHO & WHERE
Jesus, the disciples, upper room in Jerusalem

▶ WHAT IS THIS TEXT TALKING ABOUT?
The disciples' anticipated grief and uncertainty

▶ WHAT DOES THIS TEXT TEACH?
Using three images from everyday life, Jesus brings comfort to troubled hearts.

This is as personal as it gets. The world of the disciples was about to tumble out of control. Jesus's betrayal, arrest, and execution were imminent. In these chapters, Jesus speaks directly to his disciples' anticipated grief and uncertainty using images from everyday life.

The first image is architectural (John 14:1–3). The disciples were dreading the loss of personal connection with Jesus—the walks they shared, the meals they ate together. The rooms Jesus speaks about are part of a family compound shared with members of their extended family. When a girl married, she left her family group to join her husband's. Prior to their marriage, the groom went to work on adding a room to his family's compound that would become the private space for him and his bride. Jesus offered the same kind of familial expectation to his disciples: "And if

I go and prepare a place for you, I will come back and take you to be with me that you also may be where I am" (v. 3).

The second image is navigational and involves travel (vv. 4–6). Those who traveled in the ancient world did so without a GPS or physical maps. They knew the way to go because repeated trips between familiar locations created a mental map that allowed them to navigate using landmarks. If a person was traveling the road for the first time, they asked someone to come along who already had a mental map to guide them on the journey. Who would be the disciples' companion in the days ahead? When Thomas poured out his worries about disorientation, Jesus responds by saying, "I am the way and the truth and the life" (v. 6). In a world filled with uncertain crossroads, Jesus continues to be the true way to life.

The third image is agricultural (15:1–5). Loss brings uncertainty that often surfaces in the question, what am I going to do? The answer is found in a vineyard. Confusion about what to do is intimately linked to confusion about what part of the plant we are. If the disciples saw themselves as the entire plant, responsible for producing the fruit, they would quickly become frustrated. Jesus tells them they are not the vine stalk but the branches: "I am the vine; you are the branches. If you remain in me and I in you, you will bear much fruit" (v. 5). Jesus urged them to ask the right question. It was not what should they do but to whom were they connected.

Jesus weaves these images together to create a tapestry of peace: "I have told you these things, so that in me you may have peace. In this world you will have trouble. But take heart! I have overcome the world" (16:33).

For Further Reference: Psalms 16:11; 119:50; 139:1–12, 23–24; Isaiah 5:1–7; 26:3–4, 7, 12; 51:12; Jeremiah 8:18; 2 Corinthians 1:3–4

JESUS'S TRANSITION PRAYER

John 17:1–26

"For you granted him authority over all people that he might give eternal life to all those you have given him. Now this is eternal life: that they know you, the only true God, and Jesus Christ, whom you have sent." (John 17:2–3)

▶ WHO & WHERE

Jesus, upper room in Jerusalem

▶ WHAT IS THIS TEXT TALKING ABOUT?

Jesus's transition prayer

▶ WHAT DOES THIS TEXT TEACH?

On this night of transition, Jesus gave thanks for the mission he accomplished and made requests that would secure the future well-being of the church.

"Father, the hour has come" (John 17:1). This entire chapter rings with a sense of transition. The day-to-day rhythm of Jesus's life on earth was about to be shattered. Teaching in the synagogues, private conversations with the disciples, and personal acts of compassion would yield to his death and resurrection. As Jesus confronts this transition, He turns to the Father to reflect on his mission and requests that his Father provide the believers who would gather into his church what they needed.

Jesus speaks of his mission in two related parts. First, Jesus had come to bring eternal life (v. 2). Sin assured eternal death for all people. The one chance they had was Jesus, the Son of God, who brought help from outside a sin-ruined world. The successful accomplishment of his mission melded into another dimension of his quest. Second, Jesus glorified the Father who had sent him to rescue the world from its self-imposed fate (v. 4).

The bulk of Jesus's prayer touches on five gifts that the church needed going forward. Jesus's first request is for protection (vv. 11–12, 15). Jesus defended the disciples while walking with him on earth. Now that he would be transitioning back to heaven, he prayed that the Father protect them and us. Jesus's second request is for increasing joy within (v. 13). This is different than the happiness we find from the things of life. Real, lasting joy grows within as we come to know who God is and how he thinks about us. Jesus's third request is for sanctification (vv. 17–19). Right living becomes possible when we come to faith. But it is not static. As we spend time in the Word of God, our understanding of what it means to live a righteous life and our motivation for living this life grows. Jesus's fourth request is for unity (v. 23). This is more than external unity, living under the same "Christian" banner. This is a melding of thought, mind, and heart that brings believers closer to the complete unity that is known in the Father and Son relationship. And finally, Jesus's fifth request is that the mortal journey on earth may lead to an eternity in heaven (v. 24). This brings the prayer of Jesus's full circle. His mission was to give each of us "eternal life" (v. 2).

For Further Reference: Leviticus 19:2; Proverbs 18:10; Daniel 7:14; John 20:30–31; 1 Peter 1:15–16; 1 John 5:18–20

JESUS STRUGGLES IN PRAYER

Matthew 26:36–46; Mark 14:32–42; Luke 22:39–46; John 18:1

"My Father, if it is possible, may this cup be taken from me. Yet not as I will, but as you will." (Matthew 26:39)

▶ WHO & WHERE
Jesus, Peter, James, and John, Gethsemane on the Mount of Olives

▶ WHAT IS THIS TEXT TALKING ABOUT?
Jesus's struggle in prayer

▶ WHAT DOES THIS TEXT TEACH?
Jesus chose death on the cross in Jerusalem rather than escape into the wilderness.

This story incites more fear in me than any other in the Gospels, a story in which I acutely feel my eternity hanging by a thread.

Never before had Jesus looked or spoken like this. His appearance signals extreme emotional and mental distress (Matt. 26:37–38; Mark 14:34),

The name *Gethsemane* comes from a Hebrew word for an olive press, the kind used to burst the skins of olives to begin the release of their oil.

lying face down on the ground, the capillaries on his forehead bursting from the tension to produce bloody sweat (Matt. 26:39; Luke 22:44). Jesus knew he was going to die and face punishment for the sins of all people of all time (Ps. 75:8; Isa. 51:17; Jer. 25:15). And just as he was about to engage the cross, he drops this stunning request: "My Father, if it is possible, may this cup be taken from me" (Matt. 26:39).

With all that, it is easy to forget where we are. But the gospel writers won't let us. Jesus is in Gethsemane on the Mount of Olives, a place that plays a vital role in Jesus's struggle in prayer (Matt. 26:36; Mark 14:32; Luke 22:39). The two-mile (three-kilometer) long ridge called the Mount of Olives runs just east of the city of Jerusalem, between the Holy City and the Judean Wilderness. The north part of this ridge provided ideal conditions for the ridge's namesake olives. And the name Gethsemane suggest this is an industrial olive grove, a place full of *gat shemenim*, industrial-scale, olive-crushing presses.

Jesus's forebearer, King David, had walked right past the place when his son Absalom approached Jerusalem with an army intending to usurp the royal throne. Rather than subject the city to siege, David fled east, over the Mount of Olives and into the trackless folds of the wilderness (2 Sam. 15:13–31). It was the perfect place to hide from those seeking to harm him. David had blazed a trail that Jesus contemplated following.

Jesus's struggle in prayer was authentic and enhanced by its setting. When presented with a chance to do what was best for him, Jesus did what was best for us and added, "Yet not as I will, but as you will." Then, "he returned to the disciples," and he said, "Rise! Let us go! Here comes my betrayer!" (Matt. 26:39, 45–46).

For Further Reference: **2 Samuel 15:13–31; Psalms 40:6–8; 42:9–11; Isaiah 50:5; Hebrews 5:7**

THE ARREST OF JESUS

Matthew 26:47–56; Mark 14:43–52; Luke 22:47–53; John 18:2–12

"But how then would the Scriptures be fulfilled that say it must
happen in this way?" (Matthew 26:54)

▶ WHO & WHERE

Jesus, disciples, arresting party, Gethsemane on the Mount of
Olives

▶ WHAT IS THIS TEXT TALKING ABOUT?

The arrest of Jesus

▶ WHAT DOES THIS TEXT TEACH?

Jesus fostered and facilitated his own arrest, putting his mission
ahead of his own well-being.

What the arresting party expected and what they experienced were
two different things.

The arresting party made a couple of assumptions. First, they assumed
Jesus would be hiding from them. So, they contracted with an insider who
knew Jesus's movements and arranged for a signal, lest there be confusion
in the dark about which Galilean to arrest. Judas would kiss the man who
was their target. Second, they expected a fight. So, they planned the arrest
as a surprise, night operation that would minimize the number of those
who might rally to resist Jesus's arrest. But just in case things went side-
ways, they came ready for a fight with overwhelming numbers, armed with
swords and clubs.

Needless to say, the arrest did not proceed as they expected because Jesus was no ordinary suspect. Instead of changing his behavior or

Mosaic depicting the arrest of Jesus from the Basilica of the Agony (Church of All Nations, Jerusalem).

patterns to disguise his location, Jesus takes the disciples to the place they had always gone on the Mount of Olives, making him easy to locate (John 18:2). Instead of running and hiding, Jesus approached the arresting party

(Matt. 26:46). Instead of withdrawing into the crowd, Jesus stepped forward and identified himself as the man they had come to arrest (John 18:4–5). When the arresting party stepped back and fell to the ground, Jesus again identified himself and chided them for not being about their task (John 18:6–8). Peter created a distraction by pulling a knife and cutting off the ear of Malchus, the high priest's servant. But instead of using the moment's confusion to flee, Jesus ordered Peter to put away his sword and healed the man's ear (Luke 22:51). And although he had the power to summon seventy-two thousand angels to his defense (one of which would have done the job), Jesus yielded to the imperative that it must "happen in this way" (Matt. 26:53–54).

He was compliant, cooperative, even encouraging. Jesus surrendered voluntarily because he was not focused on saving himself, but the world from sin.

For Further Reference: 2 Kings 6:17; Isaiah 53:7–12; Zechariah 13:7; Acts 1:16–17; 2 Thessalonians 1:7

THE RELIGIOUS HEARINGS OF JESUS

Matthew 26:57–68; Mark 14:53–65; Luke 22:66–71; John 18:13–14, 19–24

"Again the high priest asked him, 'Are you the Messiah, the Son of the Blessed One?' 'I am,' said Jesus." (Mark 14:61–62)

▶ WHO & WHERE

Jesus, Jewish religious leaders, homes of Annas and Caiaphas in Jerusalem

▶ WHAT IS THIS TEXT TALKING ABOUT?

The religious hearings of Jesus

▶ WHAT DOES THIS TEXT TEACH?

Jesus provided the Jewish religious leaders with the evidence they lacked to advance their case for his execution.

The dissension between Jesus and the Jewish religious leaders of Jerusalem had been escalating all week. Now that they had arrested Jesus, they needed evidence to support and take action on their charges.

The pursuit of those charges takes us to the homes of Annas and Caiaphas. Rome had appointed these men as high priests. Annas was the former high priest who still had significant influence, and Caiaphas was the current high priest who chaired the Sanhedrin. There are too many irregularities in what follows for these to be official meetings of the Jewish ruling council. Rather, it appears that a group of like-minded members of the council met in the homes of the high priests to seek sustainable charges against Jesus.

The locations were designed to intimidate. The high priests lived in palatial homes in the Upper City of Jerusalem. Archaeological discoveries in this area reveal large (more than 6,000 square feet [557 square meters]), ornately decorated homes that distinguished those who lived there from ordinary people. It's unlikely Jesus had been in such a home. What is more, the houses isolated Jesus from the popular support he had felt in public places like the Temple courts.

But the efforts of the high priest ran into just the kind of problems we might expect when a verdict was reached ahead of the evidence. They secured witnesses ready to give false testimony, but their statements did not agree (Mark 14:56, 59). The focus turned to Jesus's statements about the Temple (Mark 13:1–2; John 2:19). If they could link Jesus with a plan to destroy the Temple, it would create the kind of popular uprising that Rome would not tolerate. But again, the testimony was too weak to convince.

In a panic, Caiaphas calls Jesus to testify on his own behalf. Putting Jesus under oath, he asked, "Are you the Messiah, the Son of the Blessed One?" (Mark 14:61). Jesus had been silent because there was no need to respond to unconvincing testimony. Now, Jesus not only affirmed his divine nature but calls future events to the witness stand. Quoting the language of Daniel 7:13, Jesus says all will know he is the Son of God upon his return to the earth in glory. It was blasphemy for a mortal to claim to be God.

And with that, Jesus saved the flagging hearing, giving them the evidence they needed to pronounce him guilty with the truth.

For Further Reference: **Leviticus 24:16; Deuteronomy 19:15; Psalm 2:7; Isaiah 53:7; Daniel 7:13–14; Hebrews 13:8; Revelation 1:7**

THE DENIAL OF PETER

Matthew 26:69–75; Mark 14:66–72; Luke 22:54–62; John 18:15–18, 25–27

"Then he began to call down curses, and he swore to them,
'I don't know the man!' Immediately a rooster crowed."
(Matthew 26:74)

▶ **WHO & WHERE**

Peter, home of Caiaphas

▶ **WHAT IS THIS TEXT TALKING ABOUT?**

Peter's denial of Jesus

▶ WHAT DOES THIS TEXT TEACH?

Peter's presumed anonymity and lack of familiarity with
Caiaphas's home contributed to his denial of Jesus.

Jesus had warned Peter that the loyalty test was coming (Matt. 26:33–
34; John 13:38). But an unwarranted assumption of anonymity and the
unfamiliar architectural design of the home contributed to Peter's denials.

Peter was a Galilean fisherman who suddenly and unexpectedly became immersed in a wealthy Judean world. He assumed that he could fly
below the radar. But Peter's less-refined mannerisms and distinctive Galilean accent gave him away (Matt. 26:73; Mark 14:70; Luke 22:59). Worse
yet, he had distinguished himself during Jesus's arrest by pulling his knife
and cutting off the ear of one of those in the arrest party. A relative of the
injured man had been there at the arrest and was now in the courtyard. He
identified Peter as soon as he moved into the light of the fire (John 18:26).
Peter's presumed anonymity quickly evaporated.

The location also played a role in Peter's denial. It is unlikely that Peter
had ever been inside a home like that of Caiaphas. While archaeology does
not lead us to a specific home, it does help us appreciate the kinds of homes
in the neighborhood. They were large and complex, some exceeding 6,000
square feet (557 square meters). Their floor plans were nothing like the
small homes in Galilee. The homes of Jerusalem's elite were built around an
internal, open-air courtyard surrounded by a maze of rooms and hallways.

At first, Peter waited outside, his lack of familiarity barring entry (John
18:15–16). When allowed in, Peter must have been struck by the complex-
ity of the home and its layout. It is unlikely he mapped the passageways
that led to the internal courtyard where we find him next to a fire with
those who quickly identify him as an associate of Jesus (Matt. 26:69; Mark
14:67; Luke 22:56). As his anonymity evaporated, he began to look for a
way out but made it only as far as the courtyard entrance (Mark 14:68).
Only after his third denial, when Jesus's penetrating eyes met his, did Peter

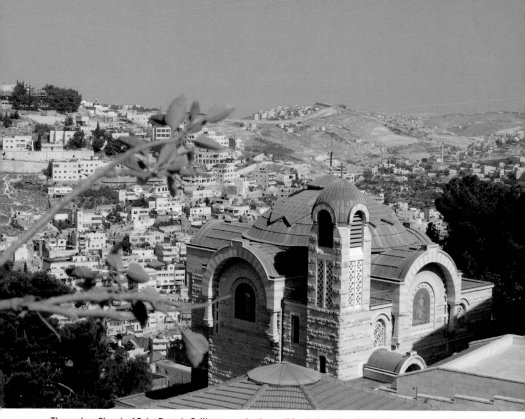

The modern Church of Saint Peter in Gallicantu marks the traditional site of Peter's denial but may rather be the place to which he fled to weep bitterly.

desperately search for and find a way out, and once outside, he "wept bitterly" (Matt. 26:75; Luke 22:62).

For Further Reference: **Acts 2:7; 4:13; James 3:14–15; 1 Peter 2:1; 1 John 2:22–23**

TRAIL OF THE BLOOD MONEY

Matthew 27:1–10

"The chief priests picked up the coins and said,
'It is against the law to put this into the treasury, since it is
blood money.' So they decided to use the money to buy the
potter's field as a burial place for foreigners." (Matthew 27:6–7)

▶ WHO & WHERE
Judas, chief priests, Hinnom Valley

▶ WHAT IS THIS TEXT TALKING ABOUT?
The blood money

▶ WHAT DOES THIS TEXT TEACH?
The trail of the blood money highlights Judas's failure to repent and links his sin to the most horrific sins of Jerusalem's past.

Follow the money. This time-tested crime investigation technique will help us decode the final actions of Judas.

First, we follow the money to the Temple (Matt. 27:5). Knowing he had violated the law by betraying an innocent man (Deut. 27:25), Judas was "seized with remorse" (Matt. 27:3). This language does not signal the godly retreat from sin we call repentance, but something less (2 Cor. 7:10). So why did this burdened man throw the coins into the Temple? This act is best understood in light of a Jewish tradition for undoing a business deal in the first century. The seller of goods or property had a limited amount of time to change their mind on the deal that was struck. During that time, the seller could return the money to the purchaser and undo the deal. But if the seller could not locate the purchaser, the seller could deposit the money in the Temple treasury, which became the equivalent of returning the money to the purchaser, thereby undoing the deal. When the chief priests refused to take the betrayal money back, Judas threw the money into the treasury in a bid to unburden his conscious. In doing so, he treated the betrayal like a business deal rather than the spiritual crisis it was for him.

Next, we follow the money to the Hinnom Valley. When the chief priests saw the tainted, blood money in the Temple, they wanted it gone. So, they quickly purchased a field associated with pottery making and made it the place for burying foreigners. But this potter's field carried a name that recalled Judas's act of betrayal—Akeldama, the Field of Blood (Acts 1:18–19).

When we follow the money to the Hinnom Valley, we join Matthew in seeing how this geography connects the impious act of Judas with the most heinous acts of the Old Testament. The Hinnom Valley that formed the western and southern boundaries of Jerusalem was used for pagan worship of all kinds, including worship that involved child sacrifice (2 Kings 23:10; Jer. 7:31–32). The betrayal of Jesus belonged in this category and became geographically linked to heinous crimes of the past when the chief priests purchased the potter's field in the Hinnom Valley.

For Further Reference: **2 Kings 23:10; Proverbs 6:16–19; Jeremiah 7:31–32; 19:1–13; Zechariah 11:12–13; Matthew 26:15; Acts 1:18–19; 2 Corinthians 7:10**

JESUS BEFORE PILATE

Matthew 27:11–26; Mark 15:1–15; Luke 23:1–25; John 18:28–19:16

"When Pilate heard this, he brought Jesus out and sat down on the judge's seat at a place known as the Stone Pavement (which in Aramaic is Gabbatha)." (John 19:13)

▶ WHO & WHERE
Jesus, Pilate, the palace of Herod the Great in Jerusalem

▶ WHAT IS THIS TEXT TALKING ABOUT?
Jesus's civil trial before Pilate

▶ WHAT DOES THIS TEXT TEACH?

Jesus did not break when brought into the intimidating and unstable setting for his civil trial.

Jesus's trial took place in a palace designed to impress and intimidate.

By this time, Pilate was the Roman governor of Judea (John 18:28). While he typically headquartered in Caesarea on the Mediterranean coast, the ever-turbulent high festivals brought him to Jerusalem—his presence was meant to quash rebellious notions. While in the Holy City, Pilate likely stayed at the luxurious palace built decades earlier by Herod the Great.

For those invited as guests, it impressed with its sophistication and refinement. According to ancient sources, the architecture of the palace and the art that filled it were too wonderful for words to capture. But for those invited for trial, this palace, complete with a judge's seat, was meant to intimidate. Here the accused was isolated from support and surrounded

The pretentious palace of Herod the Great lay just on the other side of this wall. It is the most likely location for Jesus's civil trial before Pilate.

by uniformed Roman soldiers. The Roman governor, tasked with hearing cases, delivered a decision sans a jury. And the governor's verdict was so robust that it could only be overturned by the emperor in Rome. Jesus had stepped into an impressive and intimidating space.

But the palace was also a place teetering out of control. Pilate was vicious, cruel, and insensitive to the locals. He repeatedly showed his disinterest in judicial fairness, only in outcomes that worked to his political advantage. The guilty were found innocent and the innocent were found guilty. Things were only made worse by the fact that Pilate was politically compromised. Local complaints about Pilate's abuses had reached Rome. And within a few years, the senate would remove him from his post. Jesus's trial took place before this kind of judge, a vulnerable politician who was subject to manipulation. The Jewish leadership in Jerusalem knew it and used it to get a conviction.

This judicial setting could easily have broken Jesus. The accused would disavow anything to get out of trouble, beg for mercy, and even offer the governor a bribe. Jesus did none of these. As he stood trial in this intimidating and unstable place, he listened quietly to the charges brought against him. When asked to respond, he did so briefly. And when confronted by a guilty verdict, he did not object but quietly accepted his fate.

For Further Reference: Leviticus 24:16; Isaiah 53:6–8; Acts 3:14; 2 Corinthians 5:21; Galatians 3:13

JESUS MOCKED BY THE SOLDIERS

Matthew 27:27–31; Mark 15:16–20

"And then twisted together a crown of thorns and set it on his
head." (Matthew 27:29)

▶ WHO & WHERE
Jesus, soldiers, the Antonia Fortress in Jerusalem

▶ WHAT IS THIS TEXT TALKING ABOUT?
Abuse heaped on Jesus prior to the crucifixion

▶ WHAT DOES THIS TEXT TEACH?
The soldiers' mocking of Jesus reminds us of who he is and why
he came.

Once the trial was over, the abuse began.

It appears that Jesus was moved from the palace of Herod the
Great where his trial occurred to the Roman army barracks called the Antonia Fortress (Matt. 27:27; Mark 15:16). This massive building stood on
the northwest side of the Temple campus, built to defend Jerusalem's most
vulnerable side, and provide housing for the non-Jewish Roman auxiliary
forces under the command of Pilate. On this day, these soldiers were not
defending Jerusalem from attack but preparing Jesus for crucifixion. The
condemned were typically beaten mercilessly to weaken them physically
and so diminish their resistance to crucifixion. The gospel writers spare
us the worst of the details, but both Matthew and Luke emphasize the way
these soldiers mocked the royalty of Jesus, particularly by putting a crown
of thorns on his head.

Their actions spotlight three important things about the unfolding
story. First, their dressing Jesus in royal attire, their kneeling before him,
and their acclamation, "Hail, king of the Jews!" join to recall the high crime
for which Jesus was condemned to die. Pilate had probed the charge that
Jesus was stirring rebellion against Rome by proclaiming himself a king.

Despite finding him innocent of the charge, Pilate condemned him to die. The actions of the soldiers highlight the injustice.

Second, the mock coronation stands in bold contrast to the events of Palm Sunday less than a week earlier. As Jesus entered the Holy City riding on a donkey, people called for his coronation: "Blessed is the king who comes in the name of the Lord!" (Luke 19:38). That authentic call for Jesus's coronation stands in marked contrast to this mock coronation.

Third, note the focus on the crown of thorns (Matt. 27:29; Mark 15:17). This crown recalls why Jesus was enduring it all. Thorns are first mentioned in the Bible when the Lord listed the consequences of the fall into sin (Gen. 3:17–18). The need to grow food would now be a competition with thorns and thistles. The fall into sin and thorns go hand in hand. So, the crown of thorns on Jesus's head recalls for us why he allowed all of this to happen to him. He had come to reverse the curse of Eden.

For Further Reference: Genesis 3:17–18; Psalm 22:12–16; Isaiah 53:1–7; Matthew 20:19

THE LOCATION OF JESUS'S CRUCIFIXION

Matthew 27:32–56; Mark 15:21–41; Luke 23:26–49; John 19:16–37

"They brought Jesus to the place called Golgotha (which means 'the place of the skull')." (Mark 15:22)

▶ WHO & WHERE

Jesus, Golgotha (Calvary) in Jerusalem

▶ WHAT IS THIS TEXT TALKING ABOUT?

The crucifixion of Jesus

▶ WHAT DOES THIS TEXT TEACH?

The location of Jesus's crucifixion underscores the cost of our redemption.

The story of salvation takes us to many places. None is more important than the place of Jesus's crucifixion.

The gospel writers all name the place either as "Golgotha" or "the Skull" (Matt. 27:33; Mark 15:22; Luke 23:33; John 19:17). The Aramaic "Golgotha" or Latin *Calvariae* refer to the skull or scalp. We don't know if the name refers to the shape of the natural feature where the execution took place or to the fact that it was a place associated with death. In either case, the Romans were crucifying the condemned in an abandoned rock quarry now claimed as a cemetery for those who lived in Jerusalem.

Other evidence allows us to establish the location more precisely than most other events from Jesus's life. Calvary was just outside the city walls of Jerusalem (John 19:20; Heb. 13:12) in a cemetery (John 19:41). Following the death of Jesus, the memory of the spot lingered for decades in the minds of those who remained in Jerusalem. From the first century to the present, believers have worshipped there. And a Christian church has marked the site from the fourth century to the present, the Church of the Holy Sepulchre.

It remains a powerful place to contemplate this stunning event because it underscores the cost of our salvation. While Israel was the Holy Land, Jerusalem was the Holy City. It was the city chosen by God and made his "resting place" (Ps. 132:13–14). Here the Lord expressed his presence in unique fashion at the Temple in Jerusalem—the place people came to speak with him in a way that they could not in their home villages. Jerusalem was the place where God said, "I am with you."

Since the fourth century AD, a church has stood over the location of Jesus's crucifixion and resurrection. This is called both the Church of the Holy Sepulchre and the Church of the Resurrection.

As Jesus hung on the cross, he captured the horrifying cost of our salvation with the words of Psalm 22:1. The physical and mental pain associated with crucifixion is one thing. But that was not the worst of it. In order

A WALKING TOUR OF THE GOSPELS

to save us from our sins, Jesus had to endure punishment for them. That meant experiencing all that hell had to offer. By definition, that is separation from God. Then, "about three in the afternoon Jesus cried out in a loud voice, *'Eli, Eli, lema sabachthani?'* (which means 'My God, my God, why have you forsaken me?')" (Matt. 27:46). God's own Son was abandoned by his Father in the very place where the Father promised to be with his people. That is the cost of our salvation.

For Further Reference: Genesis 3:15; Psalms 22:1–31; 34:20; 69:21; Isaiah 53:1–12; Zechariah 12:10; Hebrews 10:19–20; 13:12

THE BURIAL OF JESUS

Matthew 27:57–66; Mark 15:42–47; Luke 23:50–56; John 19:38–42

"So Joseph bought some linen cloth, took down the body, wrapped it in the linen, and placed it in a tomb cut out of rock. Then he rolled a stone against the entrance of the tomb." (Mark 15:46)

▶ WHO

Jesus, Joseph of Arimathea, Nicodemus, Mary Magdalene, the other Mary

▶ WHAT IS THIS TEXT TALKING ABOUT?

The burial of Jesus

▶ WHAT DOES THIS TEXT TEACH?

The distinctive dimensions of Jesus's burial signal that he is unique.

We often move quickly from the story of Jesus's death to his resurrection. But all four gospel writers invite us to spend time with Jesus's burial.

Several parts of the burial story follow expectations. First-century Judaism did not embalm loved ones, so burial typically took place on the day of death at a location close to where the death occurred. This is exactly what we see here as Jesus is buried on Friday using a tomb that is near the crucifixion site (John 19:41). Those caring for his remains carefully washed his body and then wrapped it in strips of linen cloth, embedding aromatics between the layers to defeat the expected smell of decomposition (John 19:39–40). All as expected.

But the unique parts of this story far outweigh the ordinary. Family typically buried their own in the family's tomb. Jesus was far from home and his immediate family and disciples were afraid of associating with Jesus's remains. So instead, a noted Jewish leader buried him in his own new tomb. That was the first unique element. Joseph of Arimathea carried

This first-century *kochim*-style tomb helps us picture the story of Jesus's burial and his resurrection.

social weight as a distinguished member of the Jewish ruling council. He used that influence to prevent the unthinkable from happening. The unclaimed remains of criminals were often tossed into the Hinnom Valley where feral dogs and birds took care of the rest.

The second unique element was the nature of the tomb itself. Archaeology from Jerusalem in this era allows us to recreate the picture. The well-to-do of the city were buried in a *kochim*-style tomb. It consisted of an expanded cave whose main room had a low stone bench on which the body was prepared for burial. Around the perimeter of this main room were key-hole shaped niches (two feet wide by seven feet long [half a meter wide by two meters long]). The wrapped body was placed into such a *koch* where it remained for a year or more. After the flesh had decayed from the bones, the family returned and placed the bones into a small stone container called an ossuary. The remains of all the family members buried in this family tomb were protected from animals and disruption by a stone that either rolled across the entrance or plugged the entry. This was not the tomb of an ordinary man much less a man convicted of a capital crime. Jesus was unique in being "assigned a grave with the wicked, and with the rich in his death" (Isa. 53:9).

The third unique element was the detachment of soldiers placed at the tomb. They were not there as an honor guard but were charged with sealing it and guarding it to keep the deceased man in his place! As we will see, they failed in their job.

For Further Reference: **Psalm 16:9–11; Isaiah 53:9; Matthew 12:38–40; Acts 2:25–31**

CHAPTER 8

Jesus's Resurrection and Ascension

THE RESURRECTION OF JESUS

Matthew 28:1–15; Mark 16:1–8; Luke 24:1–12; John 20:1–10

"Why do you look for the living among the dead? He is not here; he has risen!" (Luke 24:5–6)

▶ **WHO & WHERE**

Jesus, Mary Magdalene, Mary the mother of James, Salome, Joanna, Peter, John, tomb at Calvary

▶ **WHAT IS THIS TEXT TALKING ABOUT?**

The resurrection of Jesus

▶ **WHAT DOES THIS TEXT TEACH?**

The same Jesus who died on the cross has risen from the dead.

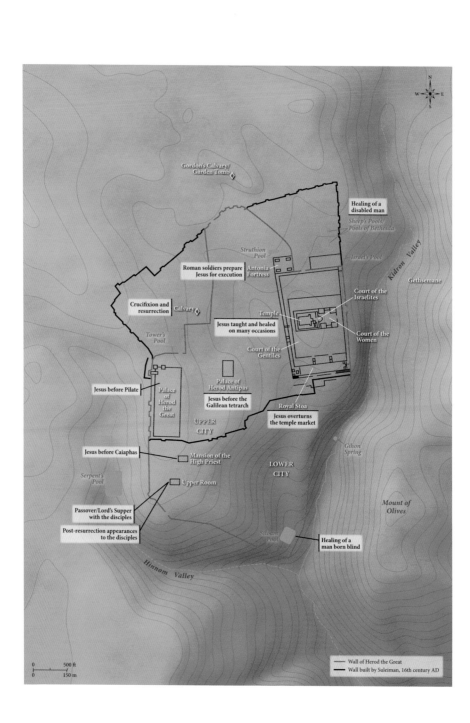

Gordon's Calvary/
Garden Tomb

Healing of a
disabled man

*Sheep's Pools/
Pools of Bethesda*

*Struthion
Pool*

Roman soldiers prepare
Jesus for execution

Antonia
Fortress

Israel's Pool

Kidron Valley

Gethsemane

Crucifixion and
resurrection

Calvary

Court of the
Israelites

Temple

Jesus taught and healed
on many occasions

Court of the
Women

*Tower's
Pool*

Court of the
Gentiles

Jesus before Pilate

Palace
of
Herod
the
Great

Palace of
Herod Antipas

Royal Stoa

Jesus before the
Galilean tetrarch

Jesus overturns
the temple market

UPPER
CITY

*Gihon
Spring*

Jesus before Caiaphas

Mansion of the
High Priest

LOWER
CITY

*Serpent's
Pool*

Upper Room

*Mount of
Olives*

Passover/Lord's Supper
with the disciples

Post-resurrection appearances
to the disciples

*Siloam
Pool*

Healing of a
man born blind

Hinnom Valley

| 0 | 500 ft |
| 0 | 150 m |

Wall of Herod the Great
Wall built by Suleiman, 16th century AD

The collection of women picking their way through the dark streets of Jerusalem were on a mission. They had stood beside Jesus during his crucifixion. They had walked with his body to the tomb. And now they would honor him by completing the burial process interrupted by the start of Sabbath.

This day would be full of surprises that began before they left their homes. Early in the morning, they felt the tremors of the violent earthquake that reminded them of the quake they felt on Friday during Jesus's crucifixion. When they arrived at the tomb, nothing was as they expected it to be. The posted guard was gone. The seal on the tomb was broken. And the massive stone blocking the tomb entry was thrown from its place. But most stunning of all, the body they had come to honor was gone. Humanity had lots of experience with death. The refrain "and so-and-so lived x-number of years, and then he died" peppers the Old Testament and the human experience. People who die stay dead. And their remains remain where last placed.

The dramatic change from the expected scene required a heavenly explanation. Angels were dispatched to offer it: "Why do you look for the living among the dead? He is not here; he has risen!" (Luke 24:5–6). The "he" was Jesus. The same man who died on the cross was alive. The absence of his body was the third element in a chain of events that Jesus had told his followers to anticipate: "The Son of Man must be delivered over to the hands of sinners, be crucified and on the third day be raised again" (v. 7).

Jesus's death on the cross and resurrection from the grave are the fundamentals of the Christian faith—one as vital as the other. His death paid the price for sin and his resurrection confirmed the Father's acceptance of the payment on our behalf. I have a problem that I cannot fix. I cannot stop sinning, which means I cannot stop dying. The same Jesus who died on the cross and rose from the grave fixed both.

For Further Reference: Psalm 16:10; Isaiah 53:10–12; Acts 2:29–32; Romans 1:1–6; 1 Corinthians 15:1–20

JESUS AND MARY MAGDALENE

John 20:11–18

"Jesus said to her, 'Mary.' She turned toward him and cried out in Aramaic, 'Rabboni!' (which means 'Teacher')." (John 20:16)

▶ WHO

Jesus, Mary Magdalene

▶ WHAT IS THIS TEXT TALKING ABOUT?

Jesus's post-resurrection appearance to Mary Magdalene

▶ WHAT DOES THIS TEXT TEACH?

Jesus's appearance to Mary Magdalene shows the deep compassion he feels for every individual experiencing the pain of personal loss.

John's Easter follows the movements of Mary Magdalene closely. She is the first person to arrive at the tomb and the last to be there.

Mary's affection for Jesus pulses at the heart of this story. Jesus had driven seven demons from her body (Luke 8:2). Mary's gratefulness led her to join those caring for Jesus's needs in life and in death. That is what roused her early that first Sunday morning to complete the burial preparation interrupted two days earlier. But when the tomb came into view, things were not as they should be—the stone blocking the entry displaced. Sensing trouble, she ran to tell Peter and John who immediately ran ahead of her to the tomb.

Mary followed but did not arrive until after these men had left. She was alone. And now the weight of the last days crashed down on her. She began to cry. John uses the Greek word here for grieving or weeping only eight times in his entire gospel. Four of the eight are here. He reserves it for describing the body-shuttering grief that accompanies the loss of a loved one. Her pain is so acute and overwhelming that she speaks to the angels at the tomb without the characteristic fear displayed by others. Mary had lost her living Jesus. Now she has lost contact with his remains.

On the first Easter Sunday morning, the stone that sealed the tomb of Jesus was violently thrown to the side.

That is when Jesus appears to her. Three things stand out in the exchange. First, he uses her personal name, "Mary." This triggered instant recognition. No one spoke her name like Jesus did. Second, Jesus allows Mary to touch his resurrected body, the first to do so. That made his return to life more real to her. And then Jesus assured her that it would not be the last time they would be together. As Mary clung to him for fear of losing him again, Jesus assured her that the time of his ascension was some time away. They would have more moments like this in the days ahead.

In all of this, we see that death and resurrection had not changed Jesus. He remains the compassionate Savior who cares about the lone individual who has experienced personal loss.

For Further Reference: **Matthew 27:56, 61; 28:1; Mark 16:1, 9–11; Luke 8:2; 24:9–10**

JESUS ON THE ROAD TO EMMAUS

Luke 24:13–35

"Were not our hearts burning within us while he talked with us on the road and opened the Scriptures to us?" (Luke 24:32)

> **WHO & WHERE**

Jesus, Cleopas, the other disciple, road to Emmaus

> **WHAT IS THIS TEXT TALKING ABOUT?**

Certainty that Jesus rose from the dead

> **WHAT DOES THIS TEXT TEACH?**

Study of the Word leads to certainty that Jesus rose from the dead.

This Easter Sunday encounter is different from the others—stories in which Jesus appeared, spoke a few words, and was quickly recognized.

The first difference is that this Easter story evolves very slowly, developing over many travel miles. It starts in Jerusalem, travels to the village of Emmaus, and then back to Jerusalem. We know where Jerusalem is located, but how about Emmaus? Given Luke's mention of seven miles (eleven kilometers), two options rise above the others, both of which lie alongside the road that travels westward from Jerusalem. If Luke is referring to the linear distance between Jerusalem and Emmaus, then we will look for Emmaus near the modern city of Abu-Ghosh. If the distance represents the round trip, then Mozah is likely where we would find first-century Emmaus. In either case, the time required to get to the village, enjoy an evening meal, and then make a nighttime return to Jerusalem all make for a story that takes hours to play out.

The second difference has to do with the way Jesus revealed himself as the risen Christ. When Jesus joined Cleopas and his friend, they were already deeply invested in a conversation that betrays their struggle. They had spent enough time with Jesus to be familiar with his powerful words and deeds and to expect that he was the one who would redeem Israel. They knew of his trial and death. They expected something special on the third day and even heard reports suggesting he was alive. They had all the parts but could not assemble them into a meaningful whole. After Jesus joined the conversation, he used the hours of travel and the time over dinner to bring it all together. Using the core of the Old Testament texts that spoke about the Messiah, he organized the details they knew into a story of suffering that led to glory.

It took all the time and distance traveled to get it done. As they arrived at the village and the evening meal began, Jesus took bread, gave thanks, broke it, and gave it to them. Then suddenly it all came together: "their eyes were opened and they recognized him, and he disappeared from their sight," and they exclaimed, "Were not our hearts burning within us while he talked with us on the road and opened the Scriptures to us?" (Luke 24:31–32).

For Further Reference: **Genesis 3:15; Deuteronomy 18:15; Isaiah 9:6–7; Daniel 7:13–14; Malachi 3:1; Mark 16:12–13; Hebrews 1:1–2; 2:10**

JESUS APPEARS TO THE TEN DISCIPLES

Luke 24:36–49; John 20:19–23

"He said to them, 'Why are you troubled, and why do doubts rise in your minds? Look at my hands and my feet. It is I myself! Touch me and see; a ghost does not have flesh and bones, as you see I have.'" (Luke 24:38–39)

▶ WHO & WHERE
Jesus, the ten disciples, upper room in Jerusalem

▶ WHAT IS THIS TEXT TALKING ABOUT?
The unique witness of the disciples

▶ WHAT DOES THIS TEXT TEACH?

To be effective witnesses for Jesus, all the disciples had to know that he had risen from the dead and fulfilled Old Testament expectations.

The effectiveness of the disciples' future teaching was intimately bound to their personal experiences with Jesus, particularly his resurrection. But to this point, we know of only two who had visited the tomb, one of whom left believing (Luke 24:12; John 20:8). This needed to change and did when Jesus appeared to them, very likely in the same upper room in which they had celebrated Passover.

The first reason Jesus made this appearance was to give convincing proof that he had risen from the dead. The evidence presented was multisensory. They saw Jesus standing among them although the door to the room was locked (John 20:19). They heard and recognized a familiar voice. They touched him, feeling the warmth of his once-dead body, examining his hands and feet that still bore marks of the crucifixion. And they watched him eat, demonstrating that Jesus was no disembodied spirit. He was the same living being with whom they had shared a Passover meal just days before in the same room. In the end, all the disciples now had a personal and persuasive experience with the risen Christ.

The second reason Jesus appeared to the disciples was to certify the vital connection between all that the disciples had witnessed and the expectations of the Old Testament. This collection of books was written by dozens of authors and poets over 1,100 years. Concerning these Scriptures, Jesus said, "This is what I told you while I was still with you: Everything must be fulfilled that is written about me in the Law of Moses, the Prophets and the Psalms" (Luke 24:44). The Law of Moses referred to the first five books of the Torah or Pentateuch. The Prophets included the historical books from Joshua to Chronicles as well as the books written by prophetic figures. The Psalms stands for the remaining books since Psalms

The traditional location of the upper room where Jesus appeared to the disciples to confirm that he had risen from the dead.

was the first and longest of the books in this category of the Hebrew Bible. The disciples did not have a new story to tell but an ongoing story to tell of a Savior from sin with deep roots in the Old Testament.

These were the essentials that made the disciples the effective witnesses they became. They personally experienced the risen Christ—saw with their own eyes, heard with their own ears, and touched with their own hands—and thus recognized that he fulfilled the expectations laid out in the Old Testament.

For Further Reference: **Psalms 16; 22; Isaiah 53; Matthew 13:10–17; John 1:1–18; 20:30–31; Acts 1:8; 10:41; 1 Corinthians 15:3–5; 1 Peter 1:10–12; 2 Peter 1:16–21; 1 John 1:1**

JESUS APPEARS FOR THOMAS

John 20:24–31

"Because you have seen me, you have believed; blessed are those who have not seen and yet have believed." (John 20:29)

▶ WHO & WHERE

Jesus, Thomas, the other disciples, upper room in Jerusalem

▶ WHAT IS THIS TEXT TALKING ABOUT?

Authentic faith in Jesus

▶ WHAT DOES THIS TEXT TEACH?

Authentic faith in Jesus is possible even if you have not had a first-person, physical encounter with the resurrected Christ.

We are Thomas. We are invited to believe this incredible story of Jesus's resurrection without a physical, firsthand experience with the resurrected Christ. Is our faith authentic without it?

Thomas was a frustrated realist. We see it in two earlier statements he makes in the gospel of John. When Jesus learned that Lazarus had died, he told the disciples that it was time to go to Judea. Knowing the risk, the realist was exasperated by this notion: "Let us also go, that we may die with him" (John 11:16). When Jesus was laying out the path ahead for the disciples following his death, the frustrated realist blurted out, "Lord, we don't know where you are going, so how can we know the way?" (14:5). It is no wonder that Thomas struggled to believe what his colleagues told him about their firsthand experience with the risen Jesus, an experience he had missed.

Jesus loved this frustrated realist and so made a second appearance to the disciples. The second experience is a near duplicate of the first. It was the same day of the week (one week later). It was in the same place. And it offered the same evidence—the familiar voice, the ability to see the wounds on Jesus's body, and the opportunity to physically touch him. Only this time the hesitant Thomas was present and believed. And through the experience, Jesus showed just how much he cared about getting this one frustrated realist on board.

But the story raises another question: is authentic faith possible for those who have not had a physical, firsthand experience with the risen Jesus? This would be the experience of nearly all the readers of John's gospel, including us. Jesus asserts not only that is faith possible but preferable. Taking God at his word is the highest form of worship: "Blessed are those who have not seen and yet have believed" (John 20:29). John confirms this by shifting our focus to the purpose of all he had written about Jesus's life: "But these are written that you may believe that Jesus is the Messiah, the Son of God, and that by believing you may have life in his name" (v. 31). That is where we live and how we believe, with a faith as authentic as that of Thomas.

For Further Reference: **Genesis 15:6; Mark 16:14; 2 Corinthians 5:7; Hebrews 10:22–23; 11:1, 6; 1 Peter 1:8–9; 1 John 1:1**

JESUS RESTORES PETER

John 21:1–25

"Take care of my sheep." (John 21:16)

▶ WHO & WHERE

Jesus, Peter, Thomas, Nathanael, James, John, and two other disciples, Sea of Galilee

▶ WHAT IS THIS TEXT TALKING ABOUT?

The new normal

▶ WHAT DOES THIS TEXT TEACH?

Jesus met with the disciples in Galilee to define their new normal.

We like to think of normal as static, but experience suggests otherwise. The old normal gets replaced by something new. As John brings his gospel to a close, we hear Jesus speak with the disciples in Galilee about their new normal.

The story begins by drawing us back into the past lives of the disciples. All lived in the district of Galilee where some fished the lake for a living. All these men became Jesus's disciples, and all abandoned him the night of his arrest. John mentions three by name, those with a past of doubting and denial—Nathanael, Thomas, and Peter (John 1:46; 18:15–18, 25–27; 20:24–25). These memories surely haunted the disciples, Peter more than the others. If only Jesus had listened when he asked him to go away from him because he was a "sinful man" (Luke 5:8).

Jesus came to assert a new normal. He meets these men on the same shoreline where he first called them from their fishing boats after the first miraculous catch of fish (Luke 5:1–11). "Friends, haven't you any fish?" he called out to them (John 21:5). Using an identical miracle, he re-calls them into service. Perhaps because Peter had sinned most publicly, we spend more time with him in this encounter with the risen Jesus. Jesus takes us back to the night of Peter's denial in two ways.

First, Jesus builds a charcoal fire. The only other time the Greek word for this kind of fire is used in the New Testament is when we see Peter trying to warm himself by such a fire just before the denial begins (John 18:18). Jesus then asks Peter three loyalty questions akin to Peter's three denials of Jesus. Location, miracle, fire, and questions all take us back into the disciples' old normal, but then Jesus flipped the script. All the disloyalty of the disciples was washed clean in the forgiveness gained on the cross and certified by the empty tomb. He treated them not as abandoned sinners but forgiven friends and family members.

Second, in the very place he first called the disciples to fish for people (Luke 5:10), Jesus then shifts to a pastoral metaphor to define both the nature and longevity of the new normal. As the Lord was a Shepherd for his people, so these students of Jesus would be under-shepherds who feed and care for the believing flock. And in speaking about both the death of Peter and John, Jesus asserted that this new normal would extend to the very end of their lives, just as our new normal in Jesus extends to the very end of our lives.

For Further Reference: Luke 5:1–11; John 1:46; 18:15–18, 25–27; 20:24–25; Acts 20:28; Hebrews 2:10–18; 1 Peter 5:2–4

THE GREAT COMMISSION

Matthew 28:16–20

"Then Jesus came to them and said, 'All authority in heaven and on earth has been given to me. Therefore go and make disciples of all nations.'" (Matthew 28:18–19)

▶ **WHO & WHERE**

Jesus, the eleven disciples, a mountain in Galilee

▶ **WHAT IS THIS TEXT TALKING ABOUT?**

The change in the disciples' status and assignment

▶ WHAT DOES THIS TEXT TEACH?

The disciples were now authorized to teach the full message of
Jesus to all nations.

Final words are important words. That makes us lean in for a closer look
at these final words of Matthew's gospel.

They speak about three changes in the lives of the disciples. First,
Jesus marks a change in their status. Within first-century Judaism, no
one was to teach unless authorized to do so by someone who already was
an authorized teacher. Jesus claimed "all authority" and now authorizes
his longtime students to function as teachers. Second, Jesus changes
the message they are to deliver. Prior to this, Jesus had severely limited
the content of what they said (Matt. 12:16; 16:20). Their message was
this simple: "The kingdom of heaven has come near" (10:7). Now they

This view from the summit of Mount Arbel is likely the one Jesus used when lifting the disciples' eyes to their new
mission that reached to every horizon.

were to share "everything" Jesus had taught them (28:20). Third, Jesus changes the scope of their mission. Prior to this, Jesus directed his disciples to speak only to those who were descendants of Abraham and Sarah, "the lost sheep of Israel" (10:5–6; 15:24). Now they were off to make disciples of all nations (28:19).

These were profound changes. And true to form, Jesus picked a location whose view complemented the content of the lesson. Matthew is not in the habit of naming mountains but often leaves tantalizing clues as to which mountain we are on. In this case, we know the mountain was in Galilee, distinguished from other rising terrain, and familiar to the disciples (26:32; 28:7, 10, 16). My best guess is that "the mountain" is Mount Arbel. It has the most distinguished profile on the Sea of Galilee. Jesus had taught the disciples here before, including the extensive lesson known as the Sermon on the Mount. And its summit comes with a commanding view. Rising 1,245 feet (380 meters) above the Sea of Galilee shoreline, the view from Mount Arbel overlooked many of the other experiences the disciples had with Jesus in the Sea of Galilee basin. What is more, it allowed the disciples to see representative of all nations walking the International Highway below them, traveling toward the horizon and the greater world beyond where they were to take the gospel.

The disciples left this mountain with a new status and a new assignment. We share both with them.

For Further Reference: Daniel 7:13–14; Mark 16:15–18; John 13:34–35; 17:20–23; Acts 1:8; Ephesians 1:20–23; Philippians 2:9–11

THE ASCENSION OF JESUS

Luke 24:50–53

"When he had led them out to the vicinity of Bethany, he lifted
up his hands and blessed them. While he was blessing them, he
left them and was taken up into heaven." (Luke 24:50–51)

▶ **WHO & WHERE**

Jesus, the eleven disciples, Mount of Olives

▶ **WHAT IS THIS TEXT TALKING ABOUT?**

The ascension of Jesus

▶ **WHAT DOES THIS TEXT TEACH?**

The location of Jesus's ascension casts it as a coronation and positions
the disciples to receive God's unique giving of the Holy Spirit.

These decades were the most consequential years of our world's
history—years when God's Son walked the earth. But now following forty days during which Jesus gave convincing proofs that he
was alive (Acts 1:3), things were about to change.

Luke describes the physical setting for the ascension in two
complimentary ways. He places it in the "vicinity of Bethany" (Luke
24:50) on the "Mount of Olives" (Acts 1:12). The Mount of Olives is a two-
mile-long (three kilometer) ridge that runs north and south, separating
Jerusalem from Bethany. It is on the summit of this ridge that ancient
churches and memorials mark the spot of the ascension. Like so many
other significant moments in Jesus's ministry, the location influences our
understanding of the event.

The Ascension Church, part of the Augusta Victoria Compound, is one of the traditional locations on the Mount of Olives that remembers Jesus's ascension.

    The first role of the location of Jesus's ascension into heaven relates to Jesus. We find him in the same place where the Palm Sunday crowd celebrated his arrival in Jerusalem just a little over a month earlier. On that day, the excited crowd called for Jesus's coronation (Luke 19:28–40). Admittedly that seemed unlikely after the Romans soldiers nailed Jesus to the cross and posted a sign above his head mocking Jesus's royal aspirations. But as Jesus rose from the Mount of Olives to be seated at the right hand of his Father, the day of his coronation had arrived (Heb. 2:5–9). The location of Jesus's anticipated coronation became the place of his realized coronation.

The second role of the location of Jesus's ascension into heaven relates to the disciples. Their preparation for ministry would not be complete until the Holy Spirit came upon them (John 16:12–15). Immediately after his resurrection, Jesus instructed the disciples to meet him in Galilee and spent time with them there. But following their time together with the risen Jesus in Galilee, the disciples returned to Jerusalem after Jesus ascended into heaven because this is where they would experience God's unique giving of the Holy Spirit (Acts 1:4–5). The Mount of Olives put them near the Temple complex. And following the ascension, the disciples joyfully returned to the Holy City where "they stayed continually at the temple, praising God" (Luke 24:53), and waited as instructed for the Spirit's coming.

That is the last thing we read in Luke's gospel. But it is the first step in the gospel message reaching us. Jerusalem became launch central: "But you will receive power when the Holy Spirit comes on you; and you will be my witnesses in Jerusalem, and in all Judea and Samaria, and to the ends of the earth" (Acts 1:8). So as Jesus's earthly story comes to a close on the Mount of Olives, our story with him is set to begin.

For Further Reference: Mark 16:19–20; Luke 19:28–40; John 16:12–15; Acts 1:1–12; Hebrews 2:5–9

Conclusion

Stories are like people: both have homes. Who we are, how we think, what we do, and how we communicate are all intimately bound to where we are from. No one can fully know us until they understand the geography that shapes us. The same is true of the stories of Jesus. And that has been the purpose of this tour, to put the stories about Jesus in their geographical and cultural homeland. The gospel writers did not exclude these vital elements of the human experience. In our walks, we have seen just how much they have to offer in understanding Jesus and the lessons he longs to teach us.

Every tour has a beginning and end. The same is true of this one. On our last night in Jerusalem, I ask the students in my study programs to reflect on how the Lord has changed them. What do they say most often? "I will never read my Bible the same way again."

I pray the same is true for you. This tour is over, but your journey has just begun.

Illustration Credits

All maps taken from *Discovery House Bible Atlas* by John A. Beck © 2015. Used by permission of Our Daily Bread Publishing, Box 3566, Grand Rapids, MI 49501. All rights reserved.

Unless otherwise indicated, photographs © John A. Beck. Used by permission.

Photographs on pages 35, 43, 55, 56, 61, 63, 87, 90, 121, 148, 170, 199, 214, 219, 246, 266, 273, 311 © Terry Bidgood. Used by permission.

Images on pages 28, 74, 232, 275 taken from *The Baker Book of Bible Charts, Maps and Time Lines*, copyright © 2016 by Baker Publishing Group. Published by Baker Books, a division of Baker Publishing Group. All rights reserved. Used by permission.

Photograph on page 25 reprinted by permission from Medioimages/Photodisc, Getty Images.

Photograph on page 33 courtesy of Charles K. Wilkinson, Wikimedia Commons.

Photograph on page 46 reprinted by permission from guter, Getty Images.

Woodcut on page 50 by Julius Schnorr von Carolsfeld, from *Die Bibel in Bildern*, 1860.

Photograph on page 96 reprinted by permission from BibleArtLibrary, Getty Images.

Photograph on page 104 reprinted by permission from Anton Ivanov, Shutterstock.

Photograph on page 108 reprinted by permission from Suprun Vitaly, Zoonar GmbH, Alamy.

Scripture Index

Help us get the word out!

Our Daily Bread Publishing exists to feed the soul
with the Word of God.

If you appreciated this book, please let others know.

- Pick up another copy to give as a gift.
- Share a link to the book or mention it
  on social media.
- Write a review on your blog, on a book-
  seller's website, or at our own site
  (odb.org/store).
- Recommend this book for your church,
  book club, or small group.

Connect with us:

- @ourdailybread
- @ourdailybread
- @ourdailybread

Our Daily Bread Publishing
PO Box 3566
Grand Rapids, Michigan 49501 USA

✉ books@odb.org